Developing Youth Football Players

HORST WEIN

HUMAN KINETICS

Library of Congress Cataloging-in-Publication Data

Wein, Horst.
  Developing youth football players / Horst Wein.
      p. cm.
  Includes bibliographical references.
  ISBN-13: 978-0-7360-6948-9 (soft cover)
  ISBN-10: 0-7360-6948-8 (soft cover)
  1. Soccer for children--Coaching. 2. Soccer for children--Training. I. Title.
  GV944.2W45 2007
  796.332083--dc22

                                                  2007010051

ISBN-10: 0-7360-6948-8
ISBN-13: 978-0-7360-6948-9

This book is a revised edition of *Developing Youth Soccer Players*, published in 2001 by Human Kinetics.

Acquisitions Editor: Jana Hunter; **Developmental Editor:** Anne Hall; **Assistant Editor:** Cory Weber; **Copyeditor:** Andy Hall; **Proofreader:** Erin Cler; **Graphic Designer:** Nancy Rasmus; **Graphic Artist:** Sandra Meier; **Cover Designer:** Keith Blomberg; **Photographer (cover):** PA Photos; **Photographer (interior):** photos on pages v, 5, 10, 93, 149, 151, 248, 253 © Horst Wein; all other photos © Human Kinetics, unless otherwise noted; **Photo Asset Manager:** Laura Fitch; **Photo Office Assistant:** Jason Allen; **Art Manager:** Kelly Hendren; **Associate Art Manager:** Alan L. Wilborn; **Illustrators:** Benjamin Echevarren/© Horst Wein; **Printer:** Versa Press

Human Kinetics books are available at special discounts for bulk purchase. Special editions or book excerpts can also be created to specification. For details, contact the Special Sales Manager at Human Kinetics.

Printed in the United States of America   10 9 8 7 6 5

The paper in this book is certified under a sustainable forestry program.

Human Kinetics
Web site: www.HumanKinetics.com

United States: Human Kinetics, P.O. Box 5076, Champaign, IL 61825-5076
800-747-4457
e-mail: humank@hkusa.com

Canada: Human Kinetics, 475 Devonshire Road, Unit 100, Windsor, ON N8Y 2L5
800-465-7301 (in Canada only)
e-mail: info@hkcanada.com

Europe: Human Kinetics, 107 Bradford Road, Stanningley, Leeds LS28 6AT, United Kingdom
+44 (0) 113 255 5665
e-mail: hk@hkeurope.com

Australia: Human Kinetics, 57A Price Avenue, Lower Mitcham, South Australia 5062
08 8372 0999
e-mail: info@hkaustralia.com

New Zealand: Human Kinetics, P.O. Box 80, Torrens Park, South Australia 5062
0800 222 062
e-mail: info@hknewzealand.com

E4130

Developing Youth Football Players

Contents

Foreword

It is a great satisfaction for me to learn that Horst Wein's Football Development Model, which has been so well accepted in Spain and other countries, is now published in this English-language edition. *Developing Youth Football Players* opens the door for a multitude of coaches and children, highly enthusiastic about football, to be exposed to his unique philosophy and highly successful method of teaching.

The valuable experience he shares in this book will serve coaches as both a teaching and learning model. Excellent drawings and photos clearly illustrate the games in his programme and reflect the art of teaching young football players.

Throughout this book, Horst Wein describes a methodology of teaching football that never limits a child's entertainment or creativity, but rather allows children to enjoy every second of the learning process. The pleasure of playing football should never be restricted by severe rules.

Young players are the cornerstone of football. They are, and always will be, the future of the sport. Much more important than winning games is the acquisition of those values inherent in football: fair play, the urge to do better and the sportive spirit.

Education, therefore, runs parallel to the technical instruction. This is how football proves its enormous social dimension.

In this way, we welcome the well-known slogan of FIFA President Joseph 'Sepp' Blatter, 'Football for everybody, everybody for football'. We also applaud his initiative to start the Goal Project, which, during the coming years, will initiate a series of activities toward developing football play and education among children.

I am happy to see FIFA, the largest football organization in the world, and the Real Federación Española de Fútbol promoting the messages in Horst Wein's *Developing Youth Football Players*. Through this approach, they foster the aim to make our sport even more popular and thus to ensure its future.

Ángel María Villar Llona
President, Real Federación Española de Fútbol
Director FIFA Football Commission
Executive Member of the Fédération Internationale de Football Associations

Introduction

A New Philosophy of Coaching Football

Whether young players choose football as a lifelong sport is determined to a high degree by the content of the training programme, the expertise and experience of the coaches, the social life in the club or school and the structure of the formative competitions. The art of developing effective training and competitive programmes for children lies in knowing which kind of practice and competition the player is ready for at any given stage of his or her physical and mental development. *Children will learn quickly, effectively and thoroughly only when the demands of the training sessions or competitions they participate in match their intellectual, psychological and motor skills.*

The *concept of readiness* (the disposition of a certain degree of *maturity*) is a prerequisite for any activity and one that should be applied in all aspects of teaching and learning. It must also be applied to children's sports activities. Coaches should ask, 'At what age is a child ready to successfully face the demands of an adult competition?' If officials were aware of the concept of readiness, children under 14 would never have been subjected to testing themselves in competitions for which they were not yet prepared. Children must be exposed to a gradual stimulation in training and to a series of progressive competitions that, over the years, allow them to advance step by step into the adult game. The art of coaching lies largely in knowing for what activity (a technical move, a tactical behaviour or a complex competition) the player is prepared for at a particular stage of physical and mental development.

All too often, children are introduced to complex sport activities for which they are not yet physically and mentally ready. Expecting a child to comprehend and respond to the complex situations in the full 11v11 football game format will only beget frustration and feelings of failure. *Developing Youth Football Players* introduces coaches to a training programme that takes into account each young player's current physical and mental development. The programme promotes the gradual development of correct technical, tactical, cognitive and physical capacities of players ages 7 to 14.

The question of maturity is also important in the matter of motor learning. Regardless of the action, adults must determine the age at which there are certain likelihoods that the child can achieve an objective. Before teaching a child to ride a bike, for example, you must first ask when children generally acquire the capacity to maintain balance on only two wheels. Experience has shown us that any attempt to teach the skill before the child is ready (before about four years of age) will fail because nature has not yet provided the means of coordination and balance.

'Training deals with the eradication of bad habits and the creation of good habits.'

—Dettmar Cramer

Unfortunately, force of habit constitutes the greatest obstacle to progress in youth football. Traditional methods are often followed blindly—adherents not giving sufficient thought to the consequences of training or the structure of competitions. To achieve better results, coaches, administrations and federations must first review the structure and organisation of their youth football programmes. *The complicated adult game has to be simplified; a logical progression of competitions must be created, designed with increasing demands that adapt perfectly to the mental and physical capacities of individual children.* Youngsters should be presented with only those exercises, games and challenges that suit their current abilities, interests and expectations. Training programmes and competitions for children should be like their shoes: They should fit perfectly and feel comfortable.

This book features the Football Development Model, an innovative system of coaching that is tailored to each age group's cognitive capacities and physical abilities. Most books on coaching young people present general instruction and drills to be applied to all children who participate, regardless of their age. In this book, however, instruction is replaced with stimulation that is fitted to the specific characteristics of children. Instead sof obliging the children to adapt to the game of football, we have adapted the game to children, thus resulting in better and more enjoyable learning of the complicated game.

This model is essentially a recipe for coaching football. It gives you the necessary ingredients of the game—and the proportions in which these ingredients have to be mixed to achieve enjoyable and effective training sessions. More importantly, it explains what skills are best taught during each stage of the evolution of young football players. All of the research has been done; you can simply apply it to your coaching programme.

Developing Youth Football Players contains nine chapters. Chapters 1 to 3 explain the developmental characteristics of children and describe how most current coaching practices actually work against players' developing minds and bodies. According to these practices, children are coached the same ways as adults, even though the adult game is much too complex for a child's mental and motor abilities. The solution to this problem is provided in chapter 2, which explains the various levels of the developmental model, including how and why it was created. Using the Football Development Model in schools and clubs will reduce the acquisition of incorrect habits that limit the performance of players at the senior level. These incorrect habits result directly from the way players have been taught and have competed at lower levels.

Chapter 4 contains basic games and exercises that make up the first level of the Football Development Model. You'll learn games and exercises for teaching young players the fundamentals, such as dribbling, passing, receiving, shooting and tackling. Level 1 also contains simplified competitions—the football decathlon and 2v2 triathlon—for players ages 7 and up.

'Because of the fact that today we are all used to instant food, instant photos, instant coffee, instant transmission of information, etc., people also expect instant success.'

—*Zig Ziglar*

Chapter 5 stimulates trainers and coaches of young football players to develop their intellectual capacities, which are still limited largely because of the authoritarian teaching style preferred by the vast majority of them. As a player´s ball skills get better and better, he or she should also perfect knowledge and thinking: not only developing muscles and tendons but also the brain.

In chapter 6, which introduces readers to the second level of the Football Development Model, the thinking and tactical awareness of players from a very early age onward is systematically developed. The emphasis is placed on a progressive stimulation of their perceptive and intellectual capacities. Their intelligence is mainly developed through the global, not analytic, method, exposing players to a series of technical-tactical simplified games in which each player has to face and resolve a series of problems that have been tailor-made to his or her physical, technical and mental capacities. This way, using a number of simplified game situations, players learn to respond to the cognitive and physical demands of the game. The simplified game preserves the contextual nature of the full game without placing too much technical demand on players in the early stages. Learning to understand the complex game of football can be best achieved through the practice of a logical progression of simplified games, with a gradual increase in the number of players on the team. Level 2 also contains competitions tailored to this age group—mini-football 3v3, the mini-football pentathlon, and the 3v3 triathlon.

Chapter 7 progresses to level 3, which pertains to players aged 10 and up. You'll learn additional simplified games for teams formed by only three players and competitions, like a 4v4 triathlon and 7v7, that gradually increase in complexity from the games in level 2. Chapter 8 describes a programme for developing young goal-keepers, and it offers exercises to enhance and develop those skills.

Chapter 9 gives you the tools for training players aged 12 years and up. This chapter presents a detailed description of level 4 in the Football Development Model. It includes more simplified games that closely link to the appropriate level of competition, 8v8 football—considered an ideal bridge for leading young athletes to the full football game. Game-orientated practice, as you find here, stimulates participants more than traditional instruction and training sessions, in which the contents are isolated from the competition.

The games and drills in chapters 4 through 9 are also complemented by a superior collection of more than 200 full-colour illustrations of particular skills, exercises or games that help you put the concepts in motion. In conclusion, the epilogue emphasises that the only way to develop healthy, happy and talented football players is to follow their natural development. To rush their development is to hinder their healthy formation and future performance.

It is time for all coaches, whether novice or experienced, to revise their ways of coaching and tailor their training sessions and competitions to the children they are entrusted with. *Developing Youth Football Players*, presented by the FIFA executive member and director of the FIFA Football Commission, Ángel María Villar Llona, is a tool you need for developing a successful football programme with satisfied young players.

The Natural Development of Young Players

'Nature decrees that children should be children before they become adults. If we try to alter this natural order, we will reach adulthood prematurely but with neither substance nor strength.'

Jean-Jacques Rousseau

All things in nature have a gestation period and must go through their proper stages to be formed. Each human being has to pass through various stages of development before finally reaching maturity. Nature does not take shortcuts; there is a natural, unhurried order to it all. Coaches, players, parents and administrators should copy nature's wisdom. Being impatient and hurrying the development of a young football player frequently results in poor performances among older players who had shown promise when they were younger. What coaches need is a training model they can perfectly tailor to their players' varying cognitive and motor abilities.

To work with, not against, an individual's developing mind and body, all youth football competitions and training programs must respect the laws of nature and take into account the actual mental and physical condition of their young participants. As children mature, the games in which they compete should gradually become more difficult and complex. *In a well-structured scheme, young football players grow at the same rate as their competitions grow in complexity and difficulty.*

Current Coaching Practices

Most players, no matter what their nationality, don't know how to tap into their potential, which remains unused and dormant. Sadly, the best coaches do not work at the grassroots level because coaching young players rarely reaps them any economic gain. Coaches with greater knowledge and experience are attracted instead to senior teams that can afford to provide them higher salaries.

This failure to attract well-qualified coaches means that young players in schools and clubs are exposed to poor quality, tedious instruction. In most cases, children are coached in the same way that adults are instructed, without taking into account the natural order or progressive development of the young player through time. The makeshift or haphazard schemes that most coaches adopt do not solve the delicate task of ensuring young players receive quality coaching. Moreover, coaching youth at the initial stages is too important for their future development to allow coaches to hastily assemble idiosyncratic methods of training.

Introducing Complex Activities Too Soon

One problem with most methods of training and competition is that they employ complex games and playing situations before children are ready for them. Even football players competing at the club level generally fail one out of three plays, so we must admit that football is a complicated game. Generally speaking, research has shown that the younger the player, the higher the percentage of failure in competition. A low success rate (fewer than 50 per cent of successful actions) is observed when beginners between eight and nine years of age compete with only seven players on a team (7v7). Players face countless difficulties and complex problems even in a game played with this pared-down team. In youth competitions with 11 players on a team, which still happens in many parts of the world, it was noted that one team lost possession of the ball four to six times in just one minute's play (that is in effectively 45 seconds' playing time)!

Young players should not be blamed for incurring this high percentage of unsuccessful actions. We must realise that all children fail frequently, not only in football but also in other physical and mental activities, if they are not brought gradually and progressively to the task. In today's training and competition, children are asked to face game situations that are simply beyond their scope at that particular stage of their psychomotor development. Subjecting children to excessively complex activities before they are ready only reinforces failure and frustration. When individuals experience frequent failure, they not only lose interest and self-esteem but may also come to feel incapable of facing situations that, in fact, are far too complex for them at the time. Stress and dropping out of the sport may result.

Demanding Too Much of Young Players

Young players struggle to overcome not only the complexity of the game but also the increasing demands placed on them within a limited amount of practice time and personal attention. Both coaches and players are challenged by ever more children becoming involved in football—but with less time and space available to them. *Teaching or learning football, as well as competing in it the traditional way does not sufficiently stimulate the bodies and minds of young players; much of their talent is left undiscovered.*

Playing the ball for a maximum of 90 seconds in a full match or being active for less than 15 minutes of a 90-minute training session doesn't allow players to develop their full potential. Yet players are still expected, and even pressured, to perform at a high level. This puts an ever-increasing demand on the youngsters' physical and mental abilities and capacities.

Using Inefficient Coaching Methods

Consider this: Many children study a foreign language over the course of eight years in school. However, if the youth then travel to a country where their mother language is not spoken, they are frequently unable to apply the knowledge they have acquired in almost a thousand hours of teaching and learning. Likewise, most recently graduated physical education teachers, after studying four years of varying sport sciences in a university physical education department, still cannot resolve the majority of the innumerable problems they encounter during their first physical education lessons. This lack of preparedness is due to having had insufficient practical applications of their studies and insufficient experience—and then having applied methods that are already out of date. The knowledge gained at universities or in national training centres has helped few coaches to confront the challenges of their profession with success. To be up to date and make use of new information (most of which tends to repeat itself about every two decades), physical education teachers (and especially those who coach future teachers) should actualize and constantly augment their knowledge and capacities to help their students learn the latest innovations of their specialisation.

The major obstacle to progress in football coaching is the strength of ease and comfort by the coaches. Because of their own inertia or sluggishness, coaches tend to continue with old habits rather than continually rethinking what has to be done and how. All too often, information is used and exercises and formative programs are applied that have already lost their validity. Many coaches have not even noticed that the information they obtained years before has already diminished in value.

Few coaches look beyond their specialty and combine, mix, or synthesise the knowledge from diverse but related sports sciences with their own teaching and learning

The tragedy of coaching young players focuses on the fact that many coaches may know a lot about the game, but they don't know their young pupils.

process. Consequently, the majority of players and coaches must continue learning from accidents, mistakes and trials rather than from the advances in various fields of sport.

Before teaching a specific sport like football, coaches should fully understand how a child, adolescent or adult learns best and then analyse the mechanisms that intervene or influence learning in each of the evolutionary stages of the student. As the young football player grows and develops, a great variety of physiological, cognitive and social-emotional changes occur. These changes directly affect the acquisition of coordination and conditional, as well as mental, capacities.

Time for a Change!

What should coaches do in these days of increasingly sedentary living habits? After 8 to 10 hours' rest overnight, children often sit for 6 more hours in school, which they reach by sitting in a bus or car. In the afternoon, after having sat down for lunch and more schooling, they may travel by bus or car to practice their favourite sport, where they mostly stand in a queue waiting for their turn, listening to the coach's instructions. Then they return home to watch television, surf the Internet, or play video games. Relatively few minutes of the day are reserved for physical stimuli or activities allowing them to use their creativity, imagination and initiative. Under these conditions, the entire tradition of coaching must be rethought and carefully revised to give players a more hands-on role in their own education.

When deciding exactly what role children should be assigned, coaches must consider the physical and emotional needs of the youngsters. They must also understand the stages of development to know at what age children are ready for certain activities. By considering all of this, coaches can provide a fun and effective football program without stress.

Promoting Active Participation

Rather than adhere to current football programs that concentrate on the execution of different skills, the modern coach should teach players to understand all aspects of the game. Too many drills will kill the young players' innate potential! Over time, coaches should carefully and progressively develop important capacities, including perception, analysis of game situations and correct decision making under stressful conditions. A coach cannot foster these qualities through verbal instruction alone. When coaches continually use verbal instruction, they become the main actors in the coaching theatre, thereby curtailing, or even killing, the active participation of the players. Usurping the players' active role is detrimental to their learning. By involving the players, on the other hand, a coach obliges *them* to think, to organise collected information and come to conclusions, to evaluate and judge, to imagine, invent, and create new moves or combinations.

In *Coaching of Performance* John Whitmore writes that a player remembers only 19 per cent of what he or she is taught three months earlier through instructing or telling, whereas he or she can recall 32 per cent of what was demonstrated and explained.

'Youth prefer to be stimulated instead of being instructed.'

—*Johann Wolfgang von Goethe*

Yet in cases where students were given the opportunity to generate the information on their own, but with the help of a teacher, fully 65 per cent of the information was memorised. That is why football players should be allowed to actively participate in the coaching and learning process: to develop as complete athletes who eventually become independent from the frequent instruction of coaches. Learning takes place best when the coach is able to transfer decisions to the players.

Allowing Children More Control

Creativity can be considered one of a human being's most elevated mental activities. Unfortunately, few coaches know how to stimulate this ability in their players. The teaching styles and rigid methods seen on most football fields tend to strangulate more than stimulate the players' capacity for fantasy, creativity and innovation.

Instead of giving young children sufficient opportunities to cultivate their innate potential during training, coaches tend to dominate everything, fearful of losing control of the situation by giving up any control to the players. *A coach's objective should be to make the others think instead of thinking for them.*

Expert coaches with a wealth of technical knowledge often have a hard time withholding their expertise. They are used to giving away their knowledge through many instructions about what, when and how to do the task, without being aware that coaching this way will limit their players' development. Giving the players solutions to memorise should be replaced by presenting them with tailor-made problems that they have to *resolve on their own.*

It is important that coaches encourage creativity to stimulate a young athlete's development.

Stimulating Players' Minds

To develop players' active involvement in the training and learning process, coaches must master the skill of posing questions. The most effective questions are open-ended ones that require descriptive answers. In contrast, closed questions with yes or no answers shut the door on the exploration of further detail. That is why coaches should concentrate on open-ended questions, ones that begin with words that seek to quantify or gather facts: *what, when, how much* or *how many.*

Through systematic questioning by the coach, the players are self-generating the information. Thanks to intelligent questions, many players become aware of problems they have never noticed before. When faced with problems presented by the coach, players have to think, examine, judge and evaluate until they find their own solutions. On the contrary, when a coach instructs or just tells players what to do in certain situations of the game, he or she does not stimulate any of these active mental processes.

Once football coaches have been convinced of the need to modify the traditional way of teaching their players, they soon discover that the process of understanding and learning football will shift increasingly to self-teaching.

10 Rules for Efficient Learning

1. Acquire good habits. Bad habits double the amount of work for the coach, because he or she must first suppress the incorrect habit and then teach the student to react correctly to the same stimulus. Just as one can learn to speak a language well or badly, one can also acquire good or bad habits and behaviours in football.

2. Confront players with problems that are within their capabilities—and also with slightly more complex and difficult activities that, after a certain number of trials, can be mastered without help from the coach. A feeling of capability and success generally nourishes and stimulates learning. When players are aware of their capability and receive some kind of reward for their success, learning will be fun and players will be encouraged to progress even further.

3. Help players learn to recognise the result of every play immediately after the action is over. Players who are conscious of the results of their play in a given game situation will be capable of later reproducing or suppressing the vivid experience in a similar game situation.

4. Teach new aspects of the game within the parameters of ones that are already known. People tend to learn more quickly when they already partially know the abilities and capacities that the coach is trying to develop.

5. Practice the individual elements of a situation to connect the stimulus and response. The first phase of learning is to recognise a game situation that is composed of various elements. To better recognise a situation, it is important to practice it many times. Apart from facilitating recognition of a situation, the repetitions tend to strengthen the connection between the stimulus and the correct answer.

6. Review and repeat material frequently. Because the loss of an ability or capacity starts right after the first practice, repetition is vital to learning. A few repetitions succeed in activating only short-term memory. Transferring information to long-term memory requires repetition of the same task.

7. Vary the exercises and games. Without varying the content of a practice, coaches risk boring the players. To avoid monotony, loss of concentration and lack of motivation in the players, which are all enemies of learning, the coach must ensure variety in the session.

8. Mix up the flow of content. The more similar the content of different parts of a training session, the higher the transference becomes between them. This is because the last thing learned is frequently superimposed on what was previously learned. Remaining on the same theme or method of presentation for even 15 to 20 minutes can lower players' concentration and interest.

9. Motivate the players, be it through praise or the choice of an activity that interests them. Motivation supports learning.

10. Stimulate both the body and the whole mind. Bulgarian scientist Lozanov discovered a 'super learning' method in the 1970s, which states that maximum learning occurs when teachers use an activity to stimulate both the left and right hemispheres of the brain. Football's traditional teaching methods often fail to adequately stimulate the right hemisphere of the brain, which harbours the creative capacities, intuition, and space- and time-orientation. Each training session should stimulate the body as well as both hemispheres of the brain.

Meeting Young People's Needs

The key to developing successful youth football players is in understanding and meeting the needs of young players rather than subjecting them to boring exercises or a game designed for adults. These are some basic, yet important, needs children have that coaches should always keep in mind.

➤ *Need for security.* During training, children need a familiar and intimate atmosphere that gives them security and confidence. Frequent changes of training site or coach or educator is not recommended. Returning to games that they are already familiar with (but with some variations) is welcomed by the kids as long as the contents of the training sessions link with something that they already know. Children require stability.

Training should always take place in a safe environment, and specific rules should be applied to ensure safety and avoid any dangerous situations.

➤ *Need for new experiences.* Nothing can be understood completely when it has not been experienced first. Coaches should allow children to experiment with tasks. Children need to discover on their own everything that surrounds them. This also applies to the world of sport and in particular to football. Kids should be stimulated with games and activities that are within their physical and mental capacities. This method of coaching allows them to develop their abilities and capacities step by step through their own discovery.

➤ *Need to be acknowledged.* Children become highly motivated when their efforts in mastering a skill or problem are praised. Through praise they are encouraged to try even harder. To children younger than 12 years old, the teacher, coach or parent is like a mirror in which they see their capacity or incapacity. That is why educators and parents have to learn to be positive, to praise the children frequently and keep critical comments to a minimum.

➤ *Need to show responsibility.* Children prefer to do things on their own without depending too much on adults. They like to reach independence as quickly as possible. The coaching methods and behaviour of the educator should consider this need, making sure that the children are frequently allowed to find solutions on their own to problems the coach presents. The educator should interfere only when the problems cannot be solved by the pupils. Youngsters can also perform the tasks of putting down or collecting cones, modifying the rules of a practice game, or choosing players for demonstrations or certain activities. Their need to demonstrate responsibility can also be stimulated in each training session by allowing them 10 minutes to freely choose what to practice, how to do it, and where and with whom to execute a determined skill or game.

Coaches who are reluctant to give up some responsibility to the children must realise that learning also takes place out of their presence. In any team game the world over, children organise their play in its logical fashion even if an adult is not available to guide them. First, they make sure that the teams are even because they want competition. They want the game to be fair and challenging, thus forcing them to play to their full potential. Second, kids don't need referees. The players take care of the rules themselves, modifying them according to conditions and the environment: no off-side, more players, bigger field and so forth. Third, teams are often composed of players of various ages. The younger players learn from the older ones, who, at the same time, are challenged by the younger players. This is how good teams are built at the senior level as well.

➤ *Need to play.* Playing games is as vital for children as sleep. Playing is necessary for the health of their bodies and minds. As children learn by playing, the central part of each training session should be the practice and understanding of simplified games. The art of coaching is to always adapt instruction to the children's ability and capacity level—not vice versa. Playing games stimulates communication and decision making; playing football without thinking can be compared to shooting without aiming.

➤ *Need to socialise.* Children instinctively look for communication with others. The older they are, the more they need company of a similar age. They love to be associated and to identify themselves with a group or team with the aim of achieving common objectives.

➤ *Need to move.* Nature wants children to be active. Youngsters have no patience to wait in queues for their turn. The rules of adult games must be modified to allow children to play the ball more often. Games with fewer players assure active participation.

➤ *Need to live in the present.* Generally, neither the past nor the future interests children very much. Their sense of time is completely different from that of adults. Children live intensely in the present, without bothering about tomorrow or yesterday, which they deem to be far away.

➤ *Need for variety.* Children crave variety, which results in less boredom and fatigue. A great variety of stimulation is fundamental to maintaining their attention level. Unless coaches frequently vary the method of presentation and its contents, most children's attention deviates. Coaches should also vary the grade of intensity of the exercises and games.

➤ *Need to be understood by adults.* Children seem to live in a different world: They have different problems, they learn differently and they don't think as logically as adults do. Their ideas, thoughts and reasoning often lack coherence. Their emotional constancy depends to a high degree on their speed of biological growth. In general, kids don't know how to use their energy well and, therefore, tire easily. They behave exactly the way they feel. For all these reasons, adults who live and work with children should know how to stimulate and guide them in their search for personality and identity.

Eliminating Anxiety

In a study conducted by Pierce and Stratton (1981), 453 youth sport participants were asked to identify the worries that bothered them so much that they might not play in the future. Most of these children indicated that not playing well (63.3 per cent) and making a mistake (62.5 per cent) were the major stressors when playing sports. Related to these anxieties, 44.2 per cent stated that their worries prevented them from playing their best and 23.6 per cent suggested that the anxiety from being worried might prevent them from playing in the future.

We all know that one main stress factor for children in a competition is the strong desire for their parents and coaches to see them winning. Pressured by the adults, the young players perceive anxiety before, during and even after the game, instead of competing mainly to have fun with friends.

Administrators, teachers, parents and other adults tend to evaluate children's abilities and capacities unrealistically high, forcing them to participate in competitions in which the young players will not do well. In turn, the unrealistic expectations thus cause the youngsters to view themselves as failures, destroying their motivation and self-esteem. But *self-esteem is the life force of the personality*, and if that is suppressed or diminished, so is the person! As a result, children perceive that they are not yet ready for, and that they will not be able to respond adequately to, the performance demands of a difficult and complex competition that was originally designed for adults a century ago.

Even before the game, children are aware of the difficulty of the task (precompetition anxiety). During the game, when they experience their limitations by making more mistakes than successful moves, the young players demonstrate even greater arousal levels. Even after the completion of the game, the children's stress level remains if they consider their completed performance inadequate.

To be more specific, the premature introduction of the 11v11 game for prepubescent children causes excessive stress, which then results in negative self-perception. This poor self-image severely hinders the learning process and motivation of the young players.

Young children learn most efficiently in nonstressful environments (Wilson 1984). Prepubescent children have to be exposed in each stage of evolution to a tailor-made competition that assures they perceive their own competence while playing a game.

Recognising the deficiencies in current practices is the first step to a more effective way of coaching football. When children's stages of development are not considered in designing a training program, a gap forms between what the football program provides them and what the children need in order to learn. It is time to challenge current coaching practices and stop subjecting children to exercises and games that are too complex to match their mental and physical development. By tailoring the game of football to fit the bodies and minds of young players, coaches develop successful football programs and happy, talented young players.

Bill of Rights for Young Football Players

1. The right to enjoyment both in practice and in competition, with a wide variety of activities that promote fun and easy learning
2. The right to play as a child and not be treated as an adult, either on or off the playing field
3. The right to participate in competitions with simplified rules, adapted to their level of ability and capacity at each stage of their evolution
4. The right to play in conditions of the greatest possible safety
5. The right to participate in all aspects of the game
6. The right to be trained by experienced and specially prepared coaches and educators
7. The right to gain experience by resolving most problems during practice themselves
8. The right to be treated with dignity by the coach, their team-mates and their opponents
9. The right to play with children of their own age with similar chances of winning
10. The right not to become a champion

A Successful Approach to Coaching Football

Planning the development of young players is like preparing for a journey. It's advisable to have a map (plan or model) to avoid getting lost and wasting time and energy.

An effective approach for coaching young players has at last been developed. In this approach, called the Football Development Model, the process has been perfectly adapted to the mental and physical levels of children from various age groups. The model, which all teachers and coaches may follow, can well replace the makeshift training and competitions that have proved ineffective in the past.

The Football Development Model is a training program that has dramatically influenced the way youngsters in more than 30 countries in Europe, Asia and South America experience the game of football. The model exposes children gradually to the difficulty and complexity of the game. However, far from being a rigid model or training plan, it allows coaches to choose from a proposed menu of whatever corresponds to his or her taste or coaching style. Instead of instructing coaches, the Football Development Model stimulates them, enabling them to find the best mix of activities for their particular group of players.

Football Development Model

Before applying the model to developing a plan for your young players, let's outline just how the model was created and exactly what it consists of.

Creating the Model

The Football Development Model takes into account everything that is known regarding a child's progressive development. It not only respects the laws of nature but also meets the expectations of the young players.

Just as children have basic needs that should be satisfied in designing a football programme, they also have certain expectations. When children play football, they are primarily interested in four things: action, personal involvement in the action, close scores and opportunities to reaffirm relationships with friends.

Because each of these factors is so important to the well-being of the children, all four were clearly in mind when designing the training and competitive programs in the Football Development Model. Numerous changes were made to more traditional training and competitive programs in order to please the children:

➤ The rules of many traditional exercises or games were simplified or modified to increase activity. We know that whenever children create their own games, they devote a good deal of effort to setting up rules that foster action. Most of the activity during their games occurs around the scoring area, and scores are so frequent that everybody scores at least once.

➤ Many exercises and games were designed specifically to increase the personal involvement of every player, allowing them to be in the centre of action frequently and therefore feel important.

➤ Changes in game rules and scoring methods helped keep game scores close and heightened challenges. In training, teams are often constructed or modified to keep game scores close enough to make the activity both interesting and challenging, even if outstanding players must accept handicaps.

➤ The organization of teams and practices was changed so that friends have opportunities to play together in a variety of ways.

Children have four phases of motor development (Gallahue 1973), and the design of the Football Development Model takes these into consideration. These four phases are

1. reflex movements—from birth until about eight months,
2. rudimentary movements—from the end of the first year of life until the end of the second,
3. fundamental movements—from the second year until about the sixth, and
4. specific or sport movements—from the sixth or seventh year onward.

By seven years of age, most children are fairly proficient (though not yet mature) in fundamental motor skills, and they start to use those basic motor skills until they improve both qualitatively and quantitatively. They also learn to vary, modify and combine them into transitional motor activities. For example, they combine running with jumping, running with throwing or kicking a ball in various ways, or running (like a sprinter, football or hockey player) with the ball under control.

This last phase of motor development is precisely where the Football Development Model begins. This ensures that the children are therefore exposed only to the level of activity that they are ready for. Children from the specific- or sport-movements phase should be exposed to the first level of the Football Development Model, then follow the suggested plan step by step and in the time line indicated.

Five Levels of Progression

The Football Development Model comprises five formation levels:

Level 1   Games for basic abilities and capacities (chapter 4)
Level 2   Games for mini-football (chapter 6)
Level 3   Games for 7v7 football (chapter 7)
Level 4   Games for 8v8 football (chapter 9)
Level 5   Games for official 11v11 football

These levels, which are illustrated more thoroughly on pages 14 and 15, represent a progressive sequence of exercises and simplified games that supply the most common game situations for an age group. There may be fewer players, reduced dimensions in the playing field, fewer or less-complicated rules, and so forth. Young players progress slowly, from one unit or game to the next one, and are continuously confronted with slightly more complex and difficult problems. They progress to the next level only after understanding and mastering the technical and tactical requirements of the previous simplified game or competition. *Their training thus becomes a developmental process of gradually increasing demands through time.*

The step-by-step approach, both for players and their coaches, is one of the keys to success in this method. Each segment is broken down into a series of small steps. These steps lead gradually and methodically to the final goal of each level of accomplishment or formation: the ability to perform well in the respective competition of that particular age group.

At the first level, youngsters aged seven years and up encounter a games program of basic abilities and capacities. These games programs include juggling and balancing the ball; dribbling; passing, receiving and shooting; and tackling. They are exposed to simplified competitions (like the football decathlon and triathlon) and a great variety of multi-lateral games. Through these games, children have sufficient opportunities to practice and discover varied motor skills before and during their acquisition of football-specific skills. Other youngsters, who at this stage of development do not get a great variety of multi-lateral motor stimuli, may later encounter a proficiency barrier. Learning increasingly complex skills may become extremely difficult for them if their fundamental skills and transitional motor activities have remained poorly developed.

Once through the different multi-lateral tasks, the children progress to the second level. This level comprises a progressive series of simplified games for teams of two players, in which the children not only experiment with and improve in the correct use of the skills learned in level 1 but also build up their capacities in communication and cooperation. The objective of this level is to understand and learn to successfully play level 2 competitive mini-football (first 3v3 without a goal-keeper, then 3v3 with a goal-keeper) and the 3v3 triathlon. All proposed activities in level 3 (simplified games of 3v3, 4v4 football triathlon and the development of young goal-keepers) lead to the capacity of playing 7v7 football across the width of the official field. At level 4, the players mainly encounter a program of simplified games for teams of four or five players. Here they will consolidate skills with the help of the activities from the first three levels. They chiefly employ corrective exercises and develop their reading of the game and their reaction skills, which allow them to perform well in 8v8 football between the penalty areas of the regular field. The developmental program for level 5, or the full game, is presented in the book *Developing Game Intelligence in Soccer* (2005) by Horst Wein.

Advantages of the Football Development Model

To further illustrate that the Football Development Model is the most effective way to stimulate young players, the following is a summary of the benefits of implementing this model. It will benefit not only your football program but also, more important, the young players themselves.

Link Between Training and Competition

Each level is composed of various corrective exercises and preparatory games specially designed to match the various tasks that competition demands among the players in each age group. Solid bridges are constructed between learning a subject and, moments later, correctly applying it in a simplified training game or in official competition. Training and competition are always seen as a unit, one being tightly linked to the other. This differs from traditional methods, which can deprive children of an efficient training and learning process that fosters understanding of the game: a process fundamental to a good performance. Instead of focusing mainly on *how* to execute a closed skill, the Football Development Model coaches children on how the skill should be best *applied*: *when*, *where* and *why*. This ensures that the players are always highly motivated, because they see the training practice always in relation to the game, not isolated from the competition (as observed all too often among youth football players).

Increase in Successful Actions

Laurence Morehouse and Leonard Gross have said that 'Practice makes perfect only if you are doing it right'. Practice doesn't make perfect if an athlete is repeating a wrong

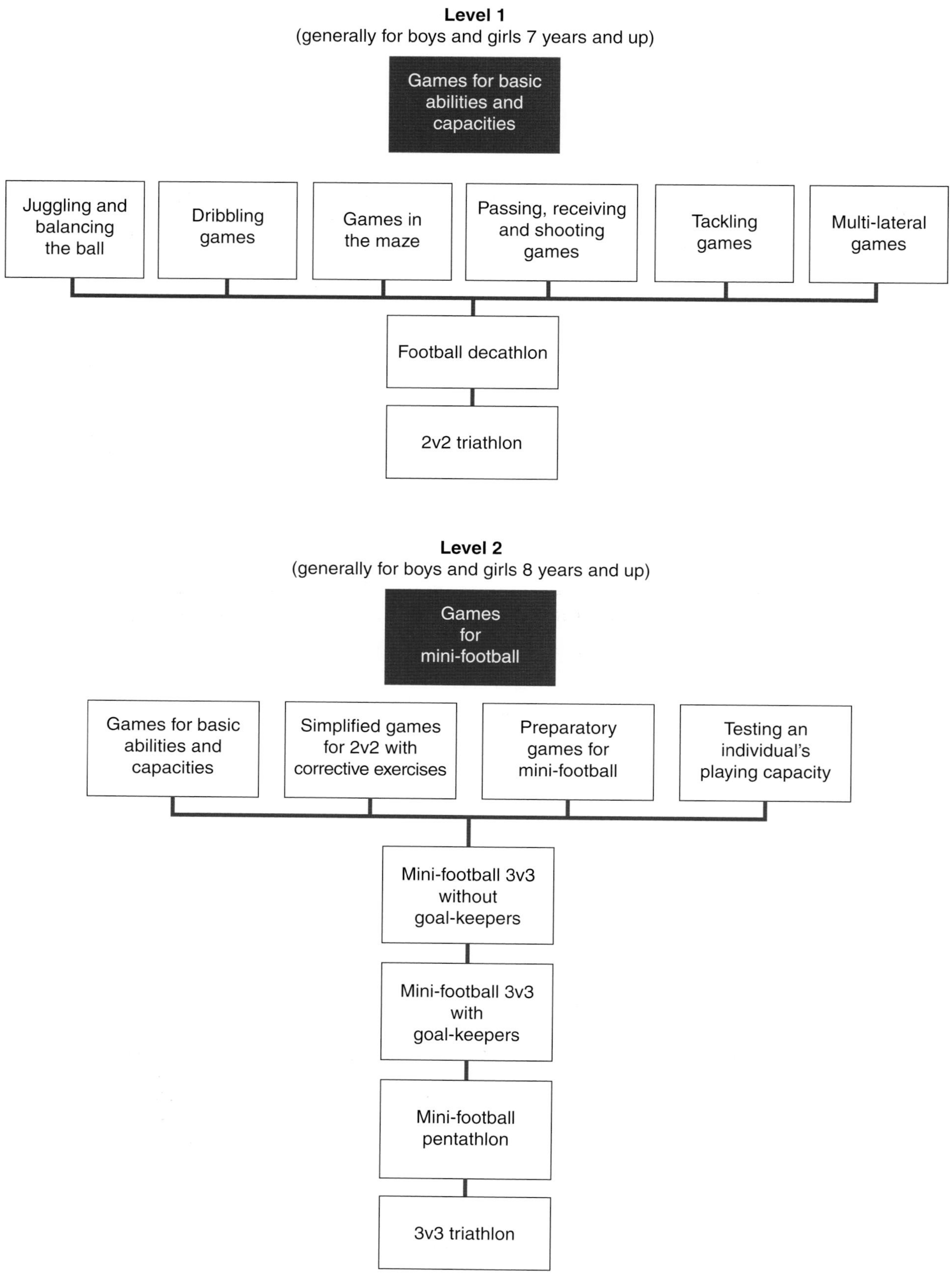

Level 1
(generally for boys and girls 7 years and up)

Games for basic abilities and capacities

| Juggling and balancing the ball | Dribbling games | Games in the maze | Passing, receiving and shooting games | Tackling games | Multi-lateral games |

Football decathlon

2v2 triathlon

Level 2
(generally for boys and girls 8 years and up)

Games for mini-football

| Games for basic abilities and capacities | Simplified games for 2v2 with corrective exercises | Preparatory games for mini-football | Testing an individual's playing capacity |

Mini-football 3v3 without goal-keepers

Mini-football 3v3 with goal-keepers

Mini-football pentathlon

3v3 triathlon

The Football Development Model contains individual exercises and simplified games as well as collective and complex game situations.

Level 3
(generally for boys and girls 10 years and up)

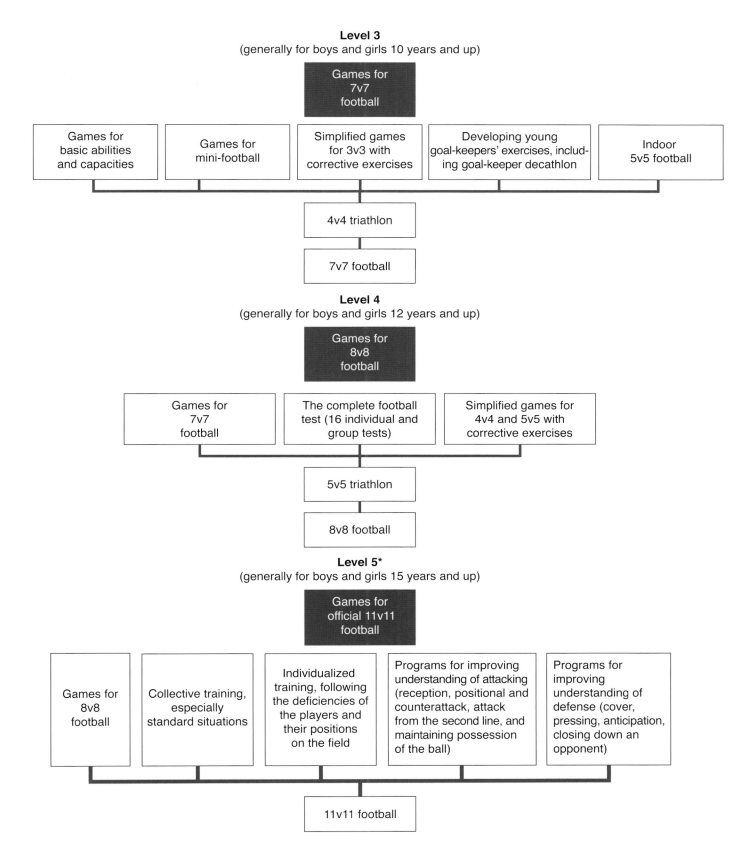

Games for
7v7
football

| Games for basic abilities and capacities | Games for mini-football | Simplified games for 3v3 with corrective exercises | Developing young goal-keepers' exercises, including goal-keeper decathlon | Indoor 5v5 football |

4v4 triathlon

7v7 football

Level 4
(generally for boys and girls 12 years and up)

Games for
8v8
football

| Games for 7v7 football | The complete football test (16 individual and group tests) | Simplified games for 4v4 and 5v5 with corrective exercises |

5v5 triathlon

8v8 football

Level 5*
(generally for boys and girls 15 years and up)

Games for
official 11v11
football

| Games for 8v8 football | Collective training, especially standard situations | Individualized training, following the deficiencies of the players and their positions on the field | Programs for improving understanding of attacking (reception, positional and counterattack, attack from the second line, and maintaining possession of the ball) | Programs for improving understanding of defense (cover, pressing, anticipation, closing down an opponent) |

11v11 football

*Information on level 5 is presented in a second volume titled *Developing Game Intelligence in Soccer*, published by Reedswain Inc., 2005.

motion or participating in poorly structured competitions, as is the case with many young players. Players who take part in competitions specially designed for their age will have far more successful actions than in the traditional game, thereby leading to an increase in self-esteem.

The game of mini-football played with only three players per team is manageable for 8-year-old beginners and, with an additional goal-keeper, for 9-year-old players. In the same way, the players under 12 years consider the seven-member team game as suitably challenging and the under-14 players understand the game with eight players per team (played in the area between the two penalty boxes of the official field). The following table provides a brief description of this progression. Each game is explained in much more detail in the following chapters.

Logical Progression of Youth Competitions							
Age at start of season	Number of players	Substitutes allowed	Ball	Duration (periods × min.)	Rules of the game	Dimensions of the pitch	Age of the referee
8	3	1	No. 4	3 × 10	No off-side 4 goals Rolling substitution	24 × 30 m.	Under 18
9	3 or 4 incl. goal-keeper	1	No. 4	3 × 10	No off-side 4 goals Rolling substitution	25 × 35 m.	Under 18
10-11	7	3	No. 4	2 × 25	Goals 6 × 2 m. Rolling substitution	35 × 55 m.	Under 20
12-13	8	3	No. 4	2 × 30	Goals 6 × 2 m. Rolling substitution	Between penalty areas	Under 21
14 and up	11	5	Official ball (No. 5)	2 × 45	Official rules	Full field	No age restriction

Enjoyment of the Game

Naturally, when players execute more successful actions, they enjoy the game more. Every two years the difficulty and complexity of the competition are increased in perfect harmony with the growing physical and intellectual capacities of the players. When young players progress with the help of the Football Development Model from so simple a base and in such small increments, the occurrence of significant failure is out of the question. Enjoyment and confidence in their capabilities become the driving force for the players' motivation and further progress. A correct use of the model reinforces success, whereas the traditional way of subjecting children to the difficulty and complexity of the full game only reinforces failure. As success reinforces success, failure reinforces failure.

Unfortunately, most people still associate great performance with pain, struggle and exhaustion. In football, the idea that learning can be fun is still novel. Whatever is enjoyable seems to be forbidden. Even though playing is the mode in which children discover their world, too often the moment they get on the training ground, the joy of discovery is quashed.

The following illustration represents the difference between the current way of coaching and the coaching method suggested by the Football Development Model. At present, most children struggle to meet the demands of a competition geared toward adults. However, with the game tailored to a child's development and gradual progress to more complex activities, the youngsters can experience much more success and, most important, they enjoy the game.

In the future, football competitions will be tailored to match a child's gradual physical and intellectual development.

Ease of Application

Players aren't the only ones who reap the benefits of the Football Development Model. The model provides coaches with a complete and effective training plan that can easily be applied to their players. Applying the Football Development Model gives even the most inexperienced football coach the ability to gradually, yet effectively, guide young players into the full game of football. The result is already known: more intelligent and complete football players.

To become more familiar with the Football Development Model, teachers can even attend a refresher coaching course. For more information, send an e-mail to horstwein@eresmas.net. In such a course, coaches learn the reasons behind a particular training and competition program for a particular age group and how to implement that program. Coaches not only acquire a detailed knowledge of the model's contents and what objectives to achieve with each exercise or simplified game, but they also become familiar with the most effective methods and coaching style to apply.

Fixed Goals

To make the model as useful as possible to the coach, it has been structured in a hierarchical order, both with overall objectives (for example, games for mini-football) and specific, partial aims (for example, dribbling games or 3v3 triathlon) for each level.

For each game or exercise, specific goals have been identified. Having the goals fixed for each category provides these benefits:

➤ Gives coaches guidelines for structuring and developing the training and learning process and allows them, after assessing the content, to add their own training programs to those proposed in the model

➤ Helps link the proposed program to the fixed goals

➤ Adds incentives for the children, allowing them to focus their efforts on some definite objective, without having to guess why they are playing some way or what they are aiming toward

➤ Allows the coach to discover whether he or she is achieving the objectives and to make any necessary alterations

With the objectives clearly defined and fixed for each category of children's football—one of the key elements of this unique teaching and learning model—the children are not exposed to a training process in which mere improvisation and intuition on the coaches' part determine content. The development model incorporates relevant sport science and motor development research in its program. That way, countless correct habits are developed in the early years of learning, resulting in the desired improvement of performance at higher levels.

Most youth coaches teach several days a week, without knowing whether they are doing it correctly or not. For them, their old habits are comfortable; they're methods that they've used frequently without much thought. When exposed to the simple and effective training programs of the Football Development Model, however, they might well double their effectiveness, doing a better job in less time and with half the effort.

Coaching Philosophy

Without the right coaching philosophy, the Football Development Model will take you only so far. Coaches should always maintain a healthy, positive attitude during training and competition.

Philosophy During Competition

These are some principles that should be applied during competition.

➤ For boys and girls between 8 and 14 years old, always consider playing well as more important than winning. While learning to play, the participants must forget about the result of the game. They should be encouraged to take some risks, despite the fact that this kind of play might allow the opponents to score. Players, parents and coaches should consider competition only as another kind of training.

➤ Mobilize all your efforts to reach victory, but never look to win at any price. Victory should never be considered the only important thing to achieve.

➤ Don't mind losing a match, because defeat is always a possibility when competing; there is no guarantee of winning. If another team beats yours, it's generally because of their better play. It should never be because your team didn't put all its efforts into the game to win it. As long as you have tried hard and played up to capability to prevent the defeat, you never should feel like losers.

➤ Winning isn't as important, nor losing as bad, as most parents believe. It all depends on what a team was able to demonstrate. Players may win after having shown a poor game played in a destructive manner—and they may lose despite having played much better than the opponents and having enjoyed every minute of the game.

➤ Learn to play in a competition as though it is a matter of practice; train with the spirit of playing an important competition.

➤ Winning is only a consequence of playing well. That is why every player has only to try to give his or her very best. The result will fall like a ripe fruit falls from the tree.

➤ In all youth categories up to 14 years, coaching to win a match is easier than coaching to play the game well. However, playing well allows you to discover new solutions to old problems, again and again. Teaching to win, on the other hand, means you restrict the game mainly to those already-known skills and tactical moves that are important for winning it (like long clearances, kick and run philosophy, pressing defence). Yet when you compete that way, in the long run you also restrict and limit the complete development of the young players.

Maintaining a Positive Attitude

A coach of young football players should conscientiously do and say things that make the young players feel good, accepted, important, happy and successful. Try these simple gestures:

➤ A warm greeting, using the player's name
➤ A smile
➤ A thumbs-up sign
➤ A pat on the back
➤ Talking with players
➤ Playing some games or activities with them
➤ Asking their advice and listening to what they say
➤ Helping them learn something new or to improve something
➤ Helping players adjust their personal objectives
➤ Attending to all their questions
➤ Showing interest in their friends, family and hobbies
➤ Providing fun and enjoyable activities
➤ Giving encouragement
➤ Praising, avoiding criticism
➤ Including the youngsters in the teaching process through effective questioning

In addition to the right coaching philosophy, a successful football programme requires organization, community support, sound promotional efforts and a safe environment. Combining the right coaching philosophy with the step-by-step progression in the Football Development Model is a surefire formula for success. The experience

'If you want to win, you almost have to forget about winning.'

—*Laurence Morehouse and Leonard Gross*

Coaching Characteristics

Certain characteristics can help a coach become well accepted by his or her young players (Halliwell 1994). Here are some of those identifiable characteristics:

- Experience and success as a player
- Experience and success as a coach
- Pleasant appearance, in physicality as well as in dress
- Healthful lifestyle (habits)
- Correct proceedings in work: punctuality and efficiency
- Good organization of training sessions, meetings and travel
- Good communication level: knows how to explain concepts and also how to listen
- Good disposition—always has time for the players
- Ample knowledge of techniques and tactics and how to coach them
- High motivation for passing knowledge on to the players
- Positive approach—encourages and motivates players with positive remarks, creates enthusiasm and praises frequently

You help players more by encouraging them than you do by correcting them.

- Knows to coach from the bench: readjusts the team's play through quick decision making, changes players shrewdly and has a sense of humour
- Can exercise leadership in the dressing room as well as on the ground during training and matches
- Self-control—emotionally stable, transmits calmness and serenity, especially when conflicts arise
- Desires to improve constantly—looks out for new exercises and games as well as for new coaching methods or styles; self-critical in coaching
- Capacity to observe, analyse and correct mistakes or wrong habits
- Honest and fair with the young players—doesn't favour any particular player, demands a lot but is fair to everybody
- Open to any suggestion—stays flexible, listens to the suggestions of players and assistants
- Demonstrates true interest in players (and for their problems off the playing field)

of success in the tailor-made competitions is a great motivator for progressing even further, but so long as the federations, clubs and schools are not aware of the need to introduce this logical progression of competitions, improvement will not take place. When more federations decide, at no expense, to provide proper annual competition for each youth category, more children will have the opportunity to play well and to enjoy the game.

Winning Matches Versus Developing Talent

The saying 'The most important thing in sport is to take part and play' has long been forgotten in most of the football clubs, as many coaches are often using their young players as a platform for climbing the social and professional ladder. The culture of winning in children's sport causes damage on a daily basis—not just to children but also to the clubs they play in. The clubs affected are those whose quality of training is determined by the fact that they stop at nothing to win, regardless of whether their teams are for youths, juniors or beginners.

Unfortunately, very few clubs measure their success based on the number of players who are capable of joining a first or representative team after years of well-planned and well-executed training. Instead of playing to win, the coaches of those clubs concentrate on playing to learn and thus become winners in the long run.

According to a U.S. survey of children who took part in organised sporting activities in the late 1990s, 14 million out of 20 million North American children stopped participating after turning 13. Today the dropout rate for young athletes is alarming. Some studies in England, for example, report that up to 70 per cent of all who participate in youth sports choose to quit. Among the reasons given for this epidemic are starting too soon, playing too often, trying and training too hard, and becoming too specialised. Perhaps bad coaching should be added to that list—as a youth who has a coach consumed with winning at all costs is surely destined to burnout. Of course, it is natural for young athletes (and all too often their parents) to want quick results. But there are no shortcuts in sport, and coaches will fail if they are unable to accept that fulfilling potential takes time. In Spanish football, also, there is a lot of concern because of the constant increase in the number of 13- to 15-year-olds who abandon federated football after having trained and competed the adult way for six or more years. This large-scale desertion is because football, originally considered by children as a simple activity to be shared with some friends, has, with the passage of time, become a bitter experience for many young people. Now as far as they are concerned, it often entails frustration, a very rigid system of competitions and critical parents. It also means for them to be held up to the high expectations of coaches whose objective is not to train young people to understand and master the progressively difficult game of football. Rather, those coaches seek to gain as many victories as possible—at any price—and hence realise the consequent prestige of being able to apply for a better-paying job in the world of football.

Many professionals who are devoted to the organization, management, research, and teaching or training of nearly every sport debate the winning versus development controversy. It is also a hot topic for discussion among many parents, who regard their children's sporting activities as a springboard to social and economic success.

The key to the problem is that regional federations still claim that there is only one way to practice sport. In those organizations, the emphasis is placed on the search for the perfect player, justifying purely competitive practice that will aid selection of model players.

Unfortunately, in such a system, the less-able players are bombarded with endless objectives and are taught by their coaches to aim at excessive targets in order to achieve the best results as early as possible. Take the following example: In any youth section of a school, club or other institution, before starting to train young people, coaches have to choose between two very different types of work ethic:

1. Trying to lead their teams to a victory in the short term—at any cost.
2. Seeking to develop the children with an age-orientated, gradual and long-term approach to the complexity and difficulty of the game of football.

Unfortunately, the size and strength of young football players continue to be the most noticeable features of many teams. It's widely known that the bigger the player, the better results a coach will obtain in training. Players' size is frequently a deciding factor for team selection, especially in competitions for very young players. It can only be countered by clearly superior ball skill. But instead of coaching those ball skills, it is much easier to rely on size. In the older age groups, size becomes less influential, but the skills, not having been worked on, are now fatally absent.

Besides looking out for winning, coaches show a tendency to overemphasise tactics. But the absence of ball skills limits the options, and the only tactics that have any hope of being successful are inevitably negative and defensive.

By continuing to put a lot of emphasis on the win–loss record of a coach, we are creating a generation of players and coaches who are afraid to take risks because of fear of failure. For them, youth football is all about winning, very often neglecting the players' development. But the best youth coach is not the one who holds a fine win–loss record, but the one who accomplishes two things. First, he or she knows how to instill a real passion for the game in young students, inspiring a young player to improve on skills away from training (a novel concept for some). Second, he or she prepares players to succeed at the next level or category of youth football. That next level might mean preparing to play successful 7v7 football within the 11-year-old age group, making that jump from the under-16 to under-18 level, or from the under-18 level to the senior club team. Notice that nowhere in that definition did we mention winning.

Of the four major areas of football, the technical, tactical, physical and psychological realms, the physical is the easiest and quickest to develop. Therefore, when we continue to judge the qualities of a youth coach due to his or her win–loss record, we are encouraging future generations of youth coaches to focus mainly on physical aspects and old-fashioned coaching styles that facilitate winning. This moves us away from skill development, coaching an understanding of the game, and the introduction of a coaching style in which the young player is an independent thinker who doesn't rely solely on commands received from his or her coach.

It is not uncommon for coaches and, more particularly, parents of 8- to 12-year-old children to be impatient for their young players to achieve good results before their time. This obsession is the driving force behind many coaches' training programs, whereby they plan and supervise practice sessions that are exclusively football orientated. Unfortunately, those coaches neglect fundamental movement skills, coordination, speed, power and endurance as well as basic requirements for any good football performance such as perception skills, decision making, creativity, and managing the parameters of space and time.

As a result, there may be rapid successes in competition, but it is only a few years before those successes become few and far between. Because of the shortcomings of early athletic development without a view to achieving long-term goals and because

Comparing Team Goals: Winning Versus Development

Objective: To win	Objective: To promote development
Usually the players chosen are physically more advanced, especially in strength. They are generally the tallest ones. Their efforts to improve, regular attendance at the training sessions and behaviour as a team member receive less attention than does their actual performance on the pitch, which guarantees a win.	Everyone plays, not just the strongest players. The coach prefers players with ball sense who have an understanding of keeping it in possession and who are intelligent. Good behaviour on and off the pitch is one of the criteria when making a selection about who will play. Putting in effort is also important.
There is little room for younger, less-able or underdeveloped players. Football is undemocratic.	Everyone has the same right to play, regardless of physique and ability. Football is democratic.
From the age of 8, excessive emphasis is placed on tactics.	Matches serve to highlight how much skill players have and allow them to gain experience in tactics.
The players rely mainly on long passes (the goal-keeper clears the ball with the foot). They play faster than their skill level allows.	All players touch the ball. They tend to make short passes and dribbles. The goal-keeper usually throws the ball in order to construct the next attack.
There is little thought given to building up the game. Usually the ball doesn't pass through midfield and goes directly to the forwards through long passes.	The ball generally advances from defence to the midfielders, with the game based on communication and cooperation.
When attacking there are few changes of direction (switches from left to right).	Often the weight of the attack is changed with the objective of creating spaces for penetration.
The coach instructs with the objective of winning the match and the championship. The player has to obey the coach, who gives orders or instructions from the side-lines.	The coach motivates the team with the aim of improving performance of each player and the team as a whole. The player decides what the next move will be rather than the coach deciding for him or her, using perception and decision-making capacities.
To win, players are taught to be disloyal, to create traps, be dishonest and to deceive opponents and the referee. The ends justify the means.	Players are taught the values of sportsmanship, honesty, respect for rules and loyalty to the team.
The game plan has been thought out by the coach as it applies to adult players. There is no time or room for flair.	The individual is allowed to introduce his or her flair, skill and imagination.
There is premature specialisation in a particular role. Always the same play and the subs rarely get an opportunity.	Everyone gets several opportunities in the competition to experience different positions in the team. Everyone plays, regardless of ability.
Young people are prematurely exposed to adults' competition instead of adapting the competition for efficient learning. It takes many years of disappointments and frustration for the children to finally develop the same correct habits that adults show in 11v11.	With the aim to assure more efficient learning of the complex game of football, the competition is adapted according to physical and intellectual abilities, at each stage of the young person's growth. More self-esteem and fun are guaranteed.
Excessive emphasis is placed on physical skill and workout, as this is the manner in which results are achieved most quickly.	The surrounding environment is respected and the players' coordination and ability to play under various conditions improve with the variety of competitions to which the children get exposed each season.
To win, during training there is an emphasis on traditional methods of teaching.	To be able to understand the game and to make fewer mistakes, the method of discovering skills and capacities in simplified games is emphasised during training.
Everything connected with football is valued more than the individual. Dubious behaviour to achieve a good result is frequently accepted.	Priority is given to the development of the person through sport. Sport is used as 'training for life'.

of early specialisation, there is a higher chance of injury. Children trained in this way are more likely to give up playing football than those who have had the advantage of training in other sports (requiring basic skills gradually leading to high achievement).

It is widely known that broad experience and development are required for football training. If it is gained at the golden age of motor learning (7 to 11 years of age), a player is able to efficiently learn and apply later the most complicated techniques and tactics that high-performance soccer requires.

To motivate football coaches to modify the structure and content of their training sessions, or their vision for the development of their pupils between the ages of 8 and 13 years, it is necessary to enrich their competition menu with football decathlons, triathlons and pentathlons. At the same time, coaches can work to change the structure of the traditional youth football competitions. It is obvious that almost all teachers or coaches prepare their young players for a football competition with football-specific exercises and simplified games that simulate situations that arise during their competitive matches. But where the competition would be a multi-lateral one, the coach will be forced to adopt a more diverse training content. So long as children's competition remains exclusively football specific, then their coaches' training will also remain only football specific.

Consequently, for the development of young players, a correct relationship between diverse, or multi-lateral, and specialised training will only be achieved when 8- to 13-year-olds are exposed to competitions that foster fundamental motor skills *as well as* football-specific skills. Through differently structured youth competitions, teachers who want to win will learn and understand that, at this early stage, the emphasis has to be on the young athletes' overall development, avoiding early specialisation.

We simply need to have a clear and better understanding of when winning and losing are important, when they get in the way of proper education and development, and when both the development of a player and his or her strong will to win could be taught at the same time in an age-appropriate way. A solution for teaching to win *and*, at the same time, ensuring a correct development of the young athletes' innate potential could be the mini-football pentathlon competition (see page 128). Additionally, coaches could stage a tournament of football triathlons that features three simplified football games as well as two more multi-lateral activities that, when combined, would form other pentathlons.

Using multi-lateral competitions in age groups will require coaches to expose young football players to *fun*damental football-specific skills and capacities as well as to *fun*damental multi-purpose activities. This way the focus is on winning and having fun, while at the same time developing a complete football player and person.

The success of youth coaches should not be judged on the number of victories but on the number of players they are able to develop each season to become members of their senior or representative squad. In the long term, developing will always outplay winning.

Coaching Age-Appropriate Football

'The football field has boundaries, but the possibility
to be creative is boundless.'

Dettmar Cramer

Coaching Players Aged 5 and 6

Football clubs should have a school of initiation for children under the age of 7 that functions as a 'sport kindergarten' for players prior to football school.

In these programs, young players would be exposed to a great variety of recreational and motor activities. This training would have the purpose of overcoming motor deficiencies and any delays that players displayed in their coordination or the control of their body as well as in their understanding of the parameters of space and time. Here the popular daily games that previous generations enjoyed in the street, the patio or at the neighbouring park would be practiced. Consider the expert opinion that future generations may be condemned to a progressively sedentary life farther away from a healthy and natural atmosphere. Yet with a programme tailor-made for young children, the negative effects of living in a modern society, with computers and televisions, would be reversed. To allow 5- and 6-year-old boys and girls to grow healthier and to be naturally more athletic, children have to be exposed to physical activity at least twice per week for the following reasons:

➤ To recognise their bodies, to know the structural and functional possibilities and limitations of their whole bodies, as well as in each of its parts, to be able to consolidate a varied repertoire of basic motor abilities: to roll, to drag, to sit up, to stop, to walk, to raise, to descend, to run, to throw, to jump, to climb, to slide, to push, to kick.

➤ To develop their psychological and social state by means of popular games such as relays, runs with a variety of obstacles and tag games; to practice basic motor skills by means of exercises with a partner with and without a ball; to build up confidence in themselves and in their physical possibilities; to learn to communicate and to express themselves verbally and with gestures; to integrate into and cooperate with small groups; to appreciate the pleasure of physical activities; to learn to take care of their bodies and respect the bodies of others; and to know and to take care of their surroundings.

➤ To know how to orientate themselves in space while being aware of their closest surroundings using movements such as up and down, ahead, behind, close, far, between and around as well as notions of relative time such as fast, slow, at the same time, after, and notions of rhythm and the combination of several movements.

➤ To have some visual experiences of the ball's movement. They must learn, with a great variety of stimuli to correctly evaluate the speed of the ball, the highest point of its flight, the possible place it will land, the spin that has been given to the ball, the bounces of different kinds of balls on different surfaces. A well-organised school of sport initiation would possess balls of various materials, sizes, weights and elasticity.

➤ To dominate and control the ball better until they have mastered ball skills and, for those children who practice at home, aspire to become a 'magician of the ball'.

➤ To learn by means of a great variety of stimuli to confidently handle not only the ball on the ground and in the air but also to simultaneously control their bodies. At this point, the ball becomes the young players' best friend.

As the players in this age group learn to control their bodies and the ball, they should regularly do the following in their practice routine:

1. Dribble the ball
   * with the right and left hand;

- with a high bounce that is controlled to reach shoulder height, the height of the hip or the knee and in mixed combinations;
- with half and complete turns;
- letting it bounce through separated legs forward and backward;
- with a hand or a foot whilst balancing one extra ball on the nape of the neck;
- with one foot and another one with the hand; and
- letting two balls bounce simultaneously, touching them with both hands at the same or different moments so that they remain in motion.

2. Pass the ball between two or more individuals with different techniques
- with a hand in a frontal shot;
- from one hand, over the head, into the other hand;
- letting it bounce with one hand against the ground;
- like a discus throw or shot put;
- with two hands like in basketball;
- as though performing an official throw-in from the competitive football game;
- with the back to the partner, throwing the ball with two hands over the head; and
- passing it through separated legs to the partner behind as in a relay.

3. Receive and then control a ball thrown into the air with two hands
- with either foot on the ground, at hip height, level with the head and over it;
- with different surfaces of the foot on the ground or at the height of the hip;
- with the thigh, the chest or the head, allowing two touches before the ball must be perfectly controlled;
- with and without having to first perform a 360-degree turn; and
- from a sitting position on the ground,
- whilst the ball is still in the air, the standing player has to receive and return a ball thrown from a partner.

4. Mini-volley, with two or three players in a team, using the passing technique of handball.

Once an acceptable level of control and coordination in the fundamental motor skills is achieved, first without and later with the ball, and once they have reached the age of 7, the children of the school of sport initiation may enter the football school of their club or municipality. Here their trainers expose them not only to other basic motor activities but also to a great variety of fundamental technical-tactical situations of football as described in this book.

Coaching Players Aged 7 to 9

Once the 5- and 6-year-old boys and girls have completed their first organised motor experiences and practiced some fundamental football-specific exercises in the sport kindergarten, they are ready to be exposed to the first two levels of the Football Development Model. From the age of 7 upwards, our aim is to introduce young boys and girls step by step to the game of football and foster their interest in this sport. However, before coaches can apply the games and exercises at these levels, they must be aware not only of the specific characteristics and needs of players of this age group but also of some important game alterations to allow better learning. Finally, they must take into consideration some general rules that will stimulate a child's talent.

Children aged 7 to 9 have some significant characteristics:

➤ They lack fine motor skills.
➤ Their movements are usually whole-body actions with little accuracy.
➤ They have short bursts of energy and enthusiasm.
➤ They are still developing coordination and they are still clumsy.
➤ They play or participate for fun and for enjoyment.
➤ Their actions are not yet automatic or programmed.
➤ They are unsure what actions lead to success at a skill.
➤ They see every detail as being important.
➤ They are uncertain in their actions and in how to achieve desired outcomes.
➤ They lack a clear idea or model of a new skill.
➤ They cannot follow too many instructions or handle too much information at one time.
➤ They are unable to use feedback effectively.

By being aware of these traits, coaches can tailor their teaching to meet young players' characteristics and needs. The table on page 29 lists additional characteristics of young children and coaching strategies that should meet the youngsters' needs.

Coaching Players Aged 10 and 11

The third level of the Football Development Model further develops players' technical and tactical abilities and capacities through a variety of simplified games for teams of three players and later for teams of four players. In addition, level 3 presents a specialised training programme for developing young goal-keepers. Before putting these programmes to work, however, coaches should understand a little more about players.

Coaching players aged 10 and 11 years old is a rewarding field of operation. At this later stage of their childhood, many sources confirm that youngsters are in a 'golden age of motor learning' (Diem lectures). Many favourable conditions exist in the biological, psychological and motor spheres at this golden age: Both the body and mind are in harmony. Leaving the dream world behind, children now strive more than ever before for realism. The world of the unreal, the incomprehensible or of fantasy declines. The children's capacity for abstraction (that is, separating the essential from the less important) develops, and this advance favours their understanding and reading of game situations. For the first time, the senses awaken to the fact that all action is submitted to certain general rules.

Prepubescent football players still have an urge for physical activity, which favours their intrinsic motivation to become more and more involved in sports. However,

Tailoring Coaching Practices to Match Characteristics of Players Aged 7 to 9

Characteristic	Coaching strategy
Boys and girls under 10 have similar characteristics when it comes to sports.	Boys and girls should train and compete together.
The children are highly motivated and enthusiastic. They like to be active.	Maintain their motivation through a wide range of exercises and games. Avoid queues and players being stationary. Listen to what players say.
Children under 10 are generally egocentric and like to possess the ball the maximum time possible. They are very concerned about themselves.	Provide everybody with a ball. Plan competitions 1v1 to make maximum use of this egocentric phase. Promote fair play.
Players have yet to establish a motor pattern that allows the skills to be executed without thinking. Their whole attention is directed toward the ball.	Allow time to learn skills. Improve the skills through repetitions and vary them before you evaluate the skill level through a competition, which demands a correct execution. Design drill practice to avoid excessive decision making.
Everybody enjoys scoring. Scoring boosts self-esteem and confidence.	Practice simplified games as well as mini-football with its variations so that everybody scores and plays the ball frequently.
Attention capacity is limited. They are unable to process a lot of information.	Change activities frequently. Mix specific football exercises or games with multi-lateral games. Almost every 15 minutes vary the content and let them complete with only one substitute. Don't talk too much; it's better to demonstrate without talking at the same time. Introduce one thing only.
They are just starting to learn how to cooperate.	Select games in which cooperation leads to winning (like mini-football). The demands on players should not exceed their stage of development. Ask questions to involve the young players mentally.
They have no clear idea of an ideal performance and therefore rely entirely on their coach.	Demonstrate to allow young players a source of feedback.
They are sensitive to criticism and failure.	Under all circumstances be positive. Praise and give rewards often to reinforce an effort or an improvement.
They are less tolerant to heat and cold than adults are.	Ensure they wear adequate clothing. They lose fluid quickly.

instead of looking to meet their insatiable or unlicensed need for movement, as happened in the years before the age of 10, the youth now strive for good performance, profiting from the fact that their movements are now more controlled and carried out more economically and with single-mindedness. Trying to emulate the sport model, youngsters can show a real dedication for continuous improvement. In fact, children aged 10 and 11 are even more motivated to practice hard when a game is organised so that they can demonstrate their abilities to their friends and to the opposing team.

What does this new level of play mean for coaches? At this stage of young football players' evolution, their teachers must make a transition from simply presenting a great variety of multi-lateral and specific football activities to preparing a more systematic, intensive and purposeful practice of technical-tactical aspects of the football game. Exercises for developing speed, coordination and aerobic resistance are to be considered the pillars of multi-lateral development, while the understanding, practice and mastering of a great variety of simplified football games (played with teams of three or four players) are the cornerstones of building their specific improvement.

Special Considerations for Beginners

When coaching young players, consider adjusting the following to better suit your players' needs and skill levels.

Ball Size

Because the official ball is oversized and too heavy for young players, many children struggle not only to handle the ball in training and competition but may even exacerbate a knee condition called Osgood-Schlatter's disease. It occurs in growing children, commonly among young athletes who run and jump. This syndrome is characterised by pain, swelling and tenderness just below the knee, over the shin bone. However, with a smaller, lighter ball, players can move more naturally and in correctly executed movement patterns. The result is that they can acquire new skills much more easily and avoid injuries.

Instead of using balls of standard size and weight for all children regardless of their age, it is better to adapt the circumference and weight of the ball to the height and strength of young football players. Players aged 7 and under should play with a No. 3 mini-ball, which weighs less than 340 grams. For young players aged 8 and above, use the No. 4 ball, which weighs between 340 and 370 grams and has a circumference of 63 to 66 centimetres and encourages better and quicker learning during practice sessions and competitions. Experience has shown that even older players (up to age 14) feel more comfortable and capable with a No. 4 ball than with the regulation ball, which might best be reserved for players aged 15 years and above. (Note: A regulation ball weighs between 400 and 454 grams and has a circumference of 68 to 71 centimetres.)

There are many advantages to using a smaller ball. Because they weigh less, the smaller balls can be passed over longer distances, allowing children to play more like adults. This undoubtedly stimulates their perceptive capacities to a higher degree. Using the No. 4 ball places higher demands on visual skills, including peripheral vision, dynamic visual acuity and vision in the depth of the field.

The No. 4 ball also makes it possible for players even farther than 15 metres away from the ball carrier to actively take part in the game. In addition, the frequently observed clustering of players around the ball, characteristic of play at these age groups, is observed less often, compared with youngsters using the official ball approved by FIFA for adults. If players don't cluster around the ball, their observation, analyses and decision making are easier; they can therefore reach a higher level of play with fewer ball losses.

During the first four years of practice with young players, a coach should often insist on players' using the less-skilled foot. Thanks to the introduction of the No. 4 ball size, all the activities presented in level 1 of the Football Development Model (as well as many exercises and games of level 2) can be carried out with the 'wrong' foot, opening a much wider range of playing options that makes the game more attractive to the players.

Playing Area

The drills and games in the first level do not require the use of an entire football field. An area approximately 20 by 40 metres is needed, that is, less than a quarter of the area of the full field or almost the size of a basketball court. When you organise a simplified game for two teams, as coach you should always take into consideration that the less skilled and capable your players are, the wider and deeper the dimensions of the playing area should be. A small area often doesn't allow the player sufficient time to observe and analyse the game situation, and then make a quick decision about what skill to execute, why to execute it, and when and where to do it best. The smaller the area, in fact, the more demands are put on skills and on attention. Needless to say, a larger playing field facilitates successful play.

If only a small playing area is available, you must reduce the number of players taking part in the game. You compensate with this reduction in numbers for the lack of space; in other words, you are still trying to tailor the game perfectly to the young players' abilities and capacities. If all the players cannot be directly involved in the practice because of limited space, the 'extras' may carry out some additional activities while they wait. For example, they might practice juggling or balancing the ball outside the training area, shooting it against a fence or wall, or even executing exercises for improving their level of coordination and balance with and without the ball. In brief, it is important for coaches to select the correct dimension of the playing area based on the technical, physical and intellectual performance levels of their players and on the number of players involved in the game.

Goal Dimensions

The size of the goals also plays an important part in the teaching and learning processes with young players. To create a game of control, the rules of many simplified games require beginners to control the ball in the opposing wide goal area (between 6 and 20 metres wide). Wild shooting is not desirable! Players should handle the ball gently and with care, without using violent movements.

Wider goals help stimulate a young player's perception. For beginners (who generally direct most of their attention toward the ball) a wider, uncovered space between the cones is much easier to detect during the dribble. In addition, using wide goal areas gives the wings the same opportunities to score as a centre-forward has, thus leading to the habit of always attacking with sufficient width. With the use of wide goals, players do not tend to cluster around the goal as is the case when goals are established only in the centre. Thanks to having wide goal areas for practice sessions, young players have greater enjoyment in the game and their self-confidence increases.

10 REQUIREMENTS FOR DEVELOPING MORE CREATIVE PLAYERS

1. Declare war against the 11v11 game. The 11v11 game, which has stunted the vigorous development of young football players for many years, should be replaced by another type of competition tailor-made for younger players.

   Games like mini-football (3v3 on four goals), 7v7 football, and 8v8 football (played between the regular pitch's penalty areas) offer the adequate frame (in terms of space, number of players, ball size and weight) for children to express their creativity and inspiration in a more healthy environment: an environment that does not contain the stress of the 11v11 game with its adult-orientated rules.

2. Use more games and fewer analytical exercises. Practicing should happen in a game context.

   Statements such as 'The game itself is the best teacher' must be rediscovered and considered in the planning of all training sessions where drills predominate. Children should be exposed to more game plays (global method) and less practice with the analytical method.

3. Let the kids play without correcting them permanently. When playing, it is not always necessary for young football players to know the specific learning objectives of a practice. The learning objectives are always important for the coach but not for the players. Players should frequently have the opportunity to just play, or play just for fun, without having any specific learning as a main objective.

Playing football without thinking is like shooting without aiming.

© PA Photos

We should not forget that one essential part of the game is its unpredictability. This explains why the game is so fascinating for kids. Friedrich Schiller states perfectly the vital meaning of playing games: 'The human feels and behaves like a human when he plays'.

4. Children should have the chance to play in all positions and in reduced space. Young football players should have the opportunity to play in various positions in order to discover the roles and functions that these positions characterise. Experimenting with play in different positions stimulates creativity. For example, 7- to 9-year-old players could perform the many variations of the mini-football game (3v3 on four goals) instead of playing 7v7 football or 11v11; 10- and 11-year-olds may participate in a 7v7 game instead of competing in the 11v11 match; and 12- to 14-year-olds could play tournaments of 8v8 football instead of championships in 11v11. The problem of positional experimentation would be solved since a competition with fewer players, in a reduced space, stimulates creativity, while the full game, on a regular football pitch, only tires the young players physically and intellectually, limiting their creative play.

5. Only those who enjoy the game can be creative individuals. Each training session should include a great variety of games, not only football-specific ones. When children play, they should have fun and be excited by the game. If young players do not identify themselves with the game proposed by the coach, the creative capacity will remain dormant. The more that players enjoy the game and the ball, the more that playing stimulates the development of a creative way of interpreting football.

Bohm and Peat (1987, pp. 255-256) maintain in *Science, Order, and Creativity* that 'the establishment of objectives and patterns of behaviour as well as the obsession of efficiency produce a rigid knowledge which blocks the free flow of thinking and movements, both necessary to lead to a creative behaviour of the player'.

6. Give players the opportunity to create their own games and rules. In a simplified game, not only should the coach ensure that the objectives are mastered, but should frequently motivate the children to create different games through modifying the rules initially proposed. The variations of mini-football with four goals, played in a reduced space, promote the young players' creativity regarding rules.

   Also, from time to time during the training session, the coach should give players 10 minutes to play freely and to do what suits them best. This could be done in any part of the training session. Once young players are familiar with the coach's style, not only will their imagination and fantasy grow, but also their sense of responsibility, personal initiative, their daring to improvise and to be creative. Also, the potential leadership qualities of some players in the group may flourish.

7. Dare to risk and improvise without fearing the consequences. Young players should not be pressured by their coach to quickly pass the ball in order to allow better team play and winning. Young players who treat the ball as their best friend and often do their own thing are frequently more creative than those who accept what the coach demands. They should be allowed to improvise their play and take risks without fearing the possible consequences of having committed a mistake or to have lost possession of the ball. That is why young players should practice and play as often as possible without the presence of coaches (in the street, in the park or in the courtyard). A coach's absence allows the players to feel more comfortable, to explore their innate potential without the fear of getting criticised when committing mistakes.

'Only those who attempt what they cannot do, will grow.'

—*Ralph Waldo Emerson*

8. Place more importance on training the right hemisphere of the brain. Once young children enter school, the left hemisphere of the brain (where logical thinking, mathematical reasoning and verbal expression are located) is mainly the one getting stimulated. Students are expected to solve tasks (generally 'closed', perfectly defined tasks) along the lines indicated by the teacher without being allowed to contribute something of their own to the solution of the task or to be creative. Nevertheless, the development of creative potential needs a systematic stimulation of the right hemisphere of the brain. That is why in school, as in football training, 'open' tasks are needed more than ever that demand young people be creative and to find a solution of their own to any given problem.

   Instead of being the sole agent in the teaching and learning process, most of the time the coach should transfer the responsibility of the situations he or she generates to young players and ask them, through systematic questioning, to solve the problems. A true master in coaching never gives the answers to problems but helps the players find and discover them on their own, guiding them to correct results. The well-structured simplified game of football itself must become the teacher, not the coach.

9. More creative coaches mean more creative players. To see more creative players on our football pitches in the future, or players who are innovative and do things in a completely different way from the norm, coaches will have to rethink the following:

While practicing or competing, coaches should not always punish the mistakes of their players, since this will restrict the players from taking risks and prevent their creativity, fantasy and imagination from flowing.

In the training sessions more space or time should be allowed for players to experiment with new moves that occur to them spontaneously. A more informal environment—as seen when football is played on the street, the beach or in a park—helps to develop more creative players.

Any flash of creative behaviour in a player should be recognised by the coach, who should do everything to encourage the player to be different and to look out for original solutions, raised by the players themselves, to the problems inherent in football.

10. The football environment is an enemy of a young player's creativity. Most of our young talent grows in an atmosphere that is noticeably hostile toward creativity. On most football fields young players are dominated by instructors, who allow relatively little freedom of movement and decision making: The opinions of young players are not taken into account. For the coach it is important to have everything under control, and, in the case of a player departing from the norms, the player is punished and called on to respect the coach's orders. Many coaches think for their players instead of stimulating them to think by themselves.

Over the years, young football players are left in no doubt about the coach's instructions and play according to the information received but without putting in their proper thoughts and personal flair. When these young players reach the age of 15 or so, it is obvious that they will face serious problems if they are requested to make their own decisions, since, for many years, they have been trained to execute only what adults have told them.

Structuring a Training Session

It is not only the quality but also the variety of the activities that determines the degree of success and acceptance of the practice session and its contents by young players. Just as someone in a restaurant orders a tasteful and varied meal after having studied the menu carefully, the coach should create an effective and enjoyable coaching session for beginners by selecting various activities from the menu. For example, at level 1 a coach chooses from a variety of games focused on basic abilities, creating a 'menu' of several courses:

Aperitif—one of the simplified games for two-player teams or, if the beginners still are not ready for that, a multi-lateral game

First course—a dribbling game with one or two variations

Second course—a game for passing, receiving or shooting

Dessert—a tackling game, a game in the maze or a test selected from the decathlon

A drink—a multi-lateral activity or simplified game for teams of not more than three players

To ensure a high level of attention from the beginners, it is best to change the proposed activity every 15 minutes. A coach should also alternate exercises and games of great intensity with those making less physical demands. The games and exercises in the Football Development Model are not to be done in any rigid order. It is up to the individual coach to put together a combination of exercises that is right for his or her players.

Coaching Players Aged 12 to 14

The fourth level of the Football Development Model is designed for players aged 12 to 14. At this stage the coach can forge a link from children to the sport for the rest of their lives. However, this can only be accomplished if the coach understands the players and exposes them to an effective and enjoyable football programme that is tailored perfectly to their desires and expectations.

The intense physical and hormonal transition induced by puberty leads to a loss of a child's balance in mobility and less responsiveness to the development of motor skills. It is therefore essential at this stage of the young players' evolution that they be exposed to collective (team) activities in which they overcome the characteristic insecurity, unsteadiness and sense of isolation.

By this time, youth players become more socially aware, more inclined to show off, and more prone to compete with their team-mates and opponents for attention. They may also want to show their independence and may even at this stage feel resentful of authority. For all these reasons, the older youths in this age group can pose special problems for the coach not only from the aspect of discipline but also in accepting what he or she teaches. However, along with these problems come a number of advantages. As the players are now much more responsive to cooperative activities with other players, this is an age group in which team play is learned with a certain ease. During this stage of their evolution, too, youths are making important decisions that may influence the formation of their character and personality.

If some of the team's players are genuine beginners and are unskilled because they have started late in playing the game, this situation can pose a problem. These late beginners may lack the elementary ball skills necessary for team play and may also not be able to learn football skills as easily as they might have been able to do some years earlier. Keeping all these characteristics in mind, here are some suggestions for coaching players aged 12 and 14:

➤ Acknowledge the players' taste for competition by using competitive exercises, especially those that require the players to attain measurable objectives, such as passing the ball at a target.

➤ Consider every player a unique individual.

➤ Encourage players as often as possible. Although this is important at all ages, and praise is always preferable to blame, players in this age group are particularly sensitive to remarks from the coach that may reduce their status in the eyes of their friends. Therefore, avoid criticizing players of this age in public!

➤ Since the players are physically bigger and may have had experience in other sports, it may be necessary to be more clear-cut and strict in applying the rules.

➤ The players are usually anxious to get into full-scale match play as often as possible, so you should explain to the players why each of the practice exercises is important for performing well in the match. This encourages them to accept the need for practice routines.

➤ Knowing *why* to do it and *what purpose* it serves is particularly important when it comes to motivating young players to overcome, with a variety of physical stimuli, their lack of coordination, balance (equilibrium), mobility, or any deficiencies in speed, resistance, and strength. In fact, these stimuli for the development of physical capacities and coordination should be interwoven in the players' football sessions as often as possible.

Toward a Different Coaching Style

Because the coach's philosophy and training programme often decide whether a child will stick with the game of football or look to other activities, coaches must strive to adapt to the sport's ever-changing demands. New knowledge appears daily, opening up possibilities we had never thought of some decades ago. What is considered valid today could already be out of date tomorrow, due to the frenetic evolution in many aspects of life. The path to success in football is always under construction. The construction has to be seen as a process, not as an objective that must be reached in a particular given time. The game of football evolves continuously, and every coach should aim to adapt to its ever-changing demands in order to stay competitive.

The creativity of the players is the source from which a coach should drink daily.

One of the principal aims in the formation of football coaches is developing people who can do new things, without blindly repeating what other generations of coaches did in the past. Striving for excellence demands more creativity, innovation and mental flexibility. Instead of teaching their players what they experienced during their past career as a player and coach, they must learn to unlock the innate and dormant potential of their players. How can coaches achieve this? First of all, the tutors of future coaches (as well as those who already train players on a daily basis) should make sure of the following:

➤ Encourage divergent thinking in their students.
➤ Let every player freely express personal opinions.
➤ Develop and apply new technical-tactical movements.
➤ Be creative to ensure success in the game.
➤ Remember that players generate most of their knowledge and experience on their own.

To sum up, coaches should use a different teaching style, one not as reliant on instructions or commands with the players obeying and being pushed into a receptive or passive role. Instead of acting as a trainer or instructor, coaches should become consultants, observers, planners, or organisers of information and skills, encouraging their players to advance and to excel until they are able to surpass the coach's own limitations.

13 Tips for Stimulating the Talent of Young Players

1. Consider the use of a No. 4 ball for training sessions and competitions. The No. 4 ball is recommended by the World Health Organization, or WHO, for health reasons, and by the world of football, to facilitate young kids' acquisition of technical skills and for them to achieve a superior tactical learning.

2. Use the many variants of mini-football with four goals (where, instead of attacking one centralised goal, the ball has to be kicked in one of two goals not less than 12 metres apart) with the purpose of systematically stimulating the perception skills. The perceptual capacity has to be considered as a base for correct decision making and for the execution of technical actions. In doing it this way, teaching football to young players sufficiently stimulates the perception skills as well as the cognitive capacities, both aspects of the game still underestimated in many countries.

3. Organise competitions regularly, each tailor-made to the mental and physical capacities of the young kids. For example, play games such as a football triathlon 3v3 or 4v4, a mini-football pentathlon, a goal-keeper decathlon, a decathlon for football players or a heptathlon. To stimulate their game intelligence, offer young talents more than a single official competition in one season. Competing in the same season in several competitions that are different from the traditional ones will improve young players' capacity for adaptation and improve the flexibility of their brains. In all these competitions, children's participation, enjoyment, recreation and fun are more important aspects than winning.

4. For children aged 10 and 11, the season should be divided into two parts. In the first half of the season, a competition is played without awarding points and without establishing a league table. In the second part of the season, a championship is played with three periods of 15 minutes and intervals of only five minutes in which the coaches may exchange comments with the players. Coaching from the side-line is forbidden.

5. In all youth football competitions, allow substitutions as in basketball, volleyball or hockey. That is, the same player may be taken off and return as often as the coach prefers. The rolling substitution generates a much better team spirit within the group of players, avoids overloads and allows better communication, since the coach may take a player off the field to give him or her any necessary technical or tactical comment.

6. To cultivate important but often-forgotten aspects of the game, such as fair play and sportsmanship toward opponents, team-mates and the referee, each team receives the opportunity to present the referee with one golden card, with the name of a player written on it, at the end of the game. The player named must always be from the opposite side. In case nobody has demonstrated good sportsmanship, no card is handed to the referee. At the end of each season, the player who received the most cards from opponents is considered sportsman of the season.

7. To diminish the percentage of anaerobic effort in a game played on the full field, convince the authorities to prohibit 11v11 competitions. Instead, competitions with three, then seven and later eight players on the field should replace the full game. The field should increase in size at the same rate as players increase in their technical, tactical and perceptual abilities, as well as in their understanding of the game.

8. Provide sufficient information on multi-purpose games to make sure that in each preparatory session the players are exposed for 30 minutes to multi-purpose motor activities that improve their level of coordination.

9. In all youth competitions, a rule should be created that allows a team that is losing with a difference of three goals (0-3, 1-4, 2-5 etc.) to introduce one additional player into the game. This rule will force the winning team to continue to try hard and play as well as they can.

(continued)

(continued)

10. Regularly supervise young players' development in the football schools of initiation. Convince coaches of the importance of using the prescribed activities as instruments to strengthen not only technical, tactical, visual, cognitive and physical capacities in the children, but also healthy habits in practicing sport.

11. Consider only those football schools of initiation that apply the philosophy and the recommendations of the national or regional body of the appropriate football federation. If they fulfill the norms imposed by a certification committee, these schools will have the right to use the badge of the federation alongside their names. This practice will attract the interest of parents and the public, and it will also garner possible benefits. These might include free insurance, discounts on sports equipment, and free access to special training seminars or camps organised by the federation. Other advantages could be help in connecting with other institutions (interchanges), the organisation of sport or cultural events, or the use of medical equipment for injury prevention.

12. Create a manual that orientates the coaches to periodical communication with the parents and informs the coaches how to let parents collaborate in the important tasks of supporting the ethical, moral, physical and intellectual growth of the players and how to leave aside the material interests that consumer society wants to impose on the world of youth football.

13. A coach of young, talented players who always wins will ultimately lose in the end. This means the coach has done everything to ensure his or her own professional future and not the future of his or her talented players. In youth football we say, 'To win one less cup in a football school means that we frequently win a more promising talent'.

4

Games for Basic Abilities

'Tomorrow's success is founded on today's preparation.'

Sir William Osler

The first level of the Football Development Model has the task of introducing children aged 7 and up to football and developing their interest and love for the game. During these decisive years of children's development, coaches must give their young players adequate training tools and stimuli to enable them to play with confidence and enjoyment. If they do not, they may convert their young charges, now full of potential, into future second-class athletes. Coaches should always aim to support the healthy development of children who start out motivated to practice their favourite sport. The less rigid and more varied their teaching style and the training programme they adopt, the more pleasant and comfortable the atmosphere will feel to children.

This chapter introduces a variety of games that form level 1 of the Football Development Model. These games are not to be played in any rigid order; instead, you can assemble a variety of games and create a training session that works best for your group of players. With adequate exposure to these games (at least twice a week), beginners quickly gain their first experiences in such basic game situations as these:

➤ Dribbling the ball
➤ Receiving, controlling, passing and shooting the ball
➤ Taking the ball away from the opponent
➤ Considering their team-mates or opponents in attack as well as in defence

Apart from exposure to special programmes focusing on the correct execution of the fundamentals in simplified game situations, the youngsters will take part in level 1 competitions, the decathlon and the 2v2 football triathlon that have been specially adapted to their motor developmental phase.

Because they are egocentric, few 7- and 8-year-old beginners are capable of successfully playing team games. Every player likes to be the protagonist and tries to keep the ball in his or her possession for as long as possible. The games and exercises in the first level have been designed with this in mind.

The games in level 1 are designed to satisfy a young player's need to possess the ball for as long as possible.

Juggling and Balancing the Ball

Young beginners, besides developing their coordination and motor skills, are introduced in the first years of practice to an array of exercises and games for learning—and then improving—the ability to juggle and manoeuvre the ball on the ground and in the air. Two training sessions a week are insufficient for players as young as 7 years to develop a ball sense that will give them an extra edge. At this age players should spend several hours a week during their leisure time juggling with different-sized balls until they learn to handle and control the ball in all possible situations. With a little creativity, all kids and their coaches can invent appropriate programmes using partners, walls, nets and other resources.

Dribbling Games

Dribbling games help players develop the ability to control the ball and also aid balance, footwork, speed, technique, change of direction and coordination. These qualities are key to further discovery of the beauty of football; they allow players to quickly reach a satisfying level of play. Although you will find the next section of games and later programmes numbered to represent a progression from easier to more difficult exercises and games, this doesn't mean that you must follow the activities in order. Presenting a more-complex problem on occasion challenges the more-talented players, while using easier exercises gives the less-talented youngsters the confidence and motivation to try harder.

1. Parallel Lines

Establish two parallel lines set 2 metres apart. Two players stand side by side on the first line, facing the second line. When the coach signals, both players dribble their ball down to the second line, then turn around and dribble it back. The first player to dribble the ball 10 times across both parallel lines wins. To maintain control of the ball while changing direction, the player should experiment with the use of different surfaces (exterior, interior, the sole and the heel) of both feet. Which technique assures the quickest turn?

VARIATIONS

- Vary the distance between both parallel lines, up to 5 metres.
- None of the players should touch their ball in between the central zone formed by the two parallel lines. Start with a zone that is only 1 metre wide and later extend it to 2 metres, 3 metres, then 4 metres.
- The ball can be played with the less-skilled foot only.

2. The Tunnel

Two players face each other at a distance of 1 metre. Player 1 has 30 seconds to pass the ball as many times as possible through the tunnel formed by the separated legs of player 2. The first player kicks the ball through his or her partner's legs and then runs behind player 2 to return kick the ball to the original side. Meanwhile, player 2 remains still and counts the number of goals scored by the opponent. Then the players switch roles, and player 2 gets 30 seconds to pass the ball. The winner is the player who, using either the left or the right foot, passes the ball more often through the tunnel formed by the opponent. In case of a tie, repeat the activity.

VARIATIONS

- The player who forms the tunnel stands in a neutral zone of 2 metres. The player with the ball passes it from outside of the zone through the opponent's legs, using either the left or right foot. The stationary player counts the number of goals scored in 30 seconds from outside of the neutral zone. Both players then alternate roles until both have competed twice. The winner is the player who scores the most goals in the two attempts. In the event of a draw, repeat the activity.
- Immediately after a goal is scored, the player who forms the tunnel changes the position of one 'goalpost' (one foot) by pivoting and changing directions.

3. Eyes Up While Dribbling

This exercise is done with three players. Player 1, the ball carrier, dribbles to player 2, who is about 20 metres away. While dribbling the ball, player 1 lifts the head as often as possible to be able to count the number of fingers shown by his team-mate (player 2) in front. The latter, after having received the ball, practices the same dribbling and lifting the head to count, but goes in the opposite direction, while player 3 indicates (twice) different number of fingers. The coach should make sure players practice dribbling the ball with either foot.

VARIATION

- Various players dribble their ball in both directions around a square (5 metres per side), going continuously into and then immediately out of it, using either foot. The goal is to avoid a clash with other players who dribble in and out of the square in the opposite direction.

4. Avoiding Collisions

To start, two players must dribble their ball to the opposite corner (about 10 metres away) while trying to avoid the other players. The players waiting at the opposite corner return the ball by dribbling along the same diagonal path. First the practice is carried out with two balls and four players, and later the intensity and difficulty are increased by using four balls and involving eight players at the same time. To avoid injuries, do not organise this game as a competition between the teams!

5. Precise Passing

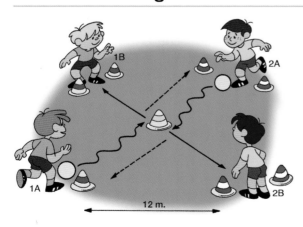

Four players pair up and form a square; the partners (players 1A and 1B and players 2A and 2B) are adjacent to one another. The two players in diametrically opposite corners (players 1A and 2A) each have a ball. At the same time, they start to dribble the ball on the left driveway, or imaginary lane that is left of the cones, until they reach the cone in the centre. From there they pass the ball on the run with the right foot, passing it to the left toward the cone goal in that direction. That goal area receiving the pass is occupied by the players' partners, players 1B and 2B, who now proceed the same way in the activity. The first pair to score 10 goals wins.

VARIATIONS

- Before executing the pass, the player has to carry out a dummy pass in the opposite direction.
- To introduce triangle play (wall passes or one-twos), the receiver has to return the ball immediately into the run of the passer who is now running into the goal opposite his or her starting position. After 10 triangular passes, both players change functions. Later on, both practice with an initial pass to the opposite side.

6. Black and White

Players line up in a row and are separated into two teams, each with a shirt or pinny of the same colour (black or white, for example). Each player has a ball for this activity. Practice this drill first without the ball, then with it. One team faces one direction, the other team faces the opposite direction. Upon the coach's signal, all players dribble a ball until they cross the far line, 12 metres away from the starting point in either direction. A team wins if all its members are first to cross the end-line with the ball under control.

VARIATIONS

- The coach designates one team (with the black shirts, for example) as dribblers. While the players with shirts of this colour try to reach the proper end-line dribbling their balls, the other team (not using balls) chases the attackers, trying to prevent them from dribbling their balls across the end-line.
- Both teams face each other from a distance of only 4 metres apart.
- Instead of defending, each of the team of nondribbling players remains at the start line and tries to hit his or her assigned (personal) opponent with the ball, which he or she kicks toward the escaping attacker.

7. Zigzag

Set up the field, dividing it with lines (see the illustration). Have the children first practice their running and turning techniques on the field without a ball. Players run from the starting line to the second line, then return to the starting line and this time run to the third line, returning to the second line before running all the way to the finish line. The turning around gives this activity its name. Next, have the players train

to dribble the ball as they run the same zigzag course. Then you can organise a competition, splitting players into two performance levels in order to motivate them all. All the lines must be passed there and back with the ball under control.

VARIATION

- Use a relay with teams of three players. Set up cones at the lines designating the course, using five cones per team, and place a ball at the first cone for each team. Player 1 on each team collects the first ball placed at the first cone (step 1) and carries it to the third cone (step 2). After its deposit, the player returns without the ball to catch the second ball from the second cone (step 3) and dribbles it two cones farther (step 4) to place it aside

the fourth cone, leap-frogging the ball left on the third cone. Continue in this fashion to the final line. After having deposited the first ball at the fifth cone, player 1 runs out of the field to touch his or her team-mate at the opposite side who does the same zigzag path through the cones, running in the opposite direction. The first team to finish its course correctly wins.

8. Changing the Square

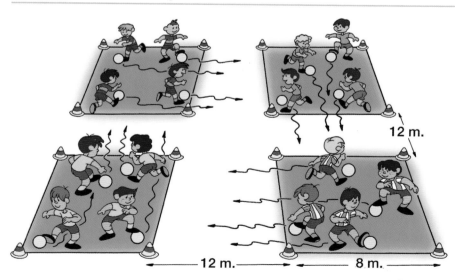

Set up teams of four youngsters each, giving each a ball. Form squares (see illustration), marking the corners with cones. The children should practice this activity first without a ball and later with a ball. Every time the coach gives a visual signal, all a team's players run (without and later with the ball) toward the next square, keeping control of their balls. As coach, give them an instruction or a visual signal to run either in a clockwise or anti-clockwise direction. (Be sure to make it clear which way to run, from what square to what square, as most very young children do not know the terms clockwise and anti-clockwise.) The team that manages to control all their balls first in the next square wins. Different teams running with the ball in opposite directions should be avoided because of the risk of head injuries through collisions!

VARIATION

- Have a defender situated between the squares. This child tries to delay the opponent's attack and conquer at least one ball. He or she then must dribble that ball into the square from which the attack was launched, the player tackled remaining to take the original defender's place.

9. Twice Around the Square

Youngsters do this activity in pairs to practice running and dribbling skills. Mark out a square (see illustration). Have players first practice the course without the ball and then with the ball. Two players located at opposite corners of the square simultaneously start out to dribble, going twice around the square in the same direction (clockwise or anti-clockwise). The first player back to his or her starting position wins. Practice and competition should be carried out in both directions to ensure that all players learn when to use the left or the right foot. The coach should explain good technique and then question them continually about the distance of the ball in relation to the feet while dribbling. Here are questions to ask: When should the ball be 'carried' close to the feet? How might an attacker save time? Which foot should be used in the change of direction when running clockwise (anti-clockwise)?

VARIATIONS

- After having completed half of their drill around the square, each player must turn around at the second cone and return to the starting point.
- Set up a course for Around the Triangle: Mark off an equilateral triangle and set up four cones along one (the base) side of it (see illustration). Players compete in pairs. Both competitors start from different locations around the triangle. As they get to the base of the triangle, they must dribble in and out of the four cones before dribbling up the next side. They learn to dribble with either foot and to execute different dribbling techniques using different surfaces of the feet.

10. Bandit

Mark the field with cones to indicate home bases, placing each cone at least 10 metres apart from one another. Form up to four teams per playing field, each team made up of just two players. Designate a home base, placing four balls there for each team or pair of players. After you give a visual signal to start, each player steals balls from other teams' home bases and deposits them at his or her own base. No tackling or defending of the home base is allowed. Whichever team has the highest number of balls after 30 seconds of play wins the game.

11. Occupying an Empty Goal

This activity is something like a football version of musical chairs, a game that most children already know. Mark off a circle about 15 metres in diameter, using about 10 cones to create the inner and outer edges of the path. These cones also designate five goals. Give each player a football. Six players at a time dribble their ball in any direction around the circle formed by the five goals. After you give a visual signal, all the players try to occupy one of the five empty goals. Whoever does not succeed loses a point.

VARIATION

• Use the same setup as above, but designate a neutral defender who makes the task of the attackers even more difficult.

12. Pivoting

One player, a receiver, stands 3 metres behind a 3-metre-wide cone goal, facing a team-mate who feeds him or her a 10-metre pass. The receiver runs toward the travelling ball with the intention of receiving and controlling it in front of the goal. Once he or she gains control, the player dribbles the ball sideward to one cone and then, with a sudden change of speed, turns toward the other cone. The player must make sure he or she is always placing himself or herself between the ball and the imaginary defender (represented by the cone goal). Once the player has rounded the goal, after one or two direction changes he or she turns and penetrates through it.

13. Staying in the Shade

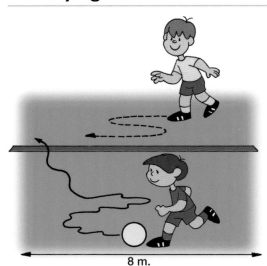

Try this at a practice when there is plenty of sun and the opportunity for objects to create shadows. Pair up children and have one be an attacker, the other a defender. Designate a line between them. Position the defender so that the sun is directly behind the youngster, producing a good shadow. The attacker tries to maintain the ball for as much time as possible in the shade of a defender, who continuously moves toward the left and right side in front of the attacker but stays beyond a line drawn between them, which the defender is not allowed to cross. It helps the children to first practice this shadowing without the ball to improve their body positioning, balance and footwork.

VARIATION

• Have the players switch roles. The attacker dribbles the ball, first slowly and then faster to either side, while the defender without the ball tries to shadow the attacker with the aim of not allowing even a ray of sun to burn the skin of the ball.

14. Practicing the Drag

Give each of the players a ball and, for each child, set up cones in a row to designate a running course (see illustration). Each player carries the ball toward a cone (representing an imaginary defender), then drags the ball square to the right side, collecting it after a distance of about 3 metres. In dragging the ball, the attacker has to change his or her speed and direction. Explain to the youngsters the idea of dummy moves and feints, and have them practice executing the dummy moves. First practice the drag from left to right, later from right to left.

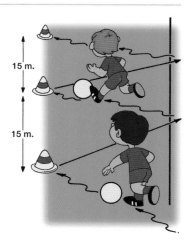

15 m.

15 m.

15. Drags From Left to Right

Position eight cones as shown in the illustration to mark off the drag areas. Explain to the children that they should experiment using different techniques to beat an opponent, including different kinds of body or foot dummies during the execution of the drags. To stimulate the young players' creativity, the coach declares the player with the finest technique (with no technical mistakes) or the most original dummy as winner.

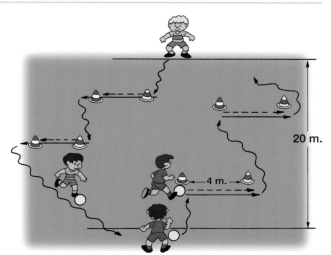

20 m.

4 m.

VARIATIONS

- Practice drags from right to left (see illustration to right). The attacker should always dribble the ball first toward the right cone before dragging it suddenly, with one touch only, toward the left one. Once the ball runs beyond the level of the left cone, it should be collected after a quick change of speed.

- Drag the first goal from left to right, and the second from right to left.

- Drag the first goal from right to left, and the second one in any direction you wish.

- Drag against 'handicapped' defenders, who remain inside the goal area (between the two cones), their right feet always keeping contact with or touching the

goal-line (see illustration to right). First the defender should be outplayed with a drag from left to right, then from right to left, and then as indicated in the last variation (with the conclusion left up to the individual player). This variation helps youngsters learn to always observe the defender before attempting to beat him or her with a drag. The defender in the second goal indicates through his or her position (putting weight clearly on one foot) on which side the attacker should beat him or her. The attacker must also learn to stay out of the defender's range of action.

16. Playing 1v1 in a 5-Metre Square

Mark off 5-metre squares with cones. Pair up the youngsters, designating an attacker and defender for each pair. To start, the attacker and defender stand at diagonally opposite corners of the square. The attacker scores when he or she manages to control the ball across one of the two red goal-lines in front of him or her. Before introducing the ball, have the children first practice the game without it, like a game of tag, to work out optimal body position, balance and good footwork.

VARIATION

- Give a visual signal for both players to run once around the square, starting from their diagonally opposite corners. The player who first completes the full turn then runs into the centre of the square to pick up the stationary ball. Using drag techniques (see previous two games), the player then dribbbles the ball across one of the two goal-lines.

17. Avoiding the Tackle

Pair the youngsters, designating an attacker and a defender. The playing field should have two lines, set about 15 metres apart. In this game, the attacker with the ball has the objective to dribble across the opposite line without losing possession to a defender. To start the play, the defender is 1 metre behind the attacker, aiming to tackle him or her from behind or from a side. The attacker, pursued by the defender, begins by running from the starting line toward the far side of the field. However, once the attacker dribbles the ball for at least 5 metres, he or she may choose to double-back and carry the ball across the starting line. In reaching either line, the attacker gets a point.

To get free of the defender behind him or her, the attacker may

- turn around, shielding the ball with his or her body;

- sell the defender a ball-stop dummy, using a backward change of speed to control the ball on the end-line in front of him or her; or
- dribble with the ball across the run of the defender, cutting off the defender's access to the ball with his or her body.

At the moment the defender crosses diagonally in front of the attacker, the defender must slow his or her speed.

18. Chasing the Dribbler

Outline a square on the playing field with four cones. Direct two players to positions outside and at opposite corners of the square. Only one of them has a ball; the other player chases the ball carrier around the square. During the first trial (level 1) the defender has to try to touch the attacker with one hand. Later (level 2), the defender has to touch the ball with either foot. For every cone reached with the ball under control, the attacker gets one point. The attacker learns to improve his or her play by dribbling the ball out of the reach of the defender whenever the latter gets near the attacker.

VARIATION

- Play this game with four players: two attackers and two defenders. Give a visual signal for each defender to start from the cone directly behind the attacker, aiming to immediately pressure him or her. The defender should try to prevent the attackers from completing a run around the square (award one point for a successful defence). Defenders and attackers switch functions until one of them scores five points.

19. Hot Pursuit

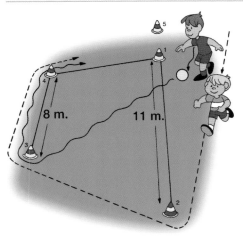

Mark off a trapezoid on the field, with four cones set at slightly uneven distances as in the illustration. A fifth cone serves to form the goal-line with the first cone. Children play in pairs, one being the attacker and one the defender. The attacker dribbles the ball around a triangle formed by three cones. As soon as the attacker begins, the defender reacts and follows, trying to prevent the attacker from keeping the ball under control as he or she reaches the goal at the end of the circuit. However, the defender has a handicap: He or she must run a longer distance (around all four cones) in order to catch the attacker. Every player attacks and defends twice. The winner is the player who, after having completed the dribble around the cones, controls the ball more often in reaching the goal-line (cones 1 and 5). In case the result is a draw, hold a playoff.

20. Tag Game

This game improves tackling and dribbling skills and can be played well by five children. Designate a rectangle for the playing field with two parallel sides twice as long as the other two. Each child has a ball. While all players are controlling their own ball, they also all try to dispossess any other player with a tackle. Any tackle that dispossesses an opponent (or plays the ball out of the square) counts as one point. In case one player loses his or her ball, that child returns to the square and continues the game until someone has reached five points.

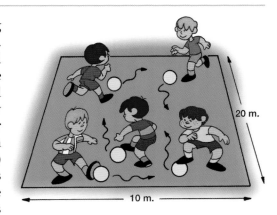

VARIATION

• Tackles count only if they are executed with the left foot.

21. Cops and Robber

Mark off a square as shown in the illustration. Group the children into threes, with one called the robber and the other two cops. Children play to see how long the robber can control the ball within the delineated playing space against both police, who also must control their footballs. The stress conditions of this game give players the chance to practice keeping their heads up while dribbling the ball, applying dummies, and applying quick changes of direction and speed, as well as improving their capacity to stay out of the reach of a defender. It is good training to play this game first without balls.

VARIATIONS

• Perform Cops and Robber as a simultaneous competition between two teams in two fields side by side. Team 1 positions its robber in the first field (A), while its two policemen chase the robber of team 2 in the second field (B). Team 2, meanwhile, positions its two cops in field A and its robber in field B. The two policemen who first catch their assigned robber are the winners.

• Use only one 22-metre square and pairs of youngsters, one pair in each area or square. Without leaving the square, the attacker tries to maintain possession of the ball for as many seconds as possible against an active defender. After five trials to establish a record, the attacker and defender switch roles. First try out this game without a ball as a game of tag, then practice with the ball to learn to systematically apply dummy moves and to protect the ball with the body against a defender. After each turn, the two competitors should have a complete rest.

22. Maintaining Ball Possession

Mark off the playing field as in the illustration, at first making it about 15 metres square and later a rectangle of 10 by 15 metres. Divide the youngsters into groups of four players: within a group, three children are attackers, each with a ball, and the fourth is the defender. None of the players may leave the playing area. The defender tries to dispossess the attackers of the ball. The attackers, in turn, try to escape or prevent the dispossession. The defender tries to get near enough to the attackers to push as many balls as possible out of the square within the playing time of 30 seconds. While dribbling, the attackers learn to lift their heads to see the defender, change speed and direction to keep away from him or her, and shield the ball in order to prevent his or her tackling successfully.

23. Cat and Mouse

Mark a 2-metre square as off limits and pair up the youngsters into cats and mice. The pair first practices the game without balls, then one ball is given to each pair. The mouse, pursued by the cat (the attacker), tries to remain in possession of the ball for 20 seconds without stepping inside the square. The cat observes the mouse's changes of direction and pursues in an attempt to dispossess the opponent. After the attacker gains possession of the ball for three rounds, the players switch so that the cat becomes the pursued mouse. To make the game more difficult as players improve, lengthen the playing time to 30 seconds and make the size of the central square only 1 metre on each side. This game helps young players recognize how perception and the capacity to execute dummies at the right moment are as essential as dribbling techniques are to winning. It also helps young players develop speed and coordination.

24. Escape

This game involves up to seven pairs of players, one member of each pair assigned to one of two teams. Each of the players should be given a ball that he or she has to dribble within the centre-circle of a pitch marked off for 7v7 (50 to 65 metres long by 30 to 45 metres wide). Once you call on one of the teams with a prearranged signal, each member of that team must then dribble his or her ball out of the circle in the centre of the field, trying to control it until getting across one of the 7v7 field's side-lines. The players of the team not called leave their balls behind and instead chase their personal opponents, trying to dispossess the ball carriers and return as many balls as possible to the centre-circle.

VARIATIONS

- As coach, give a visual signal (for instance, wave a coloured card) to define which team is to attack and which should defend.
- The attacker tries to penetrate one of the penalty areas and score, while the defender aims to tackle and return the ball to the circle in the centre of the field.
- Have as many balls available in the centre of the pitch as you have pairs of children. Once you have announced the attacking team, each attacker tries to gain possession of one ball and carry it, despite the efforts of his or her personal opponent, through one of the four or five goals you have set up with cones on different spots of the field.

25. The Challenge

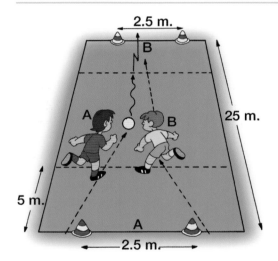

Set up a rectangular field with four cones to mark off the two goal areas; use one ball for every two youngsters. Pair up the children. Two players stand on the same goal-line (A), one on the right post (cone) and the other at the left of a 2.5-metre-wide goal. After you have given a visual signal, both should run toward a ball placed in the centre point of the playing area at a distance of 12.5 metres. The first player to gain possession of the ball must dribble it into the opponent's shooting zone and score. While player A at the left post (cone) tries to score at the far goal (B), player B at the right post must dribble it through the open goal from which he or she started (A) once he or she gains the ball. If these and other football rules are broken in the midfield outside of each shooting zone, the defender resumes the game without the ball, from half a metre behind the attacker. If the defender infringes the rules in his or her own shooting zone, the player will be penalized with a free kick from the centre of the playing area through the opponent's empty goal. Each time a goal is scored or the ball runs across any end-line, the two players change their starting places. The winner is the first player to score two goals.

Games in the Maze

There are two programme activities referred to as Games in the Maze: the Dribbling Maze Game and the Passing Maze Game. The first activity serves to stimulate the young players' capacity to watch and see. It also improves their sense of orientation, their ability to make quick decisions and their coordination, particularly dribbling technique with both feet. Because of these many skills to be developed, it is useful to have more variations of the game to ensure plenty of practice and to sustain interest. The second activity in the maze, along with its variations, helps improve communication and cooperation skills between the passer and the receiver.

1. Dribbling Maze Game

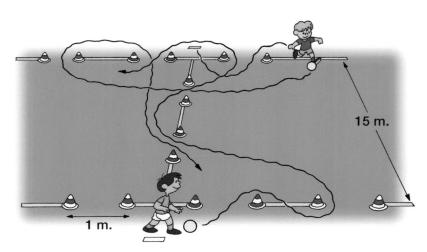

Set up the playing field according to the illustration, establishing eight goal areas that are 1 metre apart, using two cones for each goal. Pair up the children and give each a ball. Two players start simultaneously but across from each other at positions outside the maze. Their task is to dribble the ball in any direction through all eight goals of the maze without leaving any out. The winner is the player who returns to the starting point first with the ball under complete control. Have the youngsters practice without the balls at first. Later, more than two players may compete at the same time.

VARIATIONS

- Instead of goals, players waiting to be active in the game will form tunnels with their bodies. After the ball is played through a tunnel, the attacker has to jump over his or her opponent.

- Try the game as a timed activity to see which player needs less time to run through six different goals. Have the players use only the less-skillful foot or complete a full turn before dribbling the ball across a goal-line. You might also ask players to dribble the ball backward through the cone goals.

- To score, the players must pass the ball through a goal and collect it behind the goal-line by running around the posts without running through the goal (tunnel).

- To win, the player must pass through the most goals within 10 seconds.

- Set up eight goals with cones of at least three different colours. During the dribble, the players have to look out for the position of the goals with the colour you call out or designate. The winner is the first player who runs the ball through eight goals without scoring twice consecutively through the same one . The players must go from one goal of the correct colour to at least one other before returning to the same goal.

- Two or three players dribble their ball through any of the eight goals, while two or three other players enter the maze without a ball to modify the position of some cones. The goals remain the same size but change position, forcing the attackers to continuously look up and adapt to the new situation.

- Before the ball is dribbled across a goal, the attacker must complete a half turn with the ball (turn until one of the player's shoulders points toward the goal). After that, the player turns half way back (toward the left or the right) into the original position and then dribbles the ball across the goal-line. The youngster must be sure that during the pivoting motion his or her body is always placed between the goal line (two cones) and the ball, thus shielding it from an imagined opponent (cone goal).

- Three players occupy three of the eight goals, thus demonstrating to the four attackers that they can score only in one of the five unoccupied ones. The defenders may move from one to another goal but may not tackle at all. The winner will be the attacker who first scores at six of the goals without repeating the same one twice in a row.

- Four attackers play against two defenders who may tackle (unlike the previous variation, which prohibited tackling).
- To score, the attackers must slightly lift their balls with either foot above an obstacle (or an outstretched player) on each goal-line.

2. Passing Maze Game

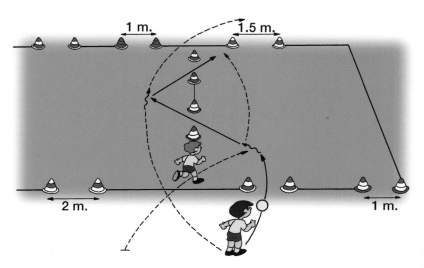

Setup the playing field as a maze as shown in the illustration, which has wider spaces between goals than for the dribbling maze game. Divide the youngsters into pairs (a passer and a receiver) who will use passing to score goals. The pair who manages to score in six different goals first will win. Make sure that the players move behind another goal immediately after they have passed to make themselves available for the next pass. Explain that before the pass is executed, the players must establish a visual agreement between passer and receiver as to where the ball will be played.

VARIATIONS

- Set up eight goals using at least three different colours of cones. During play, you should announce or designate what colour cones should be the next goal area. The pair of children that first scores eight goals wins. Players may not score in the same goal twice in a row.
- Play as in the previous variation, but limit play to 10 seconds. The winning pair is the team that manages to score most often within 10 seconds, always using a different goal for scoring.
- While a team (pair) is competing and dribbling the ball through any of the eight goals, two or three other players enter the maze without a ball to modify the position of the cone goals. This ensures that the attackers must continuously look up and adapt to the new situation.
- To score, the attackers must slightly lift the ball with either foot over an obstacle or player stretched out on each goal-line.
- Three pairs of youngsters practice simultaneously with the aim to score against two opponents who try to block the attacked goals by positioning themselves on the respective goal-lines. The defenders continuously move around the field to defend the attackers but are not allowed to tackle or intercept a pass when they are out of a cone goal. The team or pair that first scores six goals wins the competition.
- Two pairs of children try to score as many goals as possible against an active defender whose play is unlimited. Keep track of how many seconds the defender needs to touch the ball of either pair. Any goal that the attacking pairs score counts for three seconds.

Passing, Receiving and Shooting Games

Good control of the ball as it is being passed or intercepted from team-mate to team-mate is of paramount importance: It provides a team the opportunity to maintain or instigate their attacking moves. In the professional Spanish football league during the 2003-2004 season, 17.5 per cent of lost possession resulted from poor reception and ball control. This high percentage of failure is a consequence not only of technique but also of other errors occurring immediately before the ball is controlled. These are some typical errors:

➤ There is no visual agreement between the passer and receiver.

➤ The receiver does not make himself or herself available at the right moment when the passer is ready due to poor timing.

➤ The receiver waits for the ball instead of running to it.

➤ The players show poor passing skills (the ball was passed too softly, too high, imprecisely, or the pass was executed too late).

A young player should learn and apply common sense principles to a variety of techniques in order to control the ball in a particular game situation. Teach your young players the following:

1. Watch the ball carefully until it touches your feet or body. Also, pay attention to the position and movement of your team-mates and opponents before and after the execution of the control. The more experienced and confident you are, the more you can assimilate other relevant information while focusing on the ball.

2. Try to position your body in line with the ball as soon as possible. If you are an attacker, for example, it is relatively easy to receive the ball as you face the proper goal, but often this is not effective for creating a goal opportunity. It is too slow, and it limits your ability to play the ball quickly into the opponent's penalty area. Therefore, you should learn to receive and control balls from a side position as well, which allows you to perceive your team-mates' and the defenders' position and movements in the space between you and the goal.

3. Make a cushion for the ball with your feet or any other part of your body. Don't be tense. Relax and incline your playing knee or other body surface slightly forward. This helps your control. Receive the ball in a balanced position at the point of collection. Being well balanced allows more successful control with subsequent movements, and it allows a receiver to deceive any opponent nearby with a body feint.

4. While controlling the ball with the first touch, position it for the next play. If you are the receiver, you should already know what to do next before the ball is controlled. You must select how to control the ball depending on what technique you will use for the next move: a dribble, a shot or a pass. It is paramount to be able to execute an intentional or purposeful control to continue with the attack. Learning this principle of ball control well helps any player to perform considerably better.

Phases of Receiving and Controlling the Ball

The games in this section are designed to enhance the players' ability to maintain control and make accurate and well-timed passes with different techniques. The players learn to calculate and anticipate the direction and speed of the ball while receiving and controlling it, including how to read the direction and speed of an opponent's pass.

The children practice passing with either a stationary or a moving ball while disguising its direction for as long as possible from opponents. They also learn to receive the ball in the best way to exploit and utilise it for their next pass.

Phase One: Preparation

➤ Fix the ball visually and calculate its trajectory, the distance to the passer, the height of the aerial ball and its speed. These are all factors that determine the line of approach for reception as well as ball control technique.

➤ Anticipate where the first contact with the ball should take place.

➤ Select the correct line to approach the oncoming ball.

➤ Choose the most convenient surface to receive the ball.

➤ While analysing the game situation, anticipate a correct body position for the reception of the ball (lateral, frontal or with the back facing the ball but the head turned around to be able to observe the oncoming ball). Body position will determine the next move to execute.

➤ Once the trajectory of the oncoming ball is known, attention should shift away from the ball. Assess the current game situation to determine the various options available upon reception of the ball.

➤ Remain physically and mentally in balance.

Phase Two: Execution

➤ Relax the part of the body which is going to absorb the impact of the oncoming ball.

➤ Utilise the arms for balance to aid the technical-tactical execution of the reception.

➤ Knowing whether to combine feint or dummy with the reception.

➤ Know whether to receive the ball close to the feet or farther away (depending on the distance of the closest opponent).

➤ Know how to use various techniques to receive the ball, which may arrive on the ground, in the air or bouncing.

➤ Know how to bring down the ball as quickly as possible in aerial passes.

➤ Know that the next action is important in understanding the correct way to receive the ball. Should the ball be kept in possession? Should a pass, a dribble or a shot on goal be taken?

➤ Know how to adjust to imprecise passes.

1. Against the Wall

Station the youngsters near a wall, at a distance of 4 to 7 metres. Playing the ball against the wall, how many flat passes can be executed without the ball leaving the ground? To make this activity into a competition, the winner is the player who manages to execute five passes against the wall without having to move more than 1 metre away from his or her original position. For variation, use the left foot or alternate one pass with the left foot and the next one with the right foot. Insist that youngsters use different surfaces of the foot when passing. Have them repeat the activity, trying to establish a personal record time.

2. Going for Distance

Position the children at an end-line in front of a goal area. Every player shoots his or her ball from the end-line into the depth of the full pitch. Which player's ball travels farthest? Who needs fewer shots to score a goal? Have the youngsters also use their less-skillful foot and experiment in shooting with different techniques. Ask them to describe their experiences!

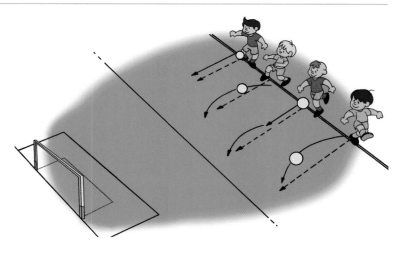

3. Accurate Passing and Control

This game can be played by individuals or as a competition with three players per team. Each player has to score from a distance of 6 to 9 metres through a 2-metre-wide goal area (marked off by cones) and then have a

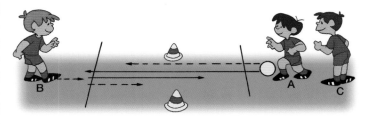

receiver (B) be able to return the pass to a third player (C). The passer (A) follows the pass to the other side and awaits a pass from the third player (C). Whoever scores 10 goals first with the passing technique you instruct them to use is the winner. With a team, the winning three players can be either those who score 10 goals first or those who score the most goals within 30 seconds.

Explore what constitutes the most efficient passing technique by using effective questioning with the players.

VARIATION

- The third player (player C) becomes a goal-keeper and defends a 4-metre-wide goal area (marked by two cones) in the centre between his or her two team-mates. An attacker who does not manage to score has to switch position with the goal-keeper. As coach you may ask the attackers to shoot stationary or moving balls. Also ask them to use the drop-kick technique or the volley shot from different distances once they know these techniques.

4. King of the Penalty

Divide the youngsters into groups of three for this game. You should have a 7v7 goal area (i.e., 5 by 2 metres) for each group playing. The three players involved start with five points each. The oldest player is the first to defend the goal area, while the other two players stand 10 metres away attempting to score goals. For every goal, the defender loses one point. When an attacker fails to score, however, he or she changes position with the goal-keeper. A player wins when the opponents have lost all their points.

VARIATION

• Indicate which technique the players must use for each set.

5. Torpedoes

This game takes 10 players and five footballs. Choose four players to line up next to each other along a line, each of them in possession of a ball. The same number of players stand facing them at a distance of 9 metres (you can move this distance back to 11 metres as the youngsters gain experience); the children in this other line do not have a ball. Two other players position themselves outside the tunnel at either end. The end players have a ball that they pass to each other through the tunnel of other players The players with a ball forming the tunnel try to calculate the direction and speed of the ball going through the tunnel from end to end. They then try to 'torpedo' it by kicking their ball at it accurately. If they miss, the player across the way will receive the pass. The kickers can use either foot. The receivers try the torpedo as it returns to the original end-player.

6. Quick Goals

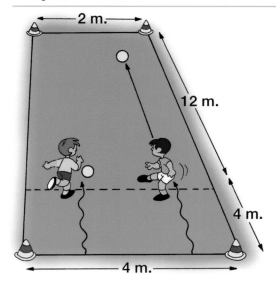

Pair up the children and give each a ball. Set up a long rectangle (see illustration), using four cones to mark the corners; the end of the rectangle serves as a goal area and should be only 2 metres wide. Give a visual signal for two players to set off from the end of the rectangle. They must dribble their ball at least to a 4-metre line and then shoot it from there through the cones at the other end of the rectangle, another 12 metres away. Racing within pairs, the player who first manages to pass the ball from any point beyond the 4-metre line between the far goalposts scores a point. The winner is the player who scores the highest number of points in five attempts.

When shooting under time pressure, the players ordinarily may choose their technique. As variations, however, you can insist they use a particular technique or even play the ball with the less-dominant foot.

7. Passing and Receiving 1v1

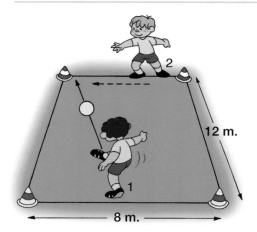

Pair up the players and mark off playing fields (see illustration) with cones. Every two players share a ball. The ends of each field should form goal areas (8 metres across). The players each stand in their own goal area, which they must defend. Player 1 tries to pass the ball along the ground from his goal-line toward the opposite goal. To avoid player 1's scoring a goal, player 2, the defender, learns to read the direction and speed of the opponent's pass. Then they reverse the action to pass the ball back to the original line.

Shots above shoulder height are disallowed and do not score. For any infringement (using hands or leaving the goal-line) a penalty is awarded from the centre of the playing area. The first player to score four goals wins the event.

VARIATIONS

- As practice, count only passes played along the ground as scoring.
- Have the children try this competition using their less-skillful foot to pass.

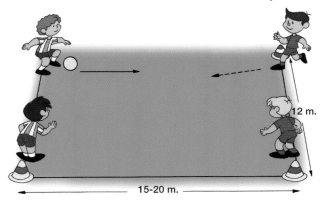

- Have the receiver start from a point 2 metres behind his or her goal-line. This helps develop the good habit of running toward the ball before controlling it.
- Have the children practice passing and receiving 2v2. Pass the ball across the opponent's goal-line from the spot where it was controlled. Depending on how much explosive power the four players have, you can mark off the goal areas to measure up to 12 metres wide and the distance between them can be increased to 15 to 20 metres in length.

8. Disguising the Pass

Several children can play this game. Set up pairs of cones to mark off two goal areas (each 2 metres wide; see the illustration). These goals should be about 11 to 13 metres from the starting line. A receiver stands behind the goals and a third player (designated as the defender) stays just in front of the goals, very close to them and facing the player who is the passer. Players have five passes to try to score a maximum number of goals in one of the two goal areas (first with a stationary ball set on the ground). A pass through one of the goals is considered valid only when the second attacker behind the defender can manage to control the well-placed pass.

As the children improve in passing, increase the distance between the goals (which is 2 metres at first). More experienced players can also practice passing with a moving ball (without indicating its direction).

9. Flat or High Passes in Pairs

To play this competition, position the children near a wall and give each pair a ball. The object is to see how many direct (first-time) passes a player can execute against a wall and then to his or her partner with or without lifting the ball from the ground. At first the players stand about 5 metres from the wall; after experience and progress, they can stand 10 to 15 metres from the wall.

Have them practice with the left foot only some of the time or alternate both feet. As another variation, have them use different passing or shooting techniques that you call out. See how many passes they can execute within a time limit, 30 seconds or one minute. This requires concentration!

VARIATIONS

- Single players assume a side position in relation to the wall, standing about 6 to 8 metres away from it. They dribble the ball parallel to the wall and pass it along the ground or in the air against it, picking up the rebounded ball on the run themselves a few metres later. This way the children simulate a triangulation initiated with a pass on the inside or outside part of the foot. They should practice standing in a direction so that the wall is to their left and then right side.
- Play 'footie-tennis' against the wall, the youngsters passing the ball alone or in pairs to hit above a line indicated on the wall. Have the children systematically use their less-skilled foot.
- Ask the players to invent other exercises for improving their ball sense and acrobatic skills.

10. Passing Around a Square

This game involves groups of five children playing on a square field marked off by four cones. Besides developing accurate passing skills, the players learn to receive the ball in a way that helps their next play (the next pass). It also teaches them to speed up the ball's movement by using appropriate positioning in relation to the nearest cone, the execution of 'purposeful controls' and hard passes. For this game, the children take turns passing the ball around the square, in either direction and with flat or high passes; you may allow each player only two or any number of ball contacts. Two players start at one corner, one with a ball. After making a pass, that player must then follow the run of the ball to the next corner of the square. The ball is then passed continuously around the square, each player following his or her pass. Use a stopwatch to time individual players or set up a timed competition between several teams at once.

VARIATION

- Add a sixth player to create competition for the five passers. At the first pass, the extra player must run twice around the square. The runner competes to be the quickest to travel around the square. The six players take turns being the runner to vie against the other five passers. All the children should take a turn at being the runner.

11. Shooting Circuit

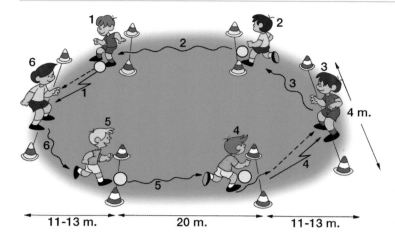

11-13 m.   20 m.   11-13 m.

Six children at a time play this game, four as passers and two as goal-keepers in the end goal areas. Mark off an area as in the illustration, using cones to designate a route around the circle of goals. At the ends of the area, place additional pairs of cones 4 metres apart to denote goals. The players dribble the length of the field (20 metres) to enter the goal area in front of them. Once the players enter the goal area they must immediately shoot at the defended goal. After the shot on goal, the attacker becomes goal-keeper; this former goal-keeper takes the ball and lines up in the next goal area at the right side. He or she then does the same as the first attacker, dribbling in the opposite direction, again on the right flank. The winner is the player who scores the highest number of goals within five minutes.

VARIATIONS

- The shot at goal is to be made from within 3 metres of the last pairs of cones.
- The attacker dribbles the ball on the left flank going clockwise, finishing the individual attack with a shot from the inside left position.
- Half way to the opposite goal area, the attacker must beat an imaginary defender—a cone goal—on either side before practicing shooting.

12. Shooting Circuit Variation

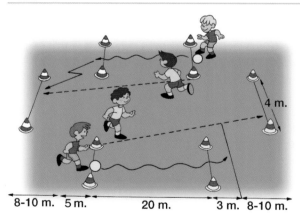

8-10 m. 5 m.   20 m.   3 m. 8-10 m.

See the previous activity. Two players compete (but more than one pair of competing youngsters can play simultaneously), one in possession of the ball and the other as a goal-keeper situated just 2 metres in front of him or her. When the attacker touches the ball, the goal-keeper tries to position himself or herself as quickly as possible at the goal in front before the attacker is able to shoot from a point within that shooting area of 3 metres. After the first attack, both players change functions and practice on the other side of the circuit. Whoever scores more goals against the opponent within five minutes wins.

VARIATIONS

- Instead of running anti-clockwise and shooting from a right-inside position, the players now reverse the direction and practice shooting from a left-inside position.

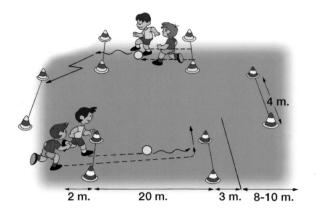

- Here the defender places himself or herself 2 metres behind the attacker to the right side. After some experience with this game, you can increase the distance to 4 metres. Once the attacker touches the ball within the first pair of cones, the defender may follow him or her with the objective to clear or take the ball before it can be shot from a point inside the shooting zone of the next undefended goal.

2 m.   20 m.   3 m.   8-10 m.

13. Precise Passing to Both Sides

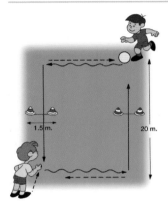

Set up the playing field with two pairs of cones marking off goal areas about midway on either side (see illustration). Pair up the players and give each pair a ball. Indicate what technique you want the players to use for passing. Player 1 starts out with a 15- to 20-metre dribble, taking him or her level with the goal cones. There, the player centres the ball through the cones still at a distance of 10 metres. Player 2, meanwhile, waits there to receive the ball behind the goal. Then the receiver (player 2) dribbles and passes along the other side. After every pass the player returns to his or her starting point (see the dotted arrow) and receives the other player's pass. Whoever first scores 10 goals wins.

1.5 m.   20 m.

VARIATIONS

- Play the same game with three players. After each pass of the ball through the centre, the passer follows the direction of the ball (see illustration's dotted and solid lines) and takes the place of the last receiver. The players take turns as indicated by the numbers in the illustration.
- The three players reverse directions and now centre from the left to the right.

10 m.

10 m.

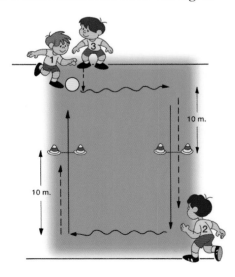

10 m.

10 m.

14. Passing With the Weaker Foot

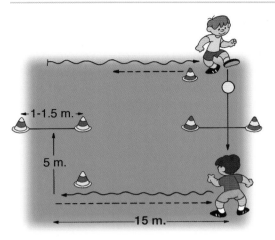

Set up a square playing field with cones to indicate goals and starting points for passes (see illustration). A pair of players uses one football for this game. After dribbling the ball the length of the field, the player must pass it while on the run through the goal area marked by cones set 1 to 1.5 metres apart. If the ball is stationary, the pass is not valid. After executing the pass from the first cone to the goal area, the player returns to the starting point and waits behind the other cones to receive the second player's pass. The winner is the player who first scores five valid goals from a distance of 5 metres.

You can change the distances, depending on the performance level of the players involved and whether you are having them use the less- or the more-skilled foot.

15. Passing Across a Wide Zone

Group the youngsters in teams of three players. Set up the field to indicate lines about 20 metres apart, and explain that the area between is a neutral zone. Two players, one with a ball, stand on one line facing a third team-mate standing on the other line. Player 1 passes the ball across the neutral zone to player 3, who should immediately return it to player 2. None of the players may step into the neutral zone to pass. After a pass, each player must follow the ball. Among the different teams, the winning one is whichever can make 10 passes across its neutral zone.

16. Passing Between Four Players

Set up a playing field that is 20 metres square. Group the youngsters in fours, giving each group one football. The four players run continuously inside the delimited area. The player in possession of the ball has to pass it as quickly as possible to the player whose name you, as coach, will call out. Each pass should preferably be received on the run. Inaccurate passes and passes that a player delays for too long count as a negative point.

VARIATIONS

- The same exercise is practiced with one defender who has the right to intercept the ball, but should never tackle the ball carrier or come very close to him or her.
- Use five attackers and two balls to play the game. The balls must be passed at the same time to different players. Declare as winner whoever is first to execute 10 precise, long (more than 10 metres) passes to all team-mates.

17. Playing 3v3 Across the Opposing End-Line

Form two teams, each of three players, and set up a square playing field that has a line down its middle. The teams face each other in the separated playing areas (like in volleyball). Without leaving the team's part of the field and without dribbling the ball, one of the three players tries to pass the ball along the ground across the opposing end-line, despite the defending efforts of the other team in their part of the playing area. No high passes are allowed. When the ball runs out of the playing area, it should be reintroduced at the spot where it went out. Touching the ball with the hands is penalized with a goal.

VARIATION

• A goal is considered valid only when the last pass from the depth of the field is a first-time (direct) pass.

18. Scoring Against One Defender

Have the children pair up and practice on either side of the 7v7 football goal. Place cones to form a 3-metre-wide goal at the top of the penalty area (at 11 metres). The defender passes the ball from the end-line toward the cones forming that goal. Once the attacker has managed to control the ball in front of the goal, he or she should score against a goal-keeper and the defender who followed his or her initial pass. Question the youngsters frequently to help them understand the best way to receive the ball (ideally, the ball should rebound into a position that allows a quick shot toward the goal), how to best play out the defender (on his or her weak side, with a well-tempered pass past the defender, through the tunnel between his or her spread legs, or when the defender is stationary and in a frontal position) and the most efficient way to defend in this situation (to close down the attacker and force him or her to score with his or her less-skillful foot).

After every attack, the two players change roles. You might later have the attacker start from 2 metres behind the goal cones to encourage his or her running toward the oncoming ball.

19. Scoring in a 2v1 Scenario

Again use a setup with a 7v7 football goal but have the children form groups of three. Have a defender and one receiver stand near the goal. Another player is positioned at the line enclosing the penalty area. In this game, at the instant a pass is made by the attacker from the edge of the penalty area to his or her team-mate, the receiver, situated on the end-line, the nearby defender tries to intercept the ball. The receiver tries to control and play the ball on his or her own or with a return pass to the attacker who started at the edge of the penalty box. This 2v1 situation finishes with the ball played out of the penalty area (by the attackers or the defender), an off-side infringement or a goal being scored despite the presence of a constant, active goal-keeper. All the players practice five times in each of the three positions. For every goal scored, both attackers gain a point.

VARIATION

- For more-advanced players, involve four youngsters (2v2, starting at the goal and the penalty area). In this variation, the attacker passes the ball from the goal-line to his or her team-mate at the top of the penalty area. Once the quick pass is made, the receiver runs toward the ball to control it—despite the active play of the defender who is initially behind him or her. At the same time both players (attacker and defender) on the goal-line move into the penalty area where they establish a 2v2 situation. The attacker's aim is to score a goal, and the defenders try to clear the ball out of the area.

20. Scoring With 3v2

Again, use a field with a 7v7 football goal. Designate three youngsters as attackers and position them about 20 metres away from the goal. They should assume the positions of inside-forward and centre-forward. Designate two youngsters as defenders and position them on either side of the goal, defended by a constant and active goal-keeper. The attackers have 10 seconds to score without running into an off-side position.

VARIATION

- One attacker, situated with the ball on an imaginary 20-metre line, passes to one of the two team-mates who are close to the end-line. Both the team-mates are marked by one of two defenders. Once the ball is passed, the three forwards try to resolve the 3v2 situation to their advantage and score a goal. At the same time the two defenders, with help from the goal-keeper, do everything to gain possession of the ball and pass it back to you, the coach, as you follow the development of the game from a position close to the third attacker.

21. Shooting 1v1

The game is played on a basketball or mini-football field (use dimensions of 20 to 25 metres by 35 to 40 metres) with 7v7 goals added (see illustration on page 66). Form two teams of two players, using just one football. One player on the team is the goal-keeper, and the other attacks or defends, depending on the game situation. Every two minutes the goal-keepers change positions with the field players.

VARIATIONS

- Use just half of the basketball field, and involve four players on each team for playing this variation. One player per team is the goal-keeper. Each team's sole attacker gets support from two team-mates, who stand beside each goalpost of the opponent's goal to play one-twos with their team-mate. They are only allowed to play the ball with one touch, and they may not enter the field. After every goal scored by any team, the attacker and the goal-keeper change positions with the two team-mates on the goalposts.

- Play the game as 3v3, with goal-keepers in the same playing area.

22. Playing 1v1 With a Shot on Goal

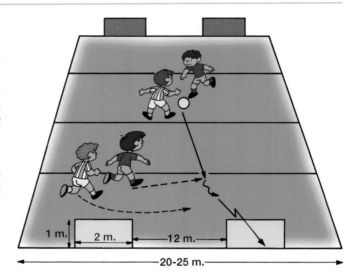

Again use a mini-football field (20 to 25 metres by 35 to 40 metres) with two goals on each end, and form two-player teams. Each player may play in only one half of the field. The aim is to score from the attacking half in one of the opposition goals. Start the game with a ball toss. Every two minutes the players of each team switch positions and functions.

1 m.　　2 m.　　12 m.

20-25 m.

23. Game of Accurate Passes

Set up two small squares (see illustration) for the playing field. Eight players participate in two groups of four, using one football. Three players are stationed in one of

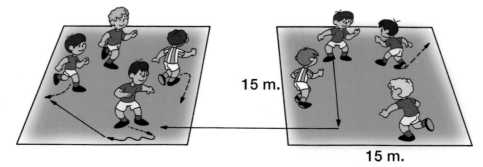

15 m.

15 m.

the squares; they maintain possession of the ball against one defender until one of them is able to pass the ball across a neutral zone (about 10 to 15 metres) to a second square. There three other players are offering themselves for a pass, which that square's defender tries to intercept. Once an attacker manages to receive and control the ball with two consecutive touches, his or her team works to return the ball to one of the three attackers in the opposite square. Count up the number of successful passes in a two-minute game. The less experienced the players are, the larger the playing area should be.

24. Header Into the Goal

2 m.

The playing area should have a 7v7 goal setup. Two players face each other at a distance of 2 metres. One of them, the goal-keeper, throws the ball in a parabola toward the forehead of the other, the attacker. The attacker does everything to score with a header against the goal-keeper, who must remain on the goal-line. If the ball is not conveniently served, the attacker may refuse to play it with his or her forehead. After five headers, the players switch positions and functions. The winner is the player who scores more goals.

Tackling Games

A smart player attempts to tackle the ball only when he or she is almost certain of success. If there is any doubt, he or she delays the tackle or executes a dummy while retreating and waiting for a more convenient instant to recover the ball.

The defender should not only exercise patience and consider what tackling methods will be most successful in particular game situations but also develop these tactics:

1. Avoid running directly toward an attacker who controls the ball.
2. Use dummies to generate an advantage.
3. Carefully observe the speed and trajectory of the ball.
4. Select the best line of approach to place him- or herself closer to the goal than the attacker.
5. Vary the method or type of tackle.
6. Avoid being flat footed before and during the tackling.
7. Make sure, in case of necessity, that a second or a third tackle could be executed.
8. Keep the legs bent before executing the tackle.
9. Reduce the speed of an attacker who has complete control over the ball.
10. Be mentally prepared to attack with possession of the ball in the event of a successful tackle.
11. Surprise the opponent (a slow tackle lacks this element of surprise).
12. Deprive the attacker of time and space, forcing the player to make mistakes.
13. Remain in a balanced position when defending, without crossing one leg over the other.

Perfect timing is vital for a successful tackle.

The tackling games in this section encourage young players to experiment with correct execution of the techniques used to dispossess an opponent of the ball—and to surprise the opponent with determination and speed. Players will learn to position themselves correctly in relation to the attacker, to tackle with precise timing and with patience. Furthermore, they'll learn to execute dummies and switch quickly to attack after making a successful tackle. By doing these activities in the progressive order you find here, players develop their defensive fundamentals step by step, before engaging in more complex situations.

I. Touch the Rope

In this first game, the children do not use a ball so that they can concentrate on learning a correct succession of movements. Pair up the children into defenders and attackers. The defender faces an attacker, who holds a rope in his or her hand; the end of the rope touches the ground 1 metre in front of this child. The defender's objective is to use just one explosive step forward in order to touch or stamp on the rope before the attacker can move it away. The defender has five chances to achieve his or her aim using either foot. Then the players swap roles. The defender quickly learns to assume an optimal basic position before tackling. In this position the legs should be sufficiently bent to keep the point of gravity sufficiently low. Apart from learning this correct succession of movements, the children experience how important quickness and surprise are for success in tackling.

2. Tackling a Loose Ball

Again group the players into pairs (defender and attacker) and mark off two lines on the field. Each defender tries to touch the stationary ball lying close to the feet of the attacker 1 metre in front of him with a quick tackle using either foot. The attacker, without looking at the ball but instead at the defender's feet, should move the ball aside in the instant the defender steps in. Players rest for five seconds between attempts. After five attempts at touching the ball, the players switch roles.

3. Tackling Twice

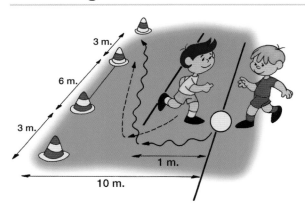

Set up the field with four cones (marking two 3-metre-wide goals with 6 metres between the goals) and two lines as in the illustration, and have the children play in pairs. The defender stands 5 metres away from the goals, about in the midway point between them. The attacker faces the defender, standing 1 or 2 metres in front of the defender with a stationary ball. At the instant the defender tries to tackle the ball with speed and surprise, the attacker plays the ball sideways, out of range of the defender, and then tries to dribble it through one of the two goal areas. As soon as the defender has failed with a frontal tackle, he or she must quickly recover the basic position and try to tackle (this time in a side position) for a second time—and prevent the attacker from controlling the ball in one of the two cone goals. Each player must defend his or her goals during five attacks. The winner is the defender who allows the attacker to score fewer goals. After each tackle, the children should rest at least 10 seconds.

4. Tackling Against a Limited Attacker

Group the children in pairs, giving each pair a football. A defender faces an attacker who dribbles the ball straight to him or her. When the attacker is about 3 metres in front of the defender, the latter steps slightly to the left until his right shoulder is in front of the right shoulder of the ball carrier, who then dribbles the ball straight to him without being allowed to dodge him.

Once the ball enters within reach, the defender, now in an optimal basic position, executes a quick and technically correct tackle. Defenders should take care to first touch the ball and not the foot of the attacker. In this activity, the defender gains experience in optical-motor assessment. The child learns to tackle at the very best moment, not too early and not too late.

VARIATIONS

- Once the attacker is within 3 metres, the defender must carry out a step-in feint. Immediately after this obvious dummy, the defender recovers, again assumes an

optimal basic position (but no longer in front of the attacker), tackles quickly and tries to surprise the opponent from a side position.

- The defender steps completely to one side, allowing the opponent to penetrate. The defender then adapts to the attacker's speed and stays with the opponent, shoulder-to-shoulder until the ideal moment for tackling. This is usually when the ball is away from the attacker's feet. Any tackling from behind should be avoided to not infringe on the game's rules. It is best to practice this activity first without a ball and then with it, and with the attacker at both sides of the defender, to help improve the basic position, the channelling of the opponent and the retreat side to side with the attacker.

5. Intercepting Passes

Gather the players in groups of four. Two players face each other at a distance of 15 metres, passing the ball between them on a line. Two defenders, at either side of the running line of the ball and always about 2 metres away from it, try to intercept the pass. The interception should be practiced from different positions (with the defender's left or right shoulder pointing to the ball carrier and with the defenders facing the passers).

6. Five Tackles

The children again work in groups of four players. Three players each dribble a ball within a small square (8 metres by 8 metres), while a fourth child without a ball has five chances to tackle. The defender's aim is to clear as many balls as possible out of the square within these five tackles.

Besides observing the attackers carefully during their dribbling, the defender must have the patience to tackle only when a good opportunity arises. Executing dummy tackles will allow the defender to achieve a higher percentage of success. The player with the most successful tackles out of five wins.

VARIATION

- All four players are in possession of a ball, and they all try to tackle the ball of any of their three opponents while controlling their own. When a player loses the ball, he or she must quickly collect it to continue participating in the game. Whoever executes the highest number of correct tackles within a given time (two minutes, for example) wins. Besides tackling, the participants learn to shield the ball by placing the body between ball and defender, to execute dummies and to lift the head during the dribble.

7. Pressing Defence 1v1

Group the players in pairs, one with and the other one without a ball, and mark off a square 15 metres per side. All pairs start the competition within this square at the same time with the tackler trying to push the attacker's ball out of the square as quickly as possible. The attacker who keeps possession of the ball the longest wins. After five attempts by the three attackers, they have to change functions with the defenders.

VARIATION

- You can involve eight players in this game, having the four defenders start from outside the square once you give a visual signal. They may follow any attacker—or you may set it up so that they may tackle only one particular (their personal) attacker. The defender who last clears a ball out of the square is the loser.

8. The Cage

Organise the youngsters in groups of five and set up a 10-metre-square field. Four of the players are attackers positioned outside the square, each with a ball. To score a point, each of the four attackers must manage to run with the ball under control through the square. The defender remains inside the square throughout the game. Call on the attackers, one after another, until they all have attacked twice. After the player inside the square has defended for these eight times, players switch positions until everyone has been a defender. The player who allows the fewest goals to be scored

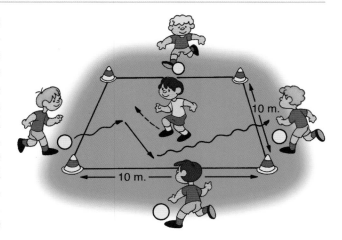

wins. As coach, you should educate the attackers waiting their turn on the side-lines around the square to spot any mistakes on the part of the defender.

9. 1v1 With Substitutes

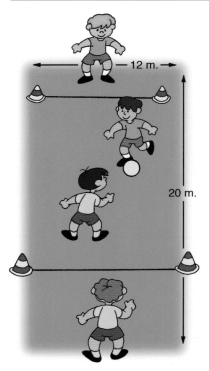

Set up a playing field 12 metres wide by 20 metres long, with goals marked by the cones at the ends. Have two youngsters stationed within the field and two waiting beyond the goals on the ends of the field. The two players within the playing area face each other until one of them is able to control the ball into the opposing goal area (12 metres wide) on the end line. After a goal is scored or after the ball has run across any goal-line, both attackers must return to their respective goal to rest. Meanwhile, the two substitutes step in from behind their respective goal areas and continue the game. The practice is over when one team (or one player) manages to score six goals.

Besides assuming a correct basic position for tackling (with the legs well bent), the defender must learn to position his or her body so that it is turned to the side and opposite the attacker's right shoulder. This position enables the defender to channel the attacker to the right and, usually, to the defender's strong foot. As coach, you should encourage the defender to execute tackling feints and to switch immediately to attack after having gained complete control over the ball. Depending on the attacker's speed and technical ability, the defender learns to use different tackling techniques.

10. Game With Four Goals

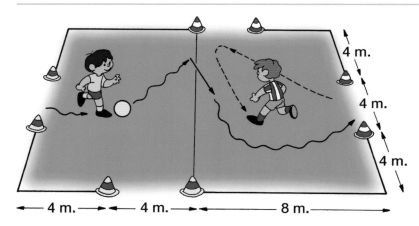

Set up a playing field as shown in the illustration, with cones set out to leave 4-metre gaps. Have two youngsters at a time play in each playing area; there should be a ball for each pair that plays. The attacker tries to dribble the ball through one of two wide goals set up to the left (or right) and opposite him or her at the other end of the playing area. The coach assigns the two goals. The player without the ball tries to defend the two assigned goals.

When the attacker starts the game, the defender in the opposite goal area should react immediately, leaving the goal and trying to prevent the opponent from scoring in either of the two goals you have assigned him or her. If the ball runs out of the playing area or if a goal is scored, the game resumes, but with the players switching roles.

After an infringement, the attacker is awarded a free dribble—with the defender no closer than 1 metre away. The defender may interfere only after the attacker resumes play. The winner is the player who scores more goals in 10 attempts.

Before putting this game to the test, have the two players experiment in tag games on the same field without using a ball. They should practice trying out the rules, how to get away from the opponent, the use of dummies, the art of channelling and employing a sudden change of direction and speed.

Games for Basic Abilities 73

11. 1v1 for Mini-Football

Use a mini-football field that is 20 to 25 metres with pairs of goals set up on either end. Six children participate, forming three pairs to practice the 1v1 situation. The game is started with the three attackers on the imaginary centre line and their respective defenders 1 metre in front of them. The object is to prevent the opponent from dribbling the ball through either of the defender's team's two goals. Once the defence is successful, a counterattack is launched, with the former attacker tackling back. To encourage a defender to channel an attacker deliberately to the right or left side, you (as coach) may award fewer points for scoring a goal on the defender's right-hand side than for scoring a goal on the left-hand side (or vice versa).

Level 1 Competitions

Decathlon and 2v2 triathlon competitions should be organised periodically as part of the training programme for beginners. At level 1, youngsters are not yet ready to compete with other clubs or institutions, which might create unnecessarily stressful situations.

Football Decathlon

The football decathlon is a simplified competition for beginners. You can also use it as a test to establish the performance level of each player compared with his or her peers. Take care in the decathlon to ensure that young players encounter the most important football fundamentals in real game situations: How to execute a skill is of no more importance than when and where to execute it.

Organising the Decathlon

There are various possibilities for organising a decathlon competition. Two of the best options are to structure the decathlon as either a two-day or 10-day competition.

Two-day competition: An unlimited number of participants run through five tests each day. You can organise the games so that the decathlon is an individual competition or a team competition. To create an individual competition, choose between these options:

- In each test a player meets a different opponent. Players draw lots to choose the pairings for each of the 10 tests. The winner of the decathlon challenge is the player who wins the most tests. If there is a draw between two or more players, use test 10 or test 2 as a tiebreaker.

- In each test a player meets the same opponent. The coach or teacher checks on the pairs to ensure that two players of very similar technical, tactical, physical and constitutional level face each other in all 10 tests. The winner of the decathlon challenge is the player who wins the most tests against his or her personal opponent.

In a team competition, two club or school teams compete, both with the same number of players. In each event, a player from one team meets a player from the other team, changing opponents for each of the 10 tests. The winning team is the one that wins the most tests.

Ten-day competition: Only one of the 10 tests will be organised during each training session, and the winner will be sought from among all the participants. If there are fewer than seven participants, have them all compete against each other until the winner is established. If there are between eight and 14 participants, divide them into two groups, the winners of which meet in the final. If there are 16 or more players, a knockout tournament is organised, and both the winners and the losers play their final rounds.

'Conditioning for winning is mainly a process of positive reinforcement.'

—Laurence Morehouse and Leonard Gross

Introducing Each Event

To introduce one of the 10 tests in the training session for the beginners do the following:

1. First prepare the playing area and select two players for demonstration. Then explain step by step the rules of the game (test), slowly demonstrating how the game develops, until all players are clear about the rules. Ask several questions of the players to be sure that the rules are understood and everybody knows how to win the test. Finally, a full demonstration of the test takes place.

2. Give all players the opportunity to practice with a chosen partner for three to five minutes to gain experience in the game (test).

3. After the practice, the beginners should explain in a short dialogue with you their first experiences for winning the test.

4. As coach, you should select who is playing against whom and where their first competition will occur.

5. The first competition takes place.

6. Discuss why one player won and the other lost the first game or test. Discover together the reasons for the win or loss.

7. Use a couple of corrective exercises to isolate an important aspect of the test (for instance the technique and tactics of tackling in the 1v1 situation, different dribbling techniques) that adversely affected the performance of the players. Then help the children practice that aspect.

8. The second competition takes place (the winners play against the winners, and the losers play the consolation round).

9. Together with the young players, work out the necessary skills and capacities to win the test. The aim is for all players to have a complete understanding of what to do in every moment of undergoing the competition game (test). That is why

one or two more corrective exercises should be practiced to help to overcome any deficiencies observed in the beginners. Sometimes taking one step backward can be the best way to advance.

10. The third competition takes place to establish the most-skillful players in this test of the decathlon.

The following 10 activities have been pulled from the current chapter to form the decathlon.

I. The Tunnel

See Dribbling Games, No. 2, for game description on page 41.

TRAINING OBJECTIVES

- To pass the ball from outside the established zone with correct speed through the open legs of an opponent and to recover it as quickly as possible.
- To use both feet to save time.
- To improve footwork and keep the centre of gravity relatively low to enhance quick changes of directions.

2. Dribbling Maze Game

See Games in the Maze, No. 1, for game description on page 53.

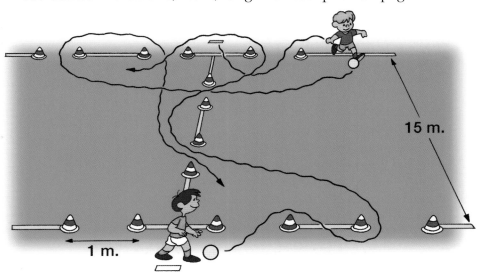

TRAINING OBJECTIVES

- To dribble the ball according to the position of the goals with the inside or outside of the right or left foot.
- To learn to collect information by raising the view (head and eyes) frequently while dribbling.
- To change the direction of the dribble.
- To find the shortest route; to mentally anticipate the next action.

3. Passing and Receiving 1v1

See Passing, Receiving and Shooting Games, No. 7, for game description on page 59.

TRAINING OBJECTIVES

- To execute passes along the ground with different techniques.
- To know how to disguise the direction of the pass.
- To receive or save the ball in a correct basic position with the legs sufficiently bent.
- To receive the ball, in motion, with either foot.
- To anticipate or read the direction of the opponent's pass.
- To enlarge the range of action of the defender.

4. Hot Pursuit

See Dribbling Games, No. 19, for game description on page 49.

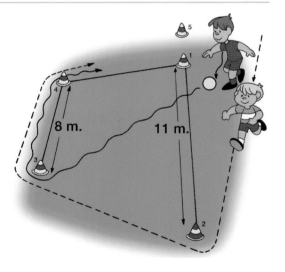

TRAINING OBJECTIVES

- To dribble the ball at high speed without losing control despite several changes of direction.
- To use the appropriate dribble technique when carrying the ball on a straight line and when changing its direction.
- To use the appropriate running technique when changing direction. After having lowered the centre of gravity, the body's weight, which rests on one leg, must be pushed with a full extension of the same leg into the new direction. At the same time, the ball is played with the other foot.
- To protect the ball with the body during the dribble when the defender is close.

5. Tackling Twice

See Tackling Games, No. 3, for game description on page 69.

TRAINING OBJECTIVES

- To assume an optimal basic position before executing the tackle.
- To know the importance of executing a tackle with the elements of speed and surprise.

- To execute a dummy move before stepping in.
- To anticipate the opponent's play, that is, the direction in which he or she is moving the ball.
- To recover the basic tackling position quickly in order to tackle a second or third time.
- As attacker, to attentively observe the preparation and execution of the opponent's tackle so as to move the ball out of that player's range of action.
- To learn to tackle at the right moment, especially when the ball is not close to the attacker's feet.

6. The Challenge

See Dribbling Games, No. 25, for game description on page 52.

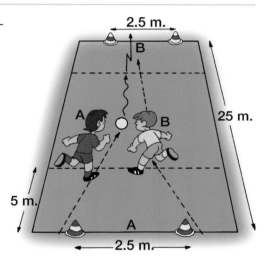

TRAINING OBJECTIVES

- To run to the ball quickly and try to gain the best position to play it first.
- To dribble and keep possession of the ball against an opponent defending from behind.
- To defend from a sideways position, not from behind, in relation to the attacker.
- To score despite the presence of an opponent.
- To change quickly from attack to defence and vice versa.
- To execute a precise pass through more than 25 metres when a penalty is awarded to the attacker.
- To avoid dribbling the ball into the range of the defender.

7. Quick Goals

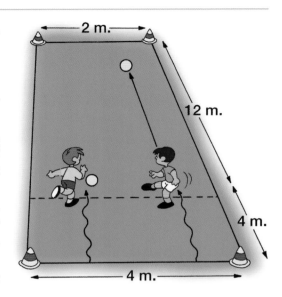

See Passing, Receiving and Shooting Games, No. 6, for game description on page 58.

TRAINING OBJECTIVES

- To accelerate with a ball from a stationary position.
- To combine two basic technical moves, such as dribbling the ball in front of the body and executing a pass or shot quickly.
- To execute the pass not only quickly and accurately but also with explosive power so that the ball travels through the goal first.
- To position the support leg at the correct level with the ball to assure accuracy.

8. Passing With the Weaker Foot

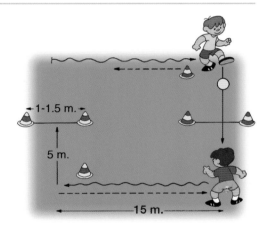

See Passing, Receiving and Shooting Games, No. 14, for game description on page 63.

TRAINING OBJECTIVES

- To ensure accuracy when passing with the less-skillful foot.
- While preparing the pass, disguise information about its moment of execution and direction.

9. Header Into the Goal

See Passing, Receiving and Shooting Games for Accurate Passes, No. 24, for game description on page 67.

TRAINING OBJECTIVES

- To provide a first experience with heading the ball.
- To motivate young players to train with several progressive exercises getting out of a sitting and kneeling position.
- To execute headers in a technically correct way in a stationary, standing position.

10. Game With Four Goals

See Tackling Games, No. 10, for game description on page 72.

TRAINING OBJECTIVES

- To raise the eyes while dribbling the ball to observe and analyse the opponent's position and play.
- To avoid dribbling the ball into the range of the defender.
- By dribbling the ball to one side, to force the defender to move in that direction; then to enter the space thus created with a sudden change of speed and direction.
- To improve the dribble technique with a change of speed and direction.
- For defenders to learn to force the attacker to dribble the ball into a desired space.
- For players to learn to use dummies while defending.

2v2 Triathlon

The triathlon competition focuses on different basic, collective situations of the football game. Players experiment not only with how to pass, dribble, receive or tackle but also with when, where and why to do it: The players must always consider the play of other team-mates as well as other defenders. By practicing the three simplified games here, players learn to read the situations and react accordingly, despite the increasing complexity of the games.

The figure on page 81 shows how a triathlon competition can be organised. In this example, teams representing Europe compete against teams representing Africa until a winner is decided. The blank spaces next to each game are for coaches to use in recording scores.

1. 2v1 With Counterattack

During the two minutes of play for each trial, two players alternately attack the 10-metre-wide goals defended by one opponent. After a successful defence, the ball is passed by the opponent to the other defender at the opposite goal, who tries to score. After having lost the ball, the attackers should tackle back in their own half of the playing area. To score, a player must dribble the ball across the opponent's goal-line. After two minutes, switch the attackers with the defenders. Free kicks or dribbles should be executed no less than 3 metres from the end-line or centre-line.

Playing time: four times, two minutes each trial, for eight minutes.

2. 2v2 With Four Intersecting Goals

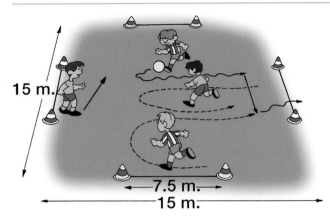

The field should have four goal areas, each 7.5 metres wide. Each team attacks the two goals assigned to it and defends the other two. The game starts with the ball toss. Free kicks and free dribbles should be executed no less than 3 metres away from the goal-lines. To score, the ball has to be dribbled across one of the opposing goals.

Playing time: three times, three minutes each trial, with one minute's rest in between trials.

3. 2v2 With Two Wide Goals

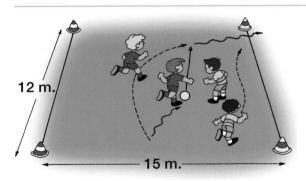

Set up the pitch to be 15 metres in length and the goal cones to be 12 metres apart. The game starts with a ball toss. Free kicks or free dribbles should be taken from no less than 3 metres from the goal-line. To score, the player must have the ball under control in the goal area.

Playing time: three trials of three minutes, with rest intervals of one minute between trials.

Europe Versus Africa

Teams	Italy	Germany	Spain	England
Names of players				

Teams	South Africa	Ghana	Nigeria	Cameroon
Names of players				

First game scores: 2v1 with counterattack (4 × 2 min.)			Second game scores: 2v2 with four intersecting goals (3 × 3 min.)			Third game scores: 2v2 with two wide goals (3 × 3 min.)		
ITA-GHA			ITA-ZAF			ITA-CMR		
DEU-ZAF			DEU-GHA			DEU-NGA		
ESP-CMR			ESP-NGA			ESP-ZAF		
GBR-NGA			GBR-CMR			GBR-GHA		

Final result: Europe _____ Africa _____ Technical delegate: _____

Note: During the triathlon, changing the composition of the team is not permitted.

The basic game situations of level 1 provide children with a solid foundation. Having played and practiced these games, the young players have had adequate stimuli to make their training both effective and enjoyable: They are starting out on the right foot. Coaches can continue to build on this foundation by exposing their players to the simplified games comprising level 2 (see chapter 6).

Developing Football Game Intelligence

'There is no greater power on the playing field than the player's intelligence.'

César Luis Menotti

Each era is characterised by certain tendencies or fashions. This also applies to football. While coaching football in the early 1950s and 1960s concentrated on improving technical skills, the following decade focused more on the physical preparation of football players, an aspect that up to then had been underestimated. After the 1990 World Cup in Italy, individual, group and team tactics were considered fundamental for achieving good results, especially against stronger teams. And now in the first decade of a new century, where is football going? What will the tendency in football coaching become in the future? Certainly, there are different views about it around the globe, but it is of interest to guess which of the various tendencies will finally come out.

To ensure frequent victories today, it is absolutely necessary to develop complete players. They must have an excellent technical ability, physical fitness and tactical knowledge; they must also be mentally prepared. But is there still something to improve in their performance that has been left behind? Which aspects of the development of a complete football player have not been considered or stimulated sufficiently in training to bring the game to a superior level?

There is one aspect of the player's performance that needs more attention in the learning and teaching process: the development of game intelligence in football. Game intelligence is the quality that allows a player to recognise and adapt to situations on the football pitch quickly in the high-pressure atmosphere of the match. Without a doubt, game intelligence is already an important criterion in evaluating the performance level of each player in many areas.

The development of the intellectual capacities of youth and adult football players is still in its infancy, largely due to the authoritarian teaching style preferred by the vast majority of trainers and coaches to shape their players. The frequent instructions and hints that the players receive from the side-line before a game and during its development are not sufficient to take the game to a higher level.

The only way to improve the standard of play in the medium and long term is, among other things, to start a systematic development of tactical awareness and thinking from a very early age with an emphasis on a progressive stimulation of perceptive and intellectual capacities. As the player's ball skills get better and better, he or she should also perfect knowledge and thinking, not only developing his or her muscles and tendons, but also the brain.

Teaching Players to Think When Playing the Game

It is well known that practicing, experimenting and observing give any child a variety of experiences. Going one step further and interpreting these experiences leads to a correct behaviour pattern when faced with different situations. But if nobody guides the child and helps him or her to interpret experiences properly, the child will never reach his or her full potential, either in life or in football. What children need is the experience of an adult to offer advice, to question almost everything and to give examples. This is not only true for everything a child experiences, for example in school or with the family, but also for the development of his or her overall performance.

Depending on the technical level of the player, all youngsters should be exposed as soon as possible during training to simplified games to gain, firsthand, knowledge and experience about the correct way to acquire tactical habits. The more knowledge the youngster acquires, the better. But subjective experiences alone are not enough. The acquisition of knowledge is much better when it is the result of a well-proven pedagogical process where the coach uses questions and demonstrations to unlock the development of knowledge so that it is clearly understood. Stimulation, encouragement or advice and an explanation or demonstration by the coach form a solid foundation in the young football player's mind for the development of game intelligence. The appropriate number of repetitions of the same game situation and the transfer of the solution to similar situations that occur in the game also build on this foundation.

Developing Game Intelligence in Young Players

Intelligence must be developed mainly through the global rather than analytic method, exposing the players to a series of technical-tactical simplified games such as 3v1, 2v1 or 3v2. Depending on the simplified game, each player has to face and resolve a series of problems that should be shaped perfectly to his or her physical, technical and mental capacities. A variety of progressive exercises and games are proposed in this book that will help to develop the youngster's tactical thinking and awareness step by step until he or she, with the coach's guidance, has discovered a number of solutions for almost every situation confronted in a football game. It does not matter whether the solution is discovered due to frequent repetition of a similar situation in training or through imagination, creativity and spontaneity. The important thing is that the player has been able to understand and read the situation and to resolve the problem successfully.

The ability for flexibility in a previously learned skill is only possible when the player has been exposed to a systematic development of his or her intellectual capacity from a very early age right through to a top performance level. Good perception, a requirement for any player, followed by a correct understanding of game situations and good decision making, culminates in a good technical execution of the mentally prepared move. All these phases of the playing action must be coached over a period of years in order to be able to raise the performance level of any player.

'Tell me, and I will forget. Show me, and I will remember. Involve me, and I will understand.'

—*Laozi*

In football, every position or role in the team requires a specific type of intelligence. The one required of a goal-keeper is totally different from that of a central defender or a forward since problems are resolved differently in defence, attack or in front of the goal. The intelligence of a player should be considered as the real driving force behind his or her performance. Often, the difference between one football player and another is the level of intelligence demonstrated in the game. His or her intelligence explains a player's success. A high performance level in football is only possible when making constant use of game intelligence. A player who is physically fit and technically proficient but without an alert mind cannot be considered a complete player. The same is true of a player who is capable of resolving problems mentally but is unable to transfer his or her brilliant ideas into actions that are beneficial to the team.

Unlocking and systematically developing a football player's game intelligence are still beyond the knowledge of many coaches and teachers. Unfortunately, there is no literature about developing this important aspect either in football or in other sports. Few coaches are prepared to modify their coaching style, which is an important prerequisite for being able to stimulate game intelligence. The continual commands and instructions given by most coaches before, during and after the match prevent most players from using their intelligence. Instead of confronting the players in training with a variety of problems to be resolved by themselves, they already receive the solutions to the problems day by day from the coach. This rigid and authoritarian coaching style does not develop intelligent players with awareness and responsibility.

To get more intelligent players on the pitch in the future, coaches need to stimulate players more and instruct less. Instead of being instructors on the football pitch, coaches should become consultants, guides or organisers of information. They should know how to complement the teaching of technical skills with the accumulation of game specific knowledge, thus achieving significant learning!

Developing game intelligence in any football player implies teaching him or her to

- ➤ read the game and understand what is happening on the pitch (for which a certain level of perception, knowledge and experience is necessary),
- ➤ draw on past experiences when confronting any given situation to come to a correct decision, and
- ➤ execute a previously devised solution quickly and with an appropriate skill level.

Apart from being able to read a situation within the game, an intelligent player can anticipate how the play is likely to develop thanks to previous information. The ability to anticipate, always the result of good perception and decision making, is a significant tool for intelligent players.

To be able to focus maximum attention on the problem at hand and decide quickly and intelligently about the next move, a player's technical skills should have been consolidated and automated beforehand. The quality of his or her game will be raised by doing so, and the player will perform at a higher level. It is necessary to make intelligence work for football in order to achieve a better game! Nobody is born with a high level of game intelligence in football. To develop their innate potential, players must be exposed daily to a progressive training program with simplified games. These games are an ideal tool to not only develop game intelligence in any player but also to hone technical and tactical skills.

What Game Intelligence Looks Like

An intelligent player does the following:

- ➤ Generally chooses the best option in less time.
- ➤ Not only looks for the best solution to the problem he or she is confronted with on the pitch by quickly prioritizing all the various alternatives, but also calculates the risk factors involved. The player rarely loses focus until he or she has resolved the situation.
- ➤ Knows in any moment of the match how to give adequate speed to the ball and to the rhythm of the team.
- ➤ Is never rushed and feels secure and confident when performing a particular move anywhere on the pitch. The player controls all the space around with his or her eyes, in front, behind and to either side, taking full advantage of both very limited space and wide open spaces. The player always appears to have time. He or she knows that rushing and doing things too quickly tend to produce errors.
- ➤ Always tries to achieve a balance between taking risks and safety. Too much risk could mean losing the ball or even the match, while playing without any risk rarely helps to turn the match in your favour. The player is brave enough to take risks!

➤ Stands out because he or she can adapt to the ever-changing situations in the game, to the referee, to team-mates, to opponents and to the pitch and weather conditions.

➤ Knows that things do not always come off. This is why his or her performance level rarely dips after making a mistake (or two or three) in a row.

➤ Has good visual-motor assessment or spatial awareness. This means a player correctly determines the distance between a team-mate, the opposition and themselves, or to the lines of the pitch and the location of the goals. These are skills acquired through many years of practice with simplified games that also sharpened his or her decision-making capacities.

➤ Knows when and where to pass the ball or when it is better to keep possession.

➤ Keeps it simple. Only a master, an outstanding player, can play simply.

➤ Knows what he or she is going to do with the ball before the player even receives and controls it.

➤ Uses creativity to the benefit of the team and team-mates.

➤ Knows how to play football without the ball, constantly making himself or herself available to the team-mates to whom he or she offers possible solutions to many situations that arise on the pitch.

➤ Is a player who contributes all his or her qualities for the good of the team. A football player who does not use intelligence to serve his or her team-mates will never succeed in the game. He or she will instead tend to perceive only a portion of the whole game, seeing plays completely isolated and never sees the big picture.

➤ Frequently asks questions and quickly learns from his or her mistakes. This player is good at memorizing a variety of plays and reproducing them.

➤ Only does what is within his or her capabilities.

➤ Knows how to pace himself or herself throughout a game. Experience allows the player to make appropriate decisions such as when to run or when it is a waste of energy.

➤ Is not affected by stress, knowing that a high level of stress tends to narrow focus and perception and also influences decision making negatively. This explains why sometimes key players do not make positive contributions in decisive matches. The pressure nullifies their usually intelligent play.

Effective Questioning

Coaching is an interaction between the coach and the players. *The teaching and learning process, therefore, is a dialogue rather than a monologue.* To enhance performance, develop this dialogue to recognise, value and use the attributes and experience of the players. Questioning demands a commitment from the coach to experiment—because most people have a natural inclination to simply tell! While most of the young players live

'As football is largely a cognitive game, it is advisable to focus learning on constructing a significant knowledge database, achieved by a balanced interaction between player, coach and situations in context.'

—*Eduardo de la Torre Navarro*

To ensure that athletes learn in an atmosphere of success, coaches should only expose players to a new exercise or game after the current one has been mastered.

in an environment dominated by telling, you as the coach help them much more by trying to involve them in the decision-making process. During the practice of simplified games ask the players to apply their knowledge and experience.

Once effective questioning is skillfully employed, it allows many game situations (previously approached through lecturing) to be tackled differently and, ultimately, more effectively. These are some suggestions to introduce more questioning in training:

➤ Develop your own sound knowledge of the simplified game and all its objectives.

➤ Use as few closed questions as possible. Open questions demand information, whereas closed questions merely call for *yes* or *no* answers.

➤ Start most of the questions with *What*, *When*, *Where* or *How much*.

➤ Ask questions that follow the interests of the player.

➤ Ask follow-up questions after listening to the various answers.

Here are examples of questions for the first simplified game, 2v1 With Two Wide Goals, found on page 94.

➤ When does the ideal moment arise for passing the ball? Explain.

➤ When should the ball carrier *not* pass the ball?

➤ What is the disadvantage of an early pass? Why?

➤ Where, ideally, should a team-mate receive the ball (in relation to the defender)?

➤ What is your opinion about the distance between the ball carrier and the receiver? Explain your opinion with more detail.

➤ Describe the target of your pass to a team-mate.

➤ What is the outcome if the pass is directed straight into the team-mate's feet?

➤ What happens when the ball arrives behind the target?

➤ What happens to the target when both attackers move forward?

➤ What happens when the defender delays his tackle and retreats?

➤ How does the speed of the pass influence the situation?

➤ Is it true that the pass has to be faster the closer the ball carrier gets to the defender? Why?

➤ What is the most natural attacking move to be carried out by the ball carrier?

➤ How might the technique of the pass vary as the ball carrier gets closer to the defender before passing?

➤ How would the defender like the attacker to play?

In the same way, you should ask numerous questions about the defence. Coaches are encouraged to revise or adapt these sample questions to the other simplified games.

Stimulating Coaching Sessions

Playing football is the best way to learn how to play the game. The teaching and learning process proceeds step by step, with each step representing a gradual increase in the level of difficulty. The players' tasks also become more complex. The different dimensions of technique, tactics and physical and mental fitness are no longer isolated but are coached in a global, integrated manner. However, football is more than the sum of technique, tactics and conditions. In a game of football, more than half of all instances of loss of possession are due to a wrong perception or decision rather than poor technique. A coach who teaches his or her players correct technique using special, frequently repeated drills is neglecting to teach them the *why, when* and *where* they need to use a technique within a given game situation. The players learn to read game situations correctly by chance, if at all.

Our players need games and drills that

➤ stimulate them technically, tactically, physically and cognitively in equal measure;

➤ promote their understanding of the game;

➤ improve their perception and decision-making ability; and

➤ help them learn to adapt quickly and securely to the constantly changing game situations in defence and attack.

Games tailored to the physical and mental capacity of players are a first step toward modernising the methods of football coaching and ensuring that coaching sessions again become as stimulating as playing street football.

In made-to-measure games, players learn to enjoy, understand and master the demands of the coaching programme at each stage of development. Through the application of different simplified games and their respective corrective exercises, the teaching and learning process advances step by step. The tasks and conditions the players should complete become more complex, while the idea of the real football game remains intact. To systematically develop game intelligence and motivate the young players at each development stage, the size of the pitch and the goals, the ways in which goals are scored, the size of the ball, the number of players, and the rules are harmonised to suit the age and level of ability of the players.

Games for Mini-Football

The game of football doesn't progress through an accumulation of many championships or tournaments but through a continuous development of original ideas.

During a football game, players face a succession of more than 100 problems that they must solve as best they can. They must correctly observe and analyse each particular game situation to make wise decisions about these problems. Once the decision is made, they must quickly carry out the appropriate technique without any loss of time. The speed in the decision-making process and in the execution of the skill frequently distinguishes skilled players from less talented or able ones.

Spectators and journalists often explain the poor performance of young players by pointing to a lack of experience. Too often, this missing experience is because the players have not been given sufficient opportunities in the learning process to read the game and respond to different game situations. Furthermore, in the beginning years of football, many young players have faced competitions that were too complex and did not allow them to gain valuable experience. A coach too often forgets in training sessions that football is played against opponents and, to a large extent, those opponents condition the players' next moves.

The traditional methods of using repetitive practices of passing, receiving or shooting drills that don't involve any opposition players have failed to take into account the contextual and cognitive nature of the game. They have tended to coach mainly *how* to do it and neglected *when* to and *why* to do it. Instead of spending excessive practice time on controlling, passing or recovering the ball, coaches should dedicate at least half of the time on understanding the game. It is essential to choose, especially when working with youths older than 10 years of age, methods that do not give priority to technique! *Instead of copying and obeying the instructions of the coach, players should learn to understand and then solve on their own the different problems in the context of a simplified game.*

Unfortunately, the decision making all too often remains with the coach, who continues to confront young players with stereotyped practices that don't demand an active participation of the right hemisphere of the brain (Thorpe, Bunker and Almond 1988).

Instead of continuing to concentrate on predictable practices, which do not help the players learn to cope with the unpredictability of game play, youth coaches should present the game to children as early as possible in order to allow them to understand and enjoy it. They will thereby cultivate such important abilities as vision, creativity, imagination, decision making and anticipation. Acquiring these and other important playing capacities does not come from practicing just isolated skills but also by participating in simple game situations in which players can learn to respond to the cognitive and physical demands of the game. The coach continuously modifies the rules and conditions of simplified games to ensure that all players gain an insight into the game they play. Assuredly, the simplified game preserves the contextual nature of the full game but without placing too great a technical demand on players still in the early stage of their playing careers.

The table on page 91 distinguishes the advantages and disadvantages of using the analytical method of coaching (concentrating on technique) or the global method of coaching (focusing on real game situations). It is clear that for success, both methods must be used in balance.

Introducing Simplified Games

Understanding the complex game of football can be best achieved through the practice of a logical progression of simplified games, with a gradual increase in the numbers of players on the teams. Just as young players are growing physically and mentally, the difficulty and complexity of the simplified games are growing as well.

Analytical Versus Global Method

	Analytical method	Global method
Characteristics	Presents one isolated aspect of the game that mainly considers the execution of a technique.	Simulates situations of the real game that are determined by the play of the opponents, the team-mates and the ball carrier.
Advantages	The coach has no difficulty in improving the few aspects that are fundamental to performance of the task. Training this way achieves quick, satisfactory results. It's easy to repeat the same situation again and again until success is ensured.	The coach focuses not only on technical aspects but also on tactical, physical and mental aspects. It takes time to achieve good performance levels.
Disadvantages	An analytic exercise emphasises only one important aspect of the game or one skill at a time. Although improvement is achieved in this particular aspect of the game or skill, it doesn't guarantee overall development.	Mastery of the fundamental skills is often neglected.
Motivation	In relation to the global method, players show lower levels of motivation.	Because of the total involvement of the young player in this activity, a high level of motivation is observed.
Capacities that affect play	*Capacities of perception:* The training situations, little modified, demand little input from the players. *Capacities of decision making:* As the tasks are already fixed and known in advance, the players are not asked to make decisions. *Capacities of skill execution:* By concentrating on only one isolated skill, the players quickly learn to execute it but without knowing where, when and why to use it.	*Capacities of perception:* Team-mates and opponents often face unpredictable situations. Therefore, the demands on perception are far greater than those when using the analytical method. *Capacities of decision making:* Following the great variety of stimuli or problems perceived, the player must first understand and then resolve them as quickly and as efficiently as possible. *Capacities of skill execution:* Less emphasis is put on skill improvement in a game.

The conclusion: Both methods have to be used in training and both are considered valid so long as they are used in balance.

The games in this chapter are called *simplified* because they have these characteristics:

➤ Reduced number of participants
➤ Reduced dimensions of the playing field
➤ Simplified rules that are flexible and adaptable to the existing conditions
➤ Limited numbers of game situations
➤ Simplification of the problems
➤ Easier contexts for coaches to be able to observe, analyse, evaluate and correct the performance of all players in the game.

These qualities that characterise the simplified games in this chapter will have a positive impact on both coaches and players for several reasons, including these:

➤ Exposing children to simplified games with teams of only two, three or four players leads to far fewer technical and tactical errors when later competing in more complex games (such as 7v7 or 8v8 football).

➤ Frequent execution of the same techniques stimulates the acquisition and perfection of skills, as does having less distraction by many other team-mates and opponents. Moreover, with fewer players, there is more time and space available, facilitating correct execution of techniques.

➤ To become a good football player, a child must learn to perceive with acuity and a wide field of vision the current game situation: the position of the ball, team-mates and opponents on the move, location of the goals and lines on the pitch. The simplified games not only aid the progressive development of perception but also enable young players to analyse game situations and make correct decisions—thanks to the football knowledge they have gained through game practice.

➤ The frequent appearance of the same basic game situations allows players to experiment with different solutions until they are able to resolve on their own the problems presented in the simplified game. Later, when the same or similar game situation reappears in a more complex competition, the player is likely to recognize it and instantly recall a good solution.

➤ The reduced number of players allows less-skilled youngsters to become intensively involved in the game.

➤ Because each team consists of just two to four players, the simplified games progressively develop the capacities of communication and cooperation between players. These are essential aspects of top football performance that have often been underestimated in the past.

➤ No premature specialisation for any playing position occurs; the simplified games make every player play defence as well as offence or attack, on the right and on the left as well as in the centre of the field. Simplified games help develop complete and intelligent football players.

Children don't need a high level of ability or specific football knowledge to enjoy training and competing with simplified games. The simplicity of the game itself immediately attracts young players and encourages them to resolve the problems they find in it. After a certain amount of practice, if the coach observes a technical or tactical deficiency that is limiting the children's playing capacity, he or she interrupts the game, isolates the problem aspect, and presents the children with corrective activities or exercises. The goal is to overcome the deficiency discovered in the global game.

For children, practice appears in a completely different light. Instead of simply working on a skill that the coach has predetermined, the child—having discovered that he or she still lacks something to win the simplified game—is motivated to learn a particular skill determined from the context of the game. The youngster *wants* to master it to a certain degree. So the mastering of a skill is perceived not so much as a prerequisite for playing a game but as a complementary part of it; the training has the clear purpose of raising the level of performance in the game in order to win it. This way drill practice does not kill the enthusiasm of the young players whose main wish is always to play and win games rather than mastering a determined skill. By using simplified games, a bridge is built between the learning of a new skill and its application in a complex game situation.

Here is a procedure to follow in a training session for introducing a simplified game to your players:

1. Decide on a problem or topic to be investigated, such as keeping possession of the ball through passes or running toward the ball when receiving.

2. Set up an appropriate simplified game form to provide the context for exploration and development of the topic.

Technically skilled players are only of value if they understand how to use their skills at the right moment in the right game situation and in the right part of the field.

3. Demonstrate the game with the players as you explain the rules step by step.

4. Give all the players several minutes to practice, during which you check whether everybody understands the rules.

5. Set up an appropriate competition for all of the teams.

6. Observe and analyse how they play.

7. Investigate, through frequent effective questioning of all players, the tactical problems and solutions. (See sections titled 'Effective Questioning'.)

8. In order to overcome the deficiencies you discover in observing the game and to convert these into correct habits, present two or three corrective exercises that all teams carry out on their competition fields. You will find these mainly in the Simplified Games for 2v2 and Corrective Games sections of this chapter.

9. When the game resumes, once again observe the level of play.

10. Intervene to further develop understanding (demonstrations are often necessary) and present more questions or corrective exercises or games.

11. Critically observe the development of the play again and evaluate the final performance.

'Drills to improve technique are certainly important, but carrying them out without any reference to real game situations is not enjoyable and unrealistic. The players always need to be aware of the relationship to real game situations if they are to be motivated and benefit from the drills.'

—*Brenda Read*

Coaching Simplified Games

- Be aware of the progression of simplified games for teams of two, three and then four players.
- Know the training or coaching objectives of every single simplified game—as well as how its grade of complexity compares with the previous and next games in the programme. This enables you as a coach to link the exercise or game with the technical-tactical experience players have gained in the previous games. And by progressing this way, the children can resolve most of the problems contained in the game on their own.
- Consider the players' abilities as well as their actual mental and physical state in order to adapt the dimensions of the playing area, the goals and the rules to their level of development.
- Objectively compare the actual playing level you find in your players with the level they should eventually achieve in their age group.
- Offer feedback and simplified games, preferably in which every player learns the result of the execution of a skill immediately after the effort and knows the reasons why he or she failed or succeeded.
- Identify any aspects that are restricting the performance levels of the players, the causes of an error and the necessary remedies (corrective exercises or games) to help youngsters form correct habits.
- Consider the motivation of every player and create a positive atmosphere during training sessions that is essential for learning. Provide every player with sufficient opportunities to experiment with successful moves; present slightly modified situations to consolidate the new experiences players have gained.
- Always consider youngsters as *active* learners during the training session: Psychologists tell us that players learn better when they are given the opportunity to resolve problems on their own without the help of their coach or teacher.

Simplified Games for 2v2

The simplified game situations in this chapter should be included as part of the young players' training to stimulate and help develop their decision-making abilities.

1st Simplified Game
2v1 With Two Wide Goals

This game's two wide goals should be set up to be 12 metres across. Despite the 2v1 aspect of the game's title, four players participate. Two players with a ball situated in the centre of the playing area alternately attack the goals, each defended by one opponent only. The objective of the attacker is to dribble the ball across the opposing goal-line despite the opponent's active defence of it.

The attack toward one goal finishes when

- the defender has touched the ball three times,
- one of the attackers has managed to dribble the ball across the goal-line,
- one attacker infringes the rules, or
- the ball runs across any end-line.

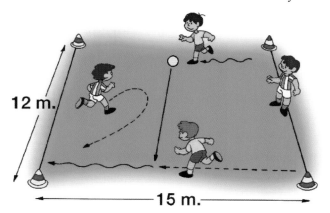

In case of an infringement of the rules by the defender, a free attack is awarded to the attacking pair. The free attack can be started with a pass or a dribble, with the defender staying no closer than 5 metres. There is no side-out or off-side.

After 10 attacks (five toward each goal) or 90 seconds of attacking, both teams switch roles and positions. The pair that scores more goals wins. In case of a draw, a tiebreaker takes place with only two attacks for every team.

VARIATION

Use the same rules, except increase the number of players to six. The goals may be set closer together as well (see illustration below). Two players attack one goal, which is defended by an opponent whose team-mate waits behind the goal without any rights to defend. The positions and roles of the two attackers and defenders are reversed as soon as a goal is scored (the ball must be dribbled across the goal-line), the ball runs behind any end-line or the defender wins the ball (after three consecutive ball touches). A third pair of players positions itself with one youngster in front and the other behind the opposite goal. The team that scores more goals in four minutes of play wins.

You can use other options to determine the winner:

- The team that manages to score with a dribble continues to alternately attack the two wide goals.
- The team that scores more goals in a row within a playing time of five minutes is the winner.

To improve the youngsters' understanding and learning, the attacking and defending roles are separated in this first simplified game. Depending on the ability level of the players, the width of the goal may have to be made wider or narrower. Once the attackers are able to score seven or more times in 10 attacks, a more difficult and complex game should be presented to them (see the following simplified games). After introducing the game, it is good to organise a practice of at least five minutes, thus allowing the players to face some of the game's potential problems without experiencing competitive pressure.

After the children have practiced one simplified game sufficiently, that activity may serve in one of the following training sessions as an internal competition in which several teams play, somewhat like a tennis tournament with the knockout system. The winners of the first matches advance to the winners' round; the group of losers determine the winners among them in a consolation tournament.

TRAINING OBJECTIVES

- Lift your head while dribbling to be able to analyse the game situations.
- Dribble the ball using different techniques.
- Know when to pass and when to dribble.
- Try dribbling past the defender after having carried out a dummy pass to the left or right.
- Pass the ball on the run toward the right or left.
- Wait for the best moment to pass (not too early and not too late) without penetrating in the range of action of the defender.
- Communicate with your team-mate before passing.
- Pass the ball with speed and accuracy.
- Adapt to the behaviour of the team-mate.
- Receive the ball from either side while you are on the run.
- Look for the correct positioning before receiving the ball.
- Execute a tackle.
- Select the best moment to tackle and know how to delay it.
- Simulate a tackle with a shift in body weight toward the ball.
- Tackle in a side-on position and look out for the 1v1 situation.
- Anticipate the attacker's play, considering both the position of the player without the ball and the dribbling technique of the ball carrier.

CORRECTIVE EXERCISES

It is important to wisely select and apply one or two corrective exercises or games after youngsters compete in the simplified game. Learning, consolidating and perfecting at least some technical, tactical or physical aspects of the simplified game are best accomplished by training outside of the context of the global game—and with the help of various specific corrective activities. It is not enough that a coach diagnose what the players did wrong. The coach must find the roots of the players' problems and apply appropriate remedies as soon as possible after the error or problem occurs. With systematic and repetitive application of corrective activities (always right after a competitive simplified game), the coach can transform the player's spontaneous or natural behaviour (often not the correct or most efficient one) into a better one (usually similar to those seen in the adult game).

Every corrective exercise or game proposed here is designed to improve only one or two aspects of the game, aspects that have negatively conditioned the performance of the four players in a previously held competition. Consider every simplified game with its specific programme of corrective exercises or games as a teaching unit. You can look on the whole programme of simplified games for two-player teams as a full season's programme, adding only one of the variations in a single training session.

1. Pass and Receive on the Run

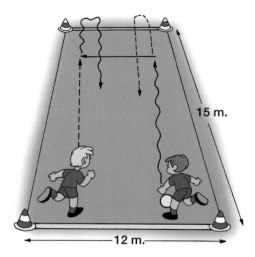

Set up goals at the ends of a field you mark off (see illustration), and pair up players. Two players on the same team, always staying more than 10 metres apart, attack the opposing goal. As a pair, they pass and receive the ball on the run. After they manage to control the ball at one empty goal, they should turn around without delay to attack the opposite goal and so on. The objective is to score 10 valid goals with 10 attacks. As a variation, the coach asks players to primarily use their less skillful foot. In another variation, two pairs start at the same time from opposite goals, trying to score 10 valid goals first. A goal is not considered valid if

- the distance between the two attackers has been less than 10 metres, or
- the player without the ball places him- or herself in front of the ball.

2. Look Left and Pass Right

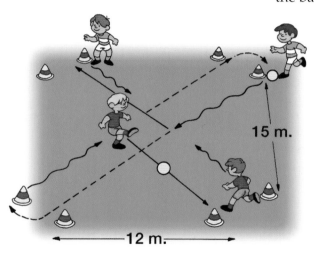

Use cones to mark off four goals as shown in the illustration. Two players from different teams dribble the ball from diagonally opposed positions to the centre of the playing area. From there, each has to pass the ball on the run toward a team-mate waiting behind the goal on the right side. Then it is the receiver's turn to dribble and pass the ball from the centre of the playing area through the goal on his or her right side to where the former passer ran. In 10 trials every player should be able to score eight times. Before actually executing the pass through the cone goal, the passer must carry out a feint or a dummy pass to the other player at the left side.

3. Reception on the Run

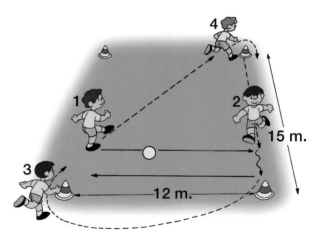

Set out four cones to mark off the corners of a playing field (see illustration). Four players occupy the areas at two cones diametrically opposite each other. Player 1, in possession of the ball, receives a visual cue from the receiver, player 2, in the upper corner of the field, then passes the ball along the goal-line toward the unoccupied cone 12 metres across from him or her. There the timed pass must be received and controlled on the run by player 2, who then returns the ball, passing it along the same goal-line back toward where player 1 had been. Player 3 awaits the pass in that corner and does the same procedure as player 1, passing to player 4, who starts from the same corner as player 2. Meanwhile, after their passes, player 1 runs behind player 4 to proceed from that corner, and player 2 runs behind player 3 to continue from that corner.

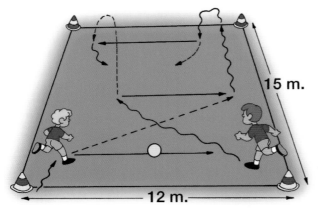

4. The Switch

Set up the pitch with four cones as in the illustration and pair up the players. Player 1 sends a pass and player 2, having received the initial horizontal pass, dribbles the ball diagonally into the position near his or her team-mate. To avoid having two players be in the same position, the team-mate moves behind the ball carrier in the opposite direction and receives the return pass as the player appears behind his or her shoulder on the right (or left) side. After every switch or dummy switch, the ball is carried across the goal-line to start the same process or combination of moves going in the opposite direction.

5. Beating the Defender

Set up the pitch with six cones; two outer cones make a wide goal area with a third cone of a different colour or design, if possible, placed inside it to represent an imaginary defender. You create two such goal areas. Call on four youngsters, giving each a ball to start. The four players each dribble a ball toward the first cone (representing the imaginary defender) placed in the centre of a goal area. They must carry out a drag going 2 metres to the right (left), again control the ball, approach and then beat the second cone in the second goal. Finally, each player should run with the ball under control across the goal-line.

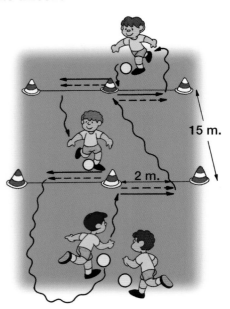

Modifying the Rules

As you coach a simplified game, it is sometimes good to change one or even two of the given rules slightly—once the players have gained experience in the practice and competition of the original game. The modification of any rule will undoubtedly vary the possible responses of the players technically, tactically or physically. Coaches should have the ability to modify the rules of any activity depending on what their intentions are in following up on the changes.

These 10 modifications of rules might be applied to the first simplified game:

1. Every team disposes of 10 attacks without time limits.

   Training objective: to understand what to do in attack as well as in defence.

2. Two attackers have 90 seconds to attack alternately both goals.

   Training objective: to consolidate experiences under fatigue conditions.

3. The right attacker may execute only one pass to the left or dribble past the defender after a dummy pass.

   Training objective: to be able to overcome the defender with a single action (a pass or a dodge with or without preceding dummy pass).

4. The left attacker may choose between a pass to the right or a dodge.

   Training objective: to know the most efficient way to resolve the 2v1 situation.

5. A goal is considered valid only when the last control of the ball was executed on the run.

   Training objective: to receive and control the ball on the run.

6. Every team uses 15 seconds for attacking both goals as often as possible with a recovery of two minutes before a new attempt is launched. Every team has four attempts to score a maximum number of goals.

   Training objective: to launch quick attacks and commit few mistakes when playing under time pressure.

7. Both attackers must also use their less-skillful foot.

   Training objective: to stimulate play with the less-skillful foot.

8. During the development of the attacks, both forwards must switch positions.

   Training objective: to use the switch systematically.

9. Both defenders may tackle in any part of the playing area. The attackers start from the centre and may score in either goal area. Attackers and defenders switch functions after 10 attacks.

   Training objective: to create an intentional 2v1 situation.

10. Each team attacks and defends two 1-metre-wide cone goals. To score, a player must control the ball inside one of the opponent's two goals, set 12 metres away from each other.

    Training objective: to ascertain the width in attack.

By asking the attackers to score with a shot into a regular goal after they have learned to control the ball in the widely set goal areas, they will gain additional experience in the conclusion of their attacks.

2nd
Simplified Game
2v1 With Counterattack

For each field, set up two wide goals (about 6 to 8 metres in width and about 15 metres away from each other). Divide the children into two-player teams. Each play lasts three minutes, during which two players of one team alternately attack the goals opposite each other. Each goal is defended by one opponent only. To score, one of the two attackers has to dribble (control) the ball across the goal-line. The attack is concluded when:

- a goal is scored,
- a defender (who has managed to gain possession of the ball) passes toward his or her team-mate in the opposite goal (after receiving the ball, the defender should dribble it into his or her goal), or

6-8 m.

15 m.

• there is an infringement by the attackers. After an infringement, a free kick is awarded to the defender, whose task is to pass the ball to the outlet player in the opposite goal.

After an infringement by a defender, the attackers choose between a pass to the team-mate or a penetrating dribble (in the event that his or her partner is marked closely). Independent of the result of the counterattack, the next 2v1 should be directed toward the opposite wide goal. The game continues for four periods—two attacking and two defending periods for each team—with each period lasting three minutes.

TRAINING OBJECTIVES

- To look up during the dribble to be able to analyse the game situation and make correct decisions.
- To pass the ball with either foot to the left and right accurately and with sufficient speed.
- To select the best moment for the pass.
- To understand whether it is more effective to pass or dribble into a less defended area.
- To execute dummies, then suddenly accelerate and dribble past a surprised defender.
- To receive and control the ball on the run and avoid receiving and controlling passes while stationary.
- To always be available for a pass, adapting to the play of the ball carrier.
- To execute a tackle in a side position both correctly and quickly.
- To adapt the tackle technique (frontal tackle, sliding tackle, tackle in a side position or tackling in retreat) to the game situation and to know which technique is the most efficient one.
- As defender, to read and anticipate the opponent's play.
- Through maintaining a correct position in relation to the ball carrier, to force that player to do what you want him or her to do.
- As defender, to use dummies to distract the opponent.
- To ensure a quick transition from playing defence to attack and vice versa; to execute a free kick as quickly as possible without indicating the trajectory of the pass.

CORRECTIVE EXERCISES

The first three corrective activities are designed to improve the defence, whereas the last three apply to the attack.

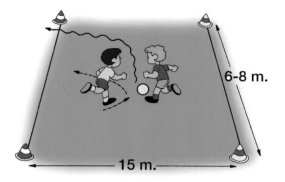

1. Tackling 1v1

Set up opposing goals about 6 to 8 metres wide. One player from each team enters the playing area, while the other two remain behind their goals (one acts as referee). They substitute for their team-mates when one scores with a dribble into the opposing goal or if the ball runs out of the playing area. Have the players draw lots to decide who gets first possession of the ball, with the defender initially at least 3 metres away. After a goal is scored, the substitute for the defender behind that goal launches the next attack against the substitute for the former attacker.

2. Best of Six Tackles

Set up a playing area of 8 by 15 metres and give a football to each of three attackers; designate a defender. The three attackers must keep possession of the ball for as long as possible without leaving the playing area. The defender may only tackle six times. How many times was the defender's tackle successful? After every player has had a turn at making six tackles, the one with the best percentage of successful tackles wins.

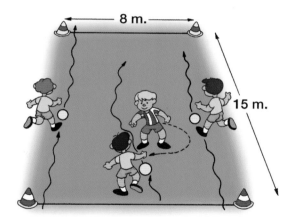

3. One Defender Versus Three Attackers

Use the same playing field as in the previous game and again use three attackers and one defender. Practice a tag game first without balls, with an attacker trying to get from one end-line to the other without getting tagged. Then give each of three attackers a football. All attackers start from one end-line with their ball with the aim of dribbling it to the opposite end-line without losing it. Meanwhile, however, the defender may tackle in any part of the playing area. Keep track of how many balls the defender was able to clear out of the area during five attacks.

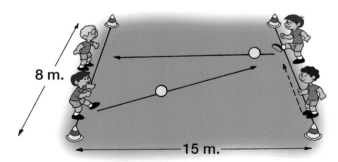

4. Three-Minute Shooting

Use the same playing field dimensions (see illustration) as in the previous two games. Form teams of two players, and have a supply of reserve balls on hand. The team that scores more goals in three minutes from their end-line is declared the winning team. In order to practice the reception and control of high and inaccurate passes, only shots below shoulder height are considered valid. As a variation, this exercise can be performed using two balls.

5. Receive and Control on the Run

Set up the field, marking lines as shown in the illustration. After you give a visual signal, one player from each team passes his or her ball from the goal-line toward a team-mate. This team-mate runs 2 metres into the field (up to the line you have indicated on the pitch), receives the ball, turns around and controls it in the wide goal before the second player of the other team can get that team's ball there. Then the players exchange roles.

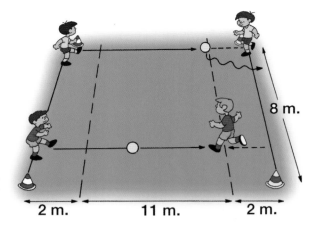

6. Relays

Form teams of four players for this competition between various teams. As coach, you should indicate what technique or foot the players will use for passing. Without leaving his or her position in one goal area, one captain passes the ball toward the opposite goal where one team-mate (player 2) receives and passes it back from his or her goal-line.

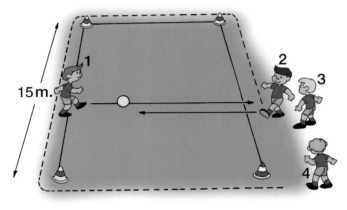

Then player 2 runs once around the playing area to rejoin his or her team-mates, now at the end of the line (see illustration). No player may enter the field. The competition finishes when player 3 has returned the ball to the captain for the second time.

3rd
Simplified Game
2v2 With Four Goals

Set up four goals that are 7.5 metres wide, as shown in the illustration. Each team of two players defends two opposite goals and attacks the other two. The game is started and restarted with a ball toss at the centre of the 15-metre square. When the ball runs out of the playing area or a player commits an infringement, a free kick or free dribble is awarded to the other team—with the opponent's and the nearest goal at least 3 metres away.

A goal is scored by a dribble across one of the two opposing goal-lines. The game continues for four periods with each period lasting three minutes.

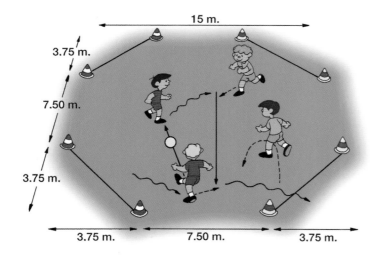

VARIATIONS

- The cones forming goal areas remain as above, but each team attacks and defends two of the goals that are side by side (rather than opposite).
- Using the same field setup, the goals are defined across the corner cones instead of across the linear cones (see the illustration). Players defend neighbouring goals.

TRAINING OBJECTIVES

- To know at any moment of the game what is going on (to read the game) in order to make correct decisions in attacks as well as in defence.
- To be capable of systematically creating a numerical superiority in attack by frequently changing direction and speed.
- To be aware of the less-controlled zones of the playing area and systematically use them to your advantage.
- As a defender, to force the attackers to play a pass to their team-mates.
- To consolidate the technical-tactical skills of attack and defence that players experienced in the first two simplified games.

CORRECTIVE EXERCISES

Choose and apply the following corrective exercises as needed to help players achieve the objectives previously outlined.

1. Change of Direction

A player from one team dribbles the ball between the two posts or cones of one goal. Meanwhile, an opponent loudly counts the number of runs completed to inform the other two players, who practice the same task in another goal area. Whichever team is first to complete six runs is the winner.

The coach should draw the players' attention to the various techniques for changing direction when arriving level with the post or cone (particularly techniques of footwork and lower-body position) and to the simultaneous change of speed. You can also arrange an individual competition between the four players.

2. 1v1

The game begins with a ball toss. The assignment of the goals is the same as in the main game 2v2 With Four Goals, but it works best to assign to each player two goals that are side by side. In case of an infringement of the rules, there is a free attack, with the defender 1 metre away. After each goal the two players are replaced by two others so they have time to recover.

◄——— 7.50 m. ———►

3. Zigzag Dribbling

Set up four 7.5-metre-wide cone goals in a circle. Two players from opposite teams start to dribble from the left post of their respective goals to the right (second) cone, return to the first and from there run to the third, back to the second, then to the fourth, back to the third and finally from there to the fifth cone (the starting point from the opponent). The winner is whoever is first to arrive at the other team's goal (fifth cone from the start). Work out the quickest way to change direction. While a player practices the dribble, the other players rest and watch the other players.

4. Slalom 8

You can use the same setup for the pitch as with the zigzag activity. Two players compete at a time, each with a ball to dribble between one goal area, making a figure eight as they dribble around the two cones. The first player to complete a figure eight five full times is declared the winner. While two players compete, the other two should rest. More advanced players should practice dribbling with the less-skilled foot only.

5. Give and Go

Again set up four goal areas using cones around an imaginary diamond shape on the pitch. Four players do the activity at a time, making up two teams. Each player occupies one goal. The two players of one team are situated in neighbouring goals (see illustration). This allows them to pass the ball anti-clockwise (go clockwise as a variation) through the goal to the team-mate. After the pass, the child runs into the opposite goal. Once there, the player establishes a visual agreement with his or her team-mate and

then receives the ball behind the goal-line before passing it again. The pair that first completes one or two rounds wins the competition. You can also have the children execute aerial passes or passes with the less-skilled foot.

6. Quick Dribbling

Once again, set up four goal areas with cones, and designate four players, giving each a football. All four youngsters start dribbling from the centre of the square. The player who first enters all four goals on the pitch with the ball under control is winner. The goal is considered valid only when the players dribble the ball from inside the pitch through the goal (see illustration).

7. Pass With the Left and Right

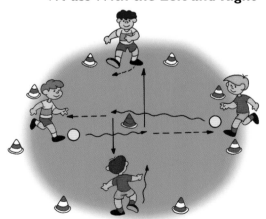

Use four goal areas, two balls, and four players. Each player occupies one goal. The two players in possession of the ball, facing each other in opposite goals, dribble their balls past the cone in the centre of the playing area. First they pass to the *right of the cone*. After having passed the cone, they must pass the ball *to the left* toward their team-mate. This game gives youngsters experience in passing the ball with the outside of the left and with the instep of the right foot. After the pass, the player positions him- or herself in the opposite goal to await the next pass from the receiver.

As a variation, the player can score a goal from the centre of the square into the goal area (3 metres wide) to the right, defended by an opponent. After a goal or control of the ball, the opponent does the same; meanwhile the first player runs straight to get situated in the opposite goal area after his or her shot. Reserve balls should be positioned close to each of the goal areas, with four substitute players collecting the balls behind the four goals as they wait for their turns. Keep track of play, counting who scores more goals.

8. 3v1

Use the same playing field with four 3-metre-wide goal areas. Designate one defender and three attackers. Using one ball, how many successive passes can be executed between the three players against the one defender in the middle without their being forced to play the ball outside of any of the four cone goals?

3 m.

4th   Simplified Game
2v1 Twice in a Game

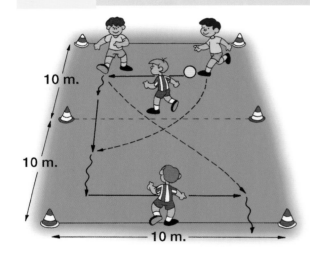

10 m.

10 m.

10 m.

For this game, set up the playing field as shown in the illustration, using six cones (having two colours of cones if possible to indicate the different end-goal areas, each 10 metres wide). Designate two teams of two players each. How many times do two attackers manage to play out, one after another, the two opponents who defend individually in front of their respective goal? To score, the attackers on each end-line must control the ball.

Use a coin toss to decide which team starts to attack and which defends individually the two goals situated in a row. No defender may tackle behind his or her goal-line, but the defenders may come forward of the goal when the team-mate in front of him or her has been passed by the attackers. An attack finishes when

- two goals are scored,
- one of the two defenders manages to take the ball away from the attackers,
- the ball runs out of the playing area, or
- one of the attackers commits an infringement of the rules.

In case of an infringement of the defenders, the same rule may be applied as in the previous games.

VARIATIONS

- Propose a time limit for the execution of the attack.
- A goal-keeper may play in the position of the second defender. He or she must defend a goal area (set the cones only 6 metres apart, as in 7v7 football). Once the attackers manage to play out the first (or last) defender, the goal-keeper may run out from the goal-line to avoid being beaten individually with a pass to the second attacker or a shot from any distance. Choosing the most appropriate moment for running out from goal is crucial for good performance by the goal-keeper.

- For more advanced players: Youngsters play 2v1 three times in front of the penalty area, with the third goal-line being part of the 11-metre-line of the 7v7 football pitch. Once all three defenders are outplayed, the two attackers practice goal scoring without any delay against a goal-keeper who defends the regular goal.

- Use three defenders, but only one of the defenders intervenes at a time. The first defender begins his or her tackling in front of the first goal-line and, in case the initial tackle is unsuccessful, retreats to also defend the second goal. The second defender, meanwhile, is situated at the top of the penalty area in the third goal and intervenes after the attackers cross the second goal. The second defender covers the back area together with the third defender, who is the goal-keeper (see the illustration).

- Use four or more defenders.

- Instead of the extra attacker always being on one side of the ball carrier, at the start of the game, the attacker positions him- or herself behind the first defender to receive a through pass. Play can go beyond the first defender either by a pass to the extra attacker or a successful dribble by the ball carrier. The second defender is not allowed to mark the team-mate of the ball carrier; he or she must remain in the goal until the ball has crossed the first goal-line (see the illustration).

TRAINING OBJECTIVES

The objectives are the same as in the first and second simplified games for 2v2.

CORRECTIVE EXERCISE

Apply the following corrective exercise to the fourth simplified game.

1. Pass or Beat the Defender

Phase One: Two players, an attacker and a defender, are situated on the goal-line. Ten metres in front of the defender, a second attacker dribbles the ball toward him or her with the intention of beating the defender individually or passing the ball to his or her team-mate on the left. With a triangular pass (direct or with no more than two ball touches), the attacker on the goal-line returns the ball immediately into the run of his or her team-mate, who is positioned behind the defender. Without leaving the goal-line, the latter tries to intercept the first or the return pass.

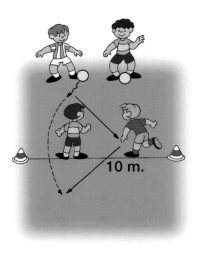

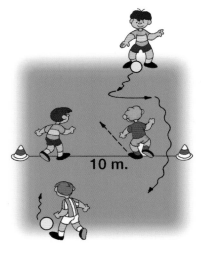

Phase Two: After completing the first attack, the second player in possession of the ball dribbles toward the goal to the former passer, beats him or her individually with or without a dummy—or passes the ball to his or her team-mate on the right. Without delay this team-mate returns the ball with a maximum of two touches to the attacker who collects it on the run behind the defender. After both attackers carry out 10 attacks alternately from the right and left sides of the goal, the four players switch positions and functions.

Phase One   **Phase Two**

5th Simplified Game
Through Passes to the Front Runners

The game is played on the mini-football field (see the illustration for the setup) with two teams formed of four players each. Two of the players must always remain in the opposing shooting zone (which is 6 metres wide), waiting for a pass from their two team-mates in the midfield. After having received and controlled the ball within their shooting zone, they try to score in either goal. Once the ball enters the shooting zone, all midfield players (attackers as well as defenders) are allowed to join the two front runners. After every goal or anytime the ball goes outside of the pitch, the defenders restart the game from the 6-metre-line with either a short pass to the team-mate or a dribble with the defenders at a distance of at least 3 metres. The game continues for four periods lasting three minutes each, with two minutes of rest between periods to work out the deficiencies of play. After each period, the midfield players switch positions and functions with the front runners.

VARIATIONS

- To improve the reception and control of lifted balls, the attackers execute aerial passes into the shooting zones.
- Only those through passes that are executed with the less-skillful foot are considered valid.
- Only those goals scored by one of the midfield players are considered valid. This rule helps all midfield players learn to support the outlet players after a successful through pass.

TRAINING OBJECTIVES

- Players learn that before a through pass is played, passer and receiver should connect visually.
- Players learn that during the dribble and reception of the ball, the ball carrier should always be aware of the positions of the two team-mates in the depth of the field and the support of the other midfield player.
- Players learn to execute a free kick quickly and before the opposing team has reorganised its defence. They understand that a through pass is preferable to a horizontal pass.
- Players learn to switch quickly from defence to attack and vice versa and to watch for the through pass immediately after having recovered the ball.
- Players learn to hide the direction of the through pass.

CORRECTIVE EXERCISES

See the last variation of the fourth simplified game on page 107 as well as the ninth simplified game on page 112. Other good activities are found in the Passing, Receiving and Shooting Games beginning on page 55, which lists exercises for improving the accuracy and speed of the pass.

6th Simplified Game
1v1 With Substitutions

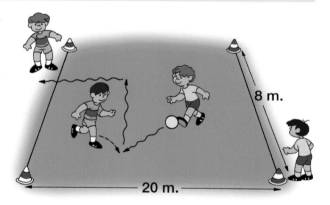

Set up a grid as shown in the illustration, and group the youngsters into two teams of two players each. Two opposing players face each other in the middle of the pitch with the objective of dribbling the ball through the opponent's goal. The younger player attacks first. After a goal or the ball goes beyond any end-line, both players must leave the playing area and position themselves behind their respective goals. Meanwhile, the two other players who have so far been behind the goals, now substitute for them, entering the pitch for a new 1v1 situation with the partner of the former defender in possession of the ball. The winning team is the pair of players who first manages to dribble the ball through the opposing goal six times.

TRAINING OBJECTIVES

There are three objectives for the attackers:

1. Keep the ball out of the defender's range of action and protect the ball with the body.
2. Vary the play, outbalance the defender and use speed (especially changes of speed).
3. Stay alert while attacking off the basic position, the positional play and the defensive actions of your opponent.

There are three objectives for the defenders:

1. Get in front of the attacker, generally, with the right shoulder facing the right one of the attacker and the defender's left foot placed slightly in front of his or her right. This position allows a defender to channel the attacker to the right side.

2. Tackle with speed and aim to surprise the attacker.

3. Use dummies to oblige the attacker to show his or her intention. (Also review the general recommendations or rules for tackling.)

CORRECTIVE EXERCISES

There are many activities to choose from for corrective exercises—for some examples refer to Dribbling Games (page 40) and Tackling Games (page 67) in chapter 4.

7th Simplified Game
Control the Ball and Beat Your Opponent

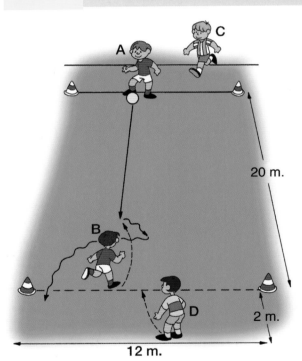

Set up the pitch as shown in the illustration, with cones set 12 metres apart to mark goal areas. The game is played between two goals at opposite ends of a pitch that is 20 metres long (or 12 meters long for younger players). Behind and parallel to the goal-lines you should draw a second line, 2 metres away from the first one. At the moment that attacker A passes the ball to B, attacker B runs quickly with defender D toward the ball to receive and control it in front of the cone goal outside the 2-metre zone. The defender is not allowed to tackle in front of the cone goal but tries to prevent the attacker from dribbling the ball through the 2-metre zone and across the back line. In case the attacker is successful, the attackers remain in attack and do the same play in the opposite direction. But if the defender gains possession of the ball, touching it three times consecutively, or if the ball runs out of the playing area, the defender gets to switch positions and function as an attacker. The pair that manages to score 10 goals wins. If you have more than four players, you may organise a tournament to establish the best team in passing, receiving under simplified conditions and dribbling with an opponent.

VARIATIONS

- Ask for aerial passes to improve the skill of receiving and controlling the ball with one or two touches. Players should know and experiment with an orientated or purposeful and planned control of the ball, anticipating during the reception their next attacking move.

- The defender may intervene beyond the goal-line, thus reducing the attacker's time and space for controlling the ball and to try to win the point.

TRAINING OBJECTIVES

- Perfect the communication skills between the passer and receiver.
- Learn to run to the ball rather than waiting for it to come to your feet to avoid the defender anticipating your play.
- Put your body between the defender and the oncoming ball before you receive and control it.
- While beating the defender, try to force him or her to move to one side; then pass the defender on the opposite side, using a change of speed and direction.
- Execute as often as possible ball control that will facilitate your next attacking move.
- As a defender, learn not to rush in to a tackle when the attacker manages to control the ball completely. Understand how it is better to move back some steps to help delay your tackle until the ball is a little loose and more available.
- Anticipate the opponent's play.
- Assume an optimal basic position before tackling; always place yourself in a correct line relative to the attacker.

CORRECTIVE EXERCISES

Choose among the Tackling Games beginning on page 40 or use the fifth corrective exercise given for the first simplified game (page 98).

8th Simplified Game
Free Kick to a Marked Attacker

6 m.

10 m.

6 m.

Four players participate: Two play inside a 10-metre square and two are stationed outside, one in front and the other behind the square. Toss a coin to determine which team attacks and which defends. The attacker outside the square executes a free kick to his or her team-mate in the centre of the square, who tries to receive the ball despite the presence and defence of an opponent.

For practice purposes the defender should position him- or herself on either side of the attacker or behind him or her; the defender may not position him- or herself in front. At the moment of executing the pass, the attacker must run toward the ball to avoid the defender anticipating the play and intercepting the ball. The attacker then tries to receive the ball, control it, and, protecting it with his or her body, pass it as quickly as possible through the wide goal to the third player behind the square. Player three now repeats the actions of the first player, passing the ball to the former defender who is closely marked by the former attacker. The attack is over when the attacker is successful (this scores one point), the ball is run out of the square or the attacker makes a rule infringement. If the defender breaks the rules, the attackers also get a point. The team or pair of players that first manages to complete 10 correct controls with subsequent pass to the player outside the square wins. After completing the first competition, both players of both teams change positions and functions.

VARIATIONS

- The receiver may return the ball to the passer, who then restarts the game from any position outside the square.
- The passer and receiver gain two points if the receiver is able to deflect the oncoming ball with one touch directly into the run of the third player.
- Practice with only three players. After every three free kicks, the players switch positions. When the defender recovers possession of the ball, he or she is asked to return it to the passer.

TRAINING OBJECTIVES

- Learn to establish mutual agreement between the passer and receiver.
- Be able to read how the defender marks his or her opponent. In case the defender marks the opponent from behind, the free kick should be directed into the attacker's feet; a marking from any side of the attacker requires a pass to the side uncovered by the defender.
- Improve the choice of the moment to pass the ball to the receiver.
- Learn to facilitate ball control. The receiver gains an optimal position in relation to the defender by putting his or her body between the defender and the ball, thus protecting the ball and not allowing the defender to anticipate the attacking play.
- Learn to select the best technique for reception, depending on the successive play. The angle of the foot in relation to the direction of the oncoming ball (90, 60 or 120 degrees) will determine whether the attacker looks first to ensure possession of the ball or to continue the attack from a side-on position as quickly as possible.
- Learn to deflect oncoming balls directly to the team-mate.
- Learn to delay the pass after receiving the ball in case playing it would be very risky.

CORRECTIVE EXERCISES

See the seventh simplified game, Control the Ball and Beat Your Opponent (page 110).

9th Simplified Game
Maintaining Ball Possession 2v1

In this game, which actually involves four players, two players try to keep possession of the ball inside a square for as long as possible, or for 15 seconds. A defender, always starting from the centre of the square, does everything to prevent them from achieving their aim. The defender's function is to play the ball out of the square while his or her team-mate outside of the square (the fourth player) counts the seconds until he or she subs in, the ball runs out of the square or the attackers infringe on the rules. In any of these cases, the defender inside the square switches positions and functions with the fourth player (and team-mate) until both have defended five times each in this 2v1 situation. After 10 trials the attackers establish their record time.

Next, both teams change functions. The previous defenders now have a chance to improve on the time of the previous attackers. Whenever a defender infringes on the rules, the time is stopped until the attackers restart the game with a pass or a dribble. If there are more than two teams, you might organise a tournament to determine which pair of players can best keep possession of the ball. Players younger than 10 years of age should play in a square that is 15 metres per side. The more advanced the players are, the smaller the playing area should be.

If you have only three players available, the attacker who loses possession of the ball three times becomes defender.

TRAINING OBJECTIVES

- Know when to pass and when to keep possession of the ball.
- Learn to continually be ready and open for a pass—to run out of the shadow of the defender—when you don't have the ball.
- While in possession of the ball keep an eye on your team-mate as well as on the defender.
- Keep the ball close to the feet to be able to pass it quickly if necessary.
- Look out and make use of the zones that the defender isn't covering. Understand that the greater the distance between the passer and receiver, the more difficult the defender's job.
- Learn to hide your intentions (the moment of the pass and its direction). Use frequent dummies or feints.
- Avoid entering the defender's range of action; learn to put your body between the ball and the defender when no pass is possible and the defender is near.
- As defender, learn to reduce the space and time at the disposal of the attackers. Show willpower until you succeed.
- Anticipate the attackers' play.
- Execute dummies to condition and direct the attacker's play.

CORRECTIVE EXERCISES

- Offer a tag game with both attackers trying to run from any direction across the playing area without getting tagged by one defender in the field's centre.
- Review the first five simplified games for teams of two players.
- Review the dribbling games Cops and Robber (page 50), Maintaining Ball Possession (page 51), Cat and Mouse (page 51) and Escape (page 51).

10th
2v2 With Two Wide Goals

Start the game with a ball toss at the centre of the playing area (set up as shown in the illustration with wide goal areas, 12 to 15 metres). Divide players into two teams of two players. To score a goal, an attacker must control the ball in the opponent's goal. The two cones of the goals are placed opposite each other at a distance (15 to 25 metres) that depends on the players' ages. Usually there are no side-lines. A rules infringement is penalised with a free kick or free dribble from a point at least 3 metres away from the opponents and their goal. The game continues for four periods each lasting three minutes.

VARIATIONS

- The same game is played using four goals, but each only 6 metres wide (see illustration). To score, the ball must be dribbled across one of the two opponents' goals.

- The youngsters play the game around an open, 6-metre-wide goal area marked off by cones. The team that does not have the ball uses one of its two players as goal-keeper, and this player may not leave the goal-line. But once that team manages to win or capture the ball, the goal-keeper may go off the line. After one successful pass between the defenders, they obtain the right to attack the goal from any side, with one former attacker defending it. A goal can be scored from any distance.

TRAINING OBJECTIVES

- In attack, learn to look out systematically for the 2v1 situation by frequently dribbling the ball straight to the other defender, who marks the second attacker. When this defender turns his or her interest to the ball carrier, the latter passes the ball to the second attacker, who stays wide and controls the ball on the run to give the defence less time to react.

- Learn the switch: After a diagonal penetration by the ball carrier, his or her teammate stays slightly back and then positions him- or herself for a pass with a sudden run behind the ball carrier (see the illustration for the first variation of the 10th simplified game on page 114).

- Review and continue to work on the coaching objectives for the previous simplified games.

Preparatory Games for Mini-Football

The following games are designed to help children focus on building the skills most important to playing successful mini-football. The players familiarise themselves with the pitch and learn how to pass the ball securely and quickly to each other, how to control and run with the ball and how to shoot accurately from inside the shooting zone. While they are practicing, the coach explains the rules of mini-football little by little.

3v0 Games

1. Attack 3v0 Without Defence

A team of three players lines up across an end-line. Two of the three begin at the two goals, with the third at centre forward. All three then progress down the field to attack the opposite goals using any combination (but everybody has to touch the ball at least once) until they are capable of scoring unopposed from any point inside the shooting area. An attack finishes

16.4 m.

5.80 m.

with a goal or the ball going across any side-line or end-line. The winner is the team that scores the most goals in 5 or 10 attacks.

2. 3v0 in Opposite Directions

Two teams of three players start from opposite ends of the pitch at the same time. Without pausing after completing their attacks, they continue until one team has scored five goals.

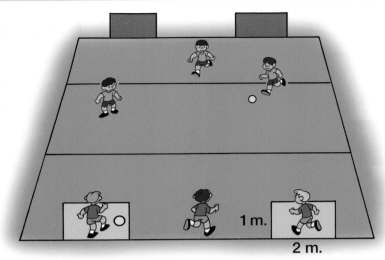

3. 3v0 in a Triangular Formation

The three players of a team must always remain in a triangular formation during the development of an attack. A goal does not count if, during the development, the players are positioned all in a line.

 **EFFECTIVE QUESTIONING**

Why must you play in a triangular formation?

- It offers more passing options.
- The opposing team has fewer opportunities to attack successfully.
- Even inaccurate passes reach their destination without the defender being able to intercept them.
- A player receiving a pass can more easily play the ball directly to the next player.
- It is easier to actively control and run with the ball.

4. 3v0 With Interchange of Positions

To score a goal, the three attackers must interchange positions during the passing move so that when they score, each of them is in a different position than when they started.

 **EFFECTIVE QUESTIONING**

Where do you have to play the ball in order to get forward as quickly as possible? Into the path of your team-mate.

Why should all the attacking positions always be occupied? Because this will eventually enable you to pull the opposing team's defence out of position.

What is the point of interchanging positions? Interchanging positions confuses the opposing team and makes it more difficult for the defenders to cover the attackers. The players learn to follow their own pass and not simply stand and wait. This creates space for the other players to push forward.

5. 3v0 Receiving on the Run

A goal only counts if all passes are taken on the run, without stopping the ball.

 EFFECTIVE QUESTIONING

Why should you pass the ball into the path of your team-mate when there is no defender in front of him or her? Because your team-mate can get forward faster if he or she runs onto the ball rather than running with it. As a result, the defenders do not have enough time to challenge.

6. 3v0 First-Time Passing

A goal only counts if each player has made a first-time pass. The players should also shoot first time.

 EFFECTIVE QUESTIONING

When and why should you pass the ball first time rather than control it? If an opponent is close to you when the pass arrives, or if an attack needs to be speeded up and you want to give the defenders less time to challenge for the ball.

When can a pass be helped on its way with your first touch? If it is played to you accurately or is played at a pace that makes it easy to deal with. A player must be available to receive the pass comfortably.

When should you hold on to the ball before passing it rather than playing a first-time pass? If the ball is passed to you inaccurately or too fast, or if no team-mate is available to receive the pass.

7. 3v0 Using the Weaker Foot

A goal only counts if the ball was passed by each player once or twice with the weaker foot.

8. 3v0 Fast Attack

This is a game between all of the teams of three players. The teams have to score a goal in the shortest possible time. Which team needs less time to reach the shooting zone and then score in either of the two goals? Each player has to touch the ball at least once. If no stopwatch is available, the game can be carried out in opposite directions. (In this case there is a risk of collisions, but it makes the players aware of others around them.)

The coach's adept questions guide the players to the best possible attacking combination. He or she especially directs their attention toward the player who starts the play and to the direction and number of passes made. After several attempts, the players learn to always start the attacks with the right winger. The winger passes the ball to the centre forward, who runs onto it in the centre of the pitch and immediately plays the left winger into the shooting zone.

3v1 Games

1. 3v1

Three players in one team start at their end-line and build up an attack on an opposing team's two goals, defended by only one player. The same player can defend all the time, or one of the two players waiting on the touchline can switch places with him or her. If the defender wins the ball, he or she must shoot as quickly as possible from any distance at one of the opposing team's goals before the three attackers can regain possession of the ball. After six attacks, another team of three defenders takes over, using rolling substitution.

VARIATIONS

- If four teams of three players are available, the coach can organise a tournament.
- Instead of one defender, a goal-keeper defends both goals.

EFFECTIVE QUESTIONING

Which attacker should have the ball when the defender challenges for it? The centre forward.

Where should the centre forward position him- or herself when a winger has the ball? If the defender challenges on the flank, the centre forward hangs back or takes up a position behind the defender, where he or she can receive a through pass (triangle formation). The attacker on the opposite flank takes up positions that take account of the off-the-ball play of the centre forward.

When must you pass the ball? Neither too early nor too late. Pass when the defender is about to challenge. If the passer's timing is good, the defender cannot recover and challenge the player who receives the ball (this is the basis of success in two against one situations). Pass the ball when you are just out of reach of the defender (illustrate the defender's reach with sliding tackles). This distance may change if a defender backs off when faced by an attacker who is running at him or her with the ball.

Why is it best if the centre forward has the ball? Because he or she is the only attacker who has the option of passing in both directions to open up scoring chances. The task of defence is at its most difficult when the defender is isolated.

What do the team-mates of the player in possession have to pay attention to? They must remain far enough away from the defender and roughly level with the player in possession so that they can run onto the ball outside the reach of the defender.

What do you do if the path to goal is free or suddenly opens up? Run with the ball toward the goal and try to score.

What do you do when you do not have the ball? Take up a good position in front of one of the goals, outside the reach of the defender.

What must you do to ensure that you can always receive a pass? Pay attention to the position of the defender relative to the player with the ball, and to the position of the third member of your team and the position of the goals. Never position yourself so that the defender is directly in line between you and the ball.

Which passes should you avoid in 3v1 situations? Avoid passes that do not gain any space so that you keep your numerical advantage and other defenders cannot intervene by tackling or intercepting.

What should the single defender do? He or she should try to make the centre forward play the ball to one of the wingers as soon as possible. On the flank the single defender has a better chance of closing down the winger who has fewer options. The defender should only challenge for the ball if the attacker lets it roll too far away from his or her foot.

What else must you watch out for when you pass? Before you come within reach of the defender, disguise the direction of the pass by feinting, using a foot or body movement. In this way you trick the defender. Now play the ball diagonally into the path of a team-mate, who receives it while level with the defender. After passing, remain involved in the play (follow the ball, overlap down the flank or take up another position to receive a pass).

2. 3v1 Continuous and Alternate Attacks Toward Both Ends

A team of three players in the middle of the pitch attacks toward each end of the pitch alternately and tries to score. At each end, the two goals are defended by only one player. After 10 attacks, the two teams swap their positions and functions. An attack ends when the defender touches the ball or when a defender gains possession and passes the ball to the team-mate in the other half, who then 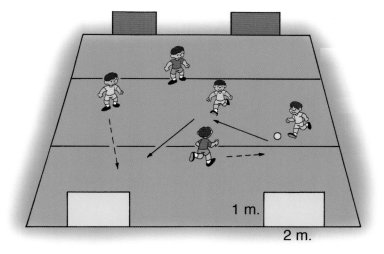 scores. The waiting third player of the defending team is substituted in for a defender who concedes a goal.

VARIATIONS

- Inside the shooting zone only one-touch passing and shooting are allowed.
- A goal can be scored also after recovering the lost ball from the defender.

3. 3v1 in a Triangular Formation

A goal only counts if the three players remain in a triangular formation during the development of an attack (they must not play in a line).

VARIATIONS

- A goal only counts if the attackers play the ball twice using the weak foot.
- A goal only counts if the attackers' passes are controlled on the run.

See also the Effective Questioning section accompanying the game 3v0 in a Triangular Formation (on page 116).

4. 3v1 Fast Attack

See rules of the games 3v0 Fast Attack (page 117) and 3v1 (page 118). The team of three players that scores a valid goal in the shortest time wins.

 EFFECTIVE QUESTIONING

Where should the ball be when the attack starts? Preferably with the centre forward.

What is the most successful way to attack in a game of 3v1? The centre forward runs with the ball at the defender. At the right moment, the centre forward plays the ball into the shooting zone, into the path of one of the wingers. The winger then shoots first time at goal.

5. 3v1 Plus One Additional Defender Supporting From Behind

Three attackers play against one defender. A second defender positioned 6 (or 4) metres behind the attackers to simulate a recovering player joins play at the attackers' first ball touch. The third player in the defending team takes a pause and replaces one of his or her team-mates when the next attack takes place. He or she waits behind the start line in a corner of the pitch for a second attack.

? EFFECTIVE QUESTIONING

What is the best way to score in this game? By running with the ball and passing it at the right moment, before the second defender can intervene. Unnecessary passes, which gain no ground, should be avoided.

Which player should have the ball when the attack starts? In order to lose as little time as possible, the centre forward should have the ball.

How does the centre forward start the attack? By passing to one of the wingers or by making a forward run with the ball? The centre forward dribbles the ball first toward the defender and only passes the ball after having him or her committed. With an initial pass the defender may have time to intervene.

What is the best time for the centre forward to pass the ball? When the defender challenges, preferably when the centre forward is just outside the reach of the defender so that the pass cannot be intercepted.

Which factors play a role in the timing of the pass? What the defender does, the direction of the second defender's run, the positions of the other two attackers and the position of the defender in relation to the two mini-goals are all factors.

Should the winger first control the ball in the shooting zone, or should he or she shoot first time? To give the defender as little time as possible to challenge, the winger should shoot first time.

6. 3v1 Plus Two Additional Defenders Supporting From Behind

The pressure on the attackers to act quickly is increased by having two additional defenders behind them. From a position 8 metres behind the attackers, the two additional defenders run back to help their team-mate. The aim of the attackers is to pass the ball with speed and accuracy to each other at the right moment, to know to make themselves available for a pass and to shoot quickly.

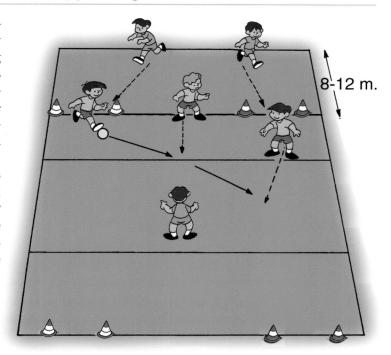

8-12 m.

? EFFECTIVE QUESTIONING

How do the two additional defenders influence the play of the attackers? If the attacker with the ball observes the two defenders behind, he or she knows which of their team-mates is farthest from a defender. When the first defender challenges, the attacker should pass the ball into the shooting zone so that the least-defended team-mate can run onto the ball and shoot first time.

Should the defenders coming from behind challenge the player in possession or try to close off his or her passing lanes? While the first defender tries to hold up the centre forward, the other two defenders should try to close off the passing lanes. The three defenders should learn to agree in advance what they intend to do.

How can the last defender influence the play of the attackers? If he or she takes no action to slow the attack and close down the passing lanes, the centre forward will not pass the ball. And, if the defender does not position him- or herself exactly in the middle but rather more to one side, the ball will be passed into the path of the attacker who is farthest away from the defender.

7. 3v1 Plus Two Defenders

Two additional defenders (one on the flank plus one behind) pressure the attackers to speed up their play. While the first defender is positioned in front of the two goals, a second defender starts off 8 metres behind the attackers. A third defender helps the first two from a number of positions—for example 10 metres from the touchlines. As soon as an attacker touches the ball, the defenders set off to prevent the attackers from scoring.

? EFFECTIVE QUESTIONING

Which attacker has the best chance of scoring? The attacker who is farthest from the three defenders when the ball is passed.

When should the centre forward pass the ball, and to whom? When the last defender is about to challenge, the centre forward should pass to the team-mate who is farthest away from the defender at the side and the defender behind him or her.

3v2 Games

1. 3v2

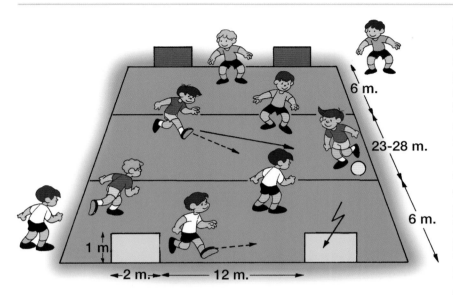

6 m.

23-28 m.

6 m.

1 m.

←2 m.→ ←——— 12 m. ———→

Different teams of three players take turns in attacking the two goals on each end-line. Initially the goals at each end are defended by a covering defender in the shooting zone and one midfielder in the centre of the field. Subsequently the restrictions of the covering defender are lifted. How many successive goals are the attackers capable of scoring against the two pairs of defenders (without losing possession or allowing the ball to go out of play)? An attack ends when a goal is scored, when the ball goes out of play, or when a defender wins the ball and passes it to the other defender or pair of defenders.

? EFFECTIVE QUESTIONING

Where do the attackers have to apply the first 2v1 situation? It is important to create a 2v1 situation or supremacy in numbers where the covering defender has difficulties assisting his or her team-mate. Therefore the player with the ball can easily steer this through the direction of his or her run at the first defender.

A two against one is most effective on the right flank because the attacker on the left flank (provided they are right footed) can disguise the direction of a pass more easily (pass with outside of right foot, or feint to pass or run in one direction and then run into the centre).

Which attacker has the best chance of scoring? Usually the attacker who makes a run down the flank does. As the defender must first of all prevent the centre forward from breaking through in the middle, the centre forward can pass to the flank after running into the middle. The defender is thus wrong-footed by the direction of the run with the ball.

If the centre forward runs with the ball toward one of the two defenders, his or her team-mate on the same flank makes a run off the ball toward the wing, thus creating a 2v1 situation. The team-mate receives the ball from the centre forward before the second defender can intervene.

What factors influence the interplay of the three attackers? The off-the-ball runs of the two team-mates of the player with the ball, the positions of the two defenders relative to each other, the positions of the defenders relative to the mini-goals and the moment when a defender first challenges for the ball are factors.

2. 3v2 Using Goal-Keeper

A team of three players attacks the two goals on each end-line of the mini-pitch. The goals are defended by a defender and a goal-keeper. The goal-keeper may not leave his or her penalty area.

 EFFECTIVE QUESTIONING

What does the player with the ball have to pay attention to before he or she passes? The player should be aware of the position of the defender and the position of the goal-keeper.

3. 3v2 Fast Attack

The team of three players that scores the fastest goal against the two defenders is the winner.

 EFFECTIVE QUESTIONING

See the questions on the fast attack games of 3v0 and 3v1 on pages 117 and 120, respectively.

4. 3v2 to 3v1

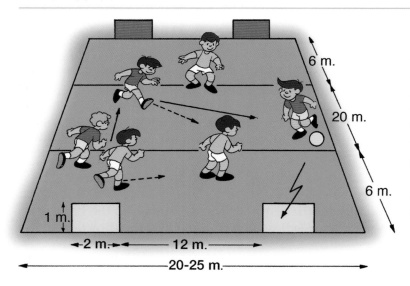

While one pair of mini-goals is guarded by two defenders, a single player defends the other pair. The three attackers first attack the goals defended by one player and then the goals defended by two players. An attack ends when one of the three defenders wins the ball and passes it to another defender, or when the ball goes out of play, or a goal is scored. After 10 attacks the teams of three swap places and tasks. The team that scores the most goals in 10 attacks is the winner.

5. 3v2 in Both Halves of the Field

After each attack against two defenders, one of the two defenders joins his or her team-mate in the other half so that two defenders always face the three attackers.

1 m

2 m. 12 m.

Testing an Individual's Playing Capacity

Ordinarily, during football sessions, you will expose the young players to a varied programme of activities, proposed in Levels 1 and 2 of the Football Development Model. For contrast and motivational challenge, however, as well as for your own checking of progress, pick three times during the season to organise a test of their capacity to play mini-football well. Before you propose the following test, group the youngsters into sets of six players and assign every boy or girl a number.

1. 1v1

Six players are paired off 1v1 and line up on opposite side-lines. One player dribbles the ball from one side-line to the other with the objective of taking the ball through one of the two cone goals or scoring in one of the mini-goals from inside the shooting zone. The opposing player, who sets off from the opposite side-line, tries to win the ball from the dribbling player and score a goal.

After a goal is scored or the ball goes over the side-line, both players remain behind their side-line while the next pair of players takes their turn. After all pairs have played, the first two players compete against each other again, but this time the second player starts with the ball.

The first player to score three valid goals is the winner and is awarded one point toward his or her test score.

EFFECTIVE QUESTIONING

What is the best way for an attacker to score in the 1v1 situation? The player penetrates into an uncovered space, running with the ball diagonally away from the defender and shielding it at the same time with his or her body. Then with a sudden change of pace and direction, the attacker runs away from the defender when the latter comes too close to him or her. Also, executing body feints or dummies with the ball (for instance stepping over the ball) may bring the attacker advantages.

What are the most common mistakes made by the attacker?

- To run at the defender and unintentionally take the ball within the defender's reach.
- To never change pace or to push the ball too far ahead.
- To neglect to screen the ball properly and give the defender the opportunity of winning it.

What should the defender do?

- Not position him- or herself directly in front of the attacker but force the attacker to head for the right or left goal.
- Shadow the attacker and wait for the best moment to challenge for the ball.

2. 2v2

Each team starts with two players on the field and one in reserve. When one of the teams scores, both teams substitute one player in rotation. Besides the obvious adjustment for the number of players on the field, the official rules of mini-football without goal-keepers apply. (See Rules of 3v3 Mini-Football Without Goal-Keepers beginning on page 127.) Each team tries to score more goals than the other team in three minutes of playing time. Each member of the winning team is awarded two points toward the total test score.

EFFECTIVE QUESTIONING

What is the most successful attacking tactic? To run diagonally with the ball toward one of the defenders and then to create a 2v1 situation with a team-mate who has made a forward run in support.

3. 3v3

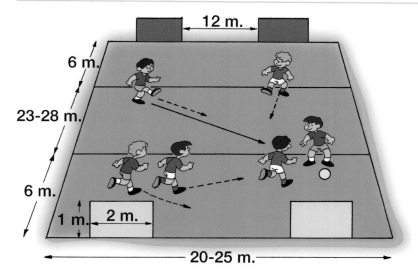

The official rules of mini-football without goal-keepers apply. (See Rules of 3v3 Mini-Football Without Goal-Keepers below.) The team that scores the most goals in three periods of three minutes playing time wins. Each member of the winning team is awarded three points toward his or her total test score.

The Winner

➤ The player with the highest total test score wins the mini-football ability test.

➤ If there is a tie between two or more players, the tie is settled by a 1v1 playoff between the two or three players. The playoff is started by throwing the ball in the air.

➤ If 12 players take part in the test, a second group of six players is formed. The top three players in each group qualify for the final round (A) and the bottom three take part in the runners-up round.

➤ If there are 18 players they are organised into three test groups. The first two players in each group qualify for the final of round A in the next training session. The numbers 3 and 4 in each group take part in the B round, and the numbers 5 and 6 take part in the C round.

Level 2 Competitions

Once 8- and 9-year-old players have been exposed to the majority of the simplified games for 2v2, they are prepared to discover the 3v3 mini-football game, which is considered an ideal competition to start the long career of any football player.

Rules of 3v3 Mini-Football Without Goal-Keepers

Field

The size of the mini-football pitch is 22 by 32 metres, or a basketball court of 14 by 26 metres can also be used. On each end-line, there are two goals measuring 2 by 1 metres. The goals are 12 metres apart (or, on a basketball court, 8 metres). The penalty area or shooting zone is marked by a line parallel to and 6 metres from the end-line. A goal is only valid if it is scored from inside the shooting zone.

Teams

A team consists of four players, three of whom are on the field. A team loses if it only has two players left. After each goal, the two teams substitute one player in a fixed sequence. The substitutions take place at the centre-line. A penalty is awarded each time an offence is committed.

Duration

A game usually lasts for three periods of 10 minutes. If several games are scheduled on the same day as part of a tournament, the games only last for two periods of 10 minutes.

Technical Rules

- There are no off-sides, corners or penalty kicks.
- Free kicks are awarded only in midfield and to defending teams in their own penalty area. Free kicks are taken by passing the ball or running with it. Free kicks must be taken at least 3 metres from the opposition's penalty area, and the opposing players must stand at least 3 metres away from the ball.
- When the ball goes out of play, it is brought back into play by passing or running with it. The opposing players must stand at least 3 metres away from the ball.
- If a defender commits an offence in his or her own penalty area, a penalty is awarded to the attackers. At a signal from the referee, an attacker runs with the ball from the centre of the pitch toward one of the opposing team's goals. At the same time the other two attackers and two defenders set off from an imaginary 5-metre line to support the attack or defend against it. The defending team's two goals are guarded by one defender, who advances toward the attacker and forces him or her to pass to a team-mate. The referee gives the start signal when all six players are in position. If several penalties are awarded, the players must take them in turn.
- If a player is guilty of unsporting behaviour, the referee asks the coach to exclude the player from the game.

Equipment

Ball: A No. 4 ball should be used.

Clothing: All the players of a team wear vests of the same colour.

Protection: All of the players should wear shin guards.

Referee

A referee is in charge of the game. There are no referee's assistants. In mini-football, referees should be under 18 years of age if possible. This ensures that new referees come up through the ranks.

3v3 Mini-Football Pentathlon

Players learn best between the ages of 7 and 12. If, at this age, the coaching programme is designed to develop their coordination as well as their football-specific skills, they will subsequently be able to master any new, complicated, technical and tactical sequences quickly and vary them to good effect. If coaches are to be persuaded to enhance their coaching methods with a multi-faceted teaching programme, our traditional games of football will have to be changed. The mini-football pentathlon is one example of this.

The five events of the mini-football pentathlon last for about one hour. The winner of the pentathlon is the team of three players (with and without substitutes) that wins at least three of the five games.

1. 3v3 With One Player Remaining Inside the Shooting Zone

1 m

←2 m.→←———— 12 m.————→

See the official rules of mini-football beginning on page 127. In this variation, one player of each team is obliged to remain in the shooting zone and cannot intervene in the midfield. After each goal the defender is replaced by a midfield player until each member of the team has played as the defender at least once during each half. A goal is scored by dribbling the ball into one of the opposing team's cone goals.

VARIATION

Instead of dribbling the ball over the goal-line, the players shoot at one of the two goals from inside the shooting zone.

EFFECTIVE QUESTIONING

Why should one of the three players stay in the shooting zone? Three players should always form a triangle so that there is a balance between defence and attack. In this way there are more passing options and there is a possibility to cover for mistakes made by team-mates.

What are the tasks of the player who hangs back behind his or her team-mates?

- He or she covers the midfield players. When the team has possession, the player's team-mates can always pass the ball back to him or her.

- He or she can launch an attack with a pass or a surprise run with the ball up-field (with another team-mate taking over the player's position), and this way create a numerical superiority in attack.

2. Coordination Relay

Each team of three or four players lines up behind one of the two cone goals on the same end-line of a mini-field. At a signal from the coach, the first player of each team

1. runs to the 6-metre line and touches it with the foot;
2. returns to his or her goal and touches a cone with the foot;
3. turns and runs round the cone in the middle of the field (jostling is an accepted part of the game);

4. jumps over a 2.5-metre-wide ditch (marked by two balls, cones or a small hurdle) on the way back to the goal; and

5. returns to the goal, where he or she touches the second cone with the foot. This is the signal for the next player to start the same sequence.

Each player should run twice. The winner is the team whose last player completes the second run first.

3. 3v3 With Through Passes to a Front Runner

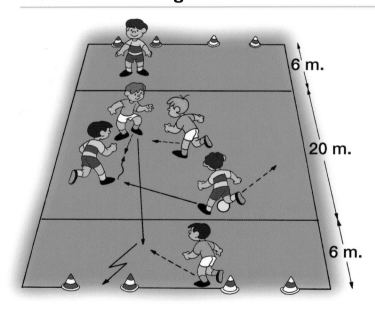

The official rules of mini-football without goal-keepers apply (see page 127). Each team has one striker (front runner) who must stay in the shooting zone, behind the opposing team's two midfielders. The striker cannot take part in the midfield play.

The coach starts the game by throwing the ball in the air. The two midfield players of each team must then try to pass the ball to their striker, making him- or herself available upfield. They are only allowed to leave the midfield when the ball is inside the shooting zone. After every two goals, the striker swaps places with one of the midfielders.

In the second half of the game, the striker is not allowed to score. When he or she receives a pass, the striker must lay the ball off to a midfielder who has made a forward run out of the midfield and is better positioned. The midfielder can then score.

? EFFECTIVE QUESTIONING

When is the best moment to play a through pass? Immediately after winning the ball, before the opposing team can regroup in defence.

What conditions must be satisfied before a successful through pass can be played? The passer and the receiver should make eye contact so that there is an understanding between them.

4. Tag Two Robbers

The cops' team stands near its goal, while the robbers' team takes up positions in the shooting zone so that they cannot be easily tagged when the first cop comes after them. When the first cop has tagged two robbers, he or she goes back to the goal and gives the next player a high five as the signal that it is now his or her turn. A robber is considered to have been tagged if he or she leaves the shooting zone. The time needed for all of the cops to tag two robbers is measured with a stopwatch. The two teams then swap places and tasks. Each team has two turns as cops. If the team that won the first round loses the second round, the team that achieved the lowest time is the winner. The content of this game can be varied to suit your coaching objectives. Tag games are good for stimulating players to learn and improve their perceptive skills, decision-making ability and coordination.

5. 3v3

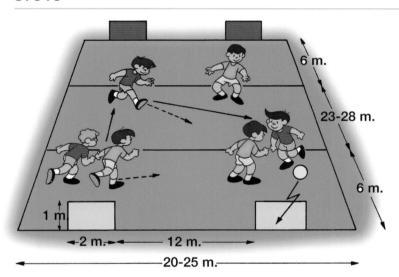

The official rules of mini-football without goal-keepers apply (see page 127). The game comprises three periods each lasting three minutes. If each team has a substitute, the length of periods is extended to five minutes.

Advantages of Using Mini-Football With Four Goals

Comparison between two competitions for players aged 8 and 9

Mini-football with 4 goals	7v7 football
Because of the two goals being situated on the wings, players are opening up their offensive play, systematically using the spaces close to the side-lines. Playing with two goals stimulates the capacity of reading and understanding the game. Stimulates the use of perception and decision-making skills before actually carrying out the planned move. Stimulates perception, imagination, fantasy and creativity more than any other traditional football competition.	Due to the position of the goal in the centre of the field, frequent conglomerations of players around the ball happen again and again, which does not stimulate the process of learning how to read the game. The development of perception skills, understanding and decision making become more difficult because of too many players being around the ball. Fewer stimuli are given for developing game intelligence, fantasy and creativity.
Sufficient space and time allow children to read and construct the mini-game, learning to develop basic communication skills. Sufficient time and space lead to fewer mistakes because analysing game situations, decision making and skill execution are easier. Because the same basic game situations appear again and again (e.g., 2v1), the young players learn very quickly.	There is less time and space available for perception, decision making and skill execution. Less time and space to play lead to more mistakes. Because 12 players are involved, the game situations are much more complex than in mini-football and don't reappear as frequently.
In mini-football the 8- and 9-year-old players are taught to treat the ball as their best friend, touching it with love and tenderness. No clearances or wild and dangerous kicking can be seen in which players harm the ball.	It is frequently seen that players clear the ball wide, far away from the danger zone. Often they play against the ball instead of with it.
Players learn to attack and defend in a triangular formation, which allows the development of better communication and collaboration. Positioning in the field is easy.	Positioning themselves in the field is often spontaneous and not a consequence of logical thinking.
Allows an all-around development of all participants because there are no fixed positions in a team that would encourage early specialisation. Everybody has to attack as well as to defend, on the left as well as on the right side of the field.	The players stick more to their assigned position in the field and don't have multi-purpose functions like in mini-football. Generally the children are already given a specific position in their team in 7v7 football.
Each player scores more than one goal in each match. All players are main actors of this dynamic game and are constantly involved.	Fewer goals are scored by fewer players.
Each player, even the weaker ones, is in a team of only three players.	The weaker players are much less involved in the game than the more talented ones.
Many ball contacts demand a permanent visual, cognitive and physical participation of each of the three players.	There are fewer ball contacts. Players take part less, physically as well as mentally, in the game than in the mini-football competition.
The play shown by the 8- and 9-year-old children is in its development more similar to 11v11 football than the 7v7 football game.	For 8- and 9-year-old children, 7v7 football is too complex, too difficult to understand and less recommendable than mini-football, which better stimulates the development of their personality and self-confidence.

Increasing Football Intelligence Through Game Variations

The following exercises are organised in increasing levels of difficulty and contain several aspects that will help prepare players for an 11v11 football game.

1. Mini-Football With One Player Remaining Inside the Shooting Zone

One player of each team stays in the penalty area and cannot advance into the midfield. After each goal this defender swaps places with a midfield player.

VARIATION

When the team is building up an attack, the defender can push forward into the midfield, provided a team-mate falls back to cover for him or her at the same time.

 EFFECTIVE QUESTIONING

Why should one of the three players remain in the shooting zone? So that there is a balance between defence and attack and there are more passing options.

What are the tasks of the player who hangs back behind his or her team-mates?

- The player who hangs back can help out if his or her team-mates make a defensive mistake and can cover the backs of the midfield players.
- He or she can take up a position to receive a back pass and can launch an attack with passes.

2. Dribbling the Ball Across One of the Two Goal-Lines

See the official rules of mini-football without goal-keepers beginning on page 127. Instead of shooting into one of the two goals from inside the shooting zone, an attacker has to dribble the ball through one of the two 6-metre-wide cone goals.

VARIATIONS

- The player who dribbles the ball over the goal-line has to demonstrate a trick, such as Zidane's spin. This variation forces the players to use the space better and create clear goal-scoring chances.
- A goal only counts if each of the three players has played the ball at least once since the moment when the team won possession.
- A goal only counts if the ball has only been played along the ground since the moment when the team won possession. This makes attacks faster and more effective.
- Between the moment when the team wins possession and the moment when it scores, at least one high pass must be played (volley). This helps the players to improve their ball control.

- A goal is only valid if all three players of the attacking team are in the defending team's half when the scorer shoots. This encourages all three players to attack as a compact unit.
- To maintain a balance between attack and defence, one of three attackers must be in his or her own half of the field when a goal is scored. The player is then in position to slow down an opposing counterattack if his or her team loses possession.

3. Make It, Take It

After scoring, the attackers immediately attack the other two goals at the other end of the field. The defending team cannot pressure them inside the shooting zone in which they have just scored. This means that the defenders can only defend the counterattack in the midfield. The team that scores the most goals in sequence is the winner. This variation is especially good for improving the players' concentration.

 ### EFFECTIVE QUESTIONING

What do we learn when we have to attack the goal at the opposite end immediately after scoring a goal?

- You learn how to quickly adjust to a new situation and play the ball out of a crowded zone to give your team more time and space to create a scoring chance.
- You learn how to control the pace of the play (you can speed up the play or slow it down).

What is the best way for the attacking team to score several times in succession? Immediately after scoring, the scorer should not try to run with the ball but should play it to a team-mate who has made a run into space in midfield. All of the players who helped in the move that led to the goal should put distance between themselves and the ball and run into space in the opposing team's half of the field.

4. Mini-Football With a Handicap

After each goal, the scoring team loses a player and must play until the next goal with one player less than the other team (2v3). If the team with three players scores, the third player of the other team comes back into the game while the scoring team loses a player (3v2). If a team with two players scores, it again loses a player and must then play 1v3.

This variation on mini-football without goal-keepers is played for three periods of two minutes with two pauses of one minute, in which the coach discusses with the players any errors that may have been made.

 ### EFFECTIVE QUESTIONING

Why do we play mini-football with a handicap? So that you learn how to adjust to different game situations and how to continuously read the game. Initially you play 3v3, then 2v3 or 3v2, or even 1v3 or 3v1.

5. Mini-Football With Three Teams

A team of three players takes up positions in the middle of the field and attacks the mini-goals on both end-lines alternately. Each set of two goals is defended by a team of three players. One defender is a goal-keeper and stays close to both goals, while another defender can only defend being on the 6-metre line. The third defender can move and defend freely within his or her own half of the field.

VARIATIONS

- All three defenders can move and defend freely in their own half of the field. After 10 attacks (five at each end), the attackers swap places with one of the defending teams. This is repeated until all of the teams have played once as attackers.
- The attackers lose their right to attack if a shot misses the goal or they lose possession. When the defenders win the ball, they must pass it at least once to acquire the right to carry out the next attack.

EFFECTIVE QUESTIONING

How does the goal-keeper's position in front of the two goals influence the build-up play of the three attackers? Give examples for the different positions of the goal-keeper in front of the two goals. The players should attack the goal farther away from the keeper (preferably using a long through pass). When the ball is in the opposition's half, the goal-keeper observes the play from a position midway between the two goals so that he or she can quickly defend the goal that is attacked.

6. Through Passing to a Front Runner

Each team positions a striker (front runner) in the opponent's shooting zone. The striker expects to receive an accurate through pass from one of the two team-mates, who are not allowed to leave the midfield. The striker controls the ball (preferably standing side-on to the goals in order to see them) and shoots at one of the goals. As the players' skills become more proficient, the coach may not only ask the striker to stand side-on but can also ask the players to use different passing techniques with the right or left foot. Otherwise a goal will not count.

EFFECTIVE QUESTIONING

When is the best moment to play a through pass? Immediately after winning the ball, before the opposing team has time to regroup defensively.

What conditions must be satisfied before a successful through pass can be played? The passer and the receiver should have a visual agreement (eye contact) so that there is an understanding between them. The receiver should always receive and control the ball standing side-on to the goals, which allows him or her to see what is going on behind.

Is it better to pass along the ground or in the air? Why? Passing along the ground is better, because high passes complicate the play and slow it down. High passes result in more mistakes.

VARIATIONS

- To improve receiving and controlling the ball, the ball has to be passed through the air to the striker.
- The midfielders can only enter the shooting zone after the ball has been passed into it. This forces the striker to receive, control and orientate the ball versus a space where there is no opponent.
- The striker is not allowed to score. This means that one of the two midfielders must quickly offer him- or herself upfield in the shooting area where he or she receives the ball from the striker and then scores.

 ### EFFECTIVE QUESTIONING

What do we have to do to score a goal? One of the two midfielders must make a forward run into the shooting zone and call for the ball.

Which of the two midfielders should make the forward run? Usually this will be the player who is closest to the striker. In some game situations a switch of flanks is better, because the midfielder who is farther away then has a free run at the goal.

Why do the two midfielders not both make forward runs? If the defenders win the ball, they will be able to counterattack, because no one is covering in midfield.

7. Retaining Possession in 3v2 Situations

Each team must have one player in its own shooting zone. The other two players remain in the midfield. Each team tries to keep possession of the ball for six seconds, being pressured by two opponents. Once the three attackers manage to retain the possession of the ball for the given time, the player in the shooting zone may move upfield and score together with the two midfielders against the three opponents, set up in a 2:1 formation. Once his or her team loses possession, one of the three attackers returns to the shooting zone. Meanwhile, the other two players now defend against the three new attackers who keep possession of the ball before they are being allowed to attack.

VARIATIONS

- With the exception of the following rules, the official rules of mini-football without goal-keepers apply (see page 127). A team has to pass the ball four times in succession before it can attack the opposing team's goals. The defender behind can push up into midfield when his or her team has managed to pass the ball four times in succession.
- To improve specific skills, only successful passes with the weaker foot, passes over 10 metres and first-time passes are counted.

 ### EFFECTIVE QUESTIONING

What do the players have to do between winning the ball and scoring?

- Secure possession.
- Build up an attack in the direction of the shooting zone.

- Pass the ball into the path of a team-mate whenever possible.
- Shoot.

What is the best way to retain possession?

- Avoid unnecessary 1v1 situations.
- Pass the ball to the feet of a team-mate whenever possible.
- Run into space, look for free space and use it.

8. Attacking Diagonally Opposite Goals

Each team attacks two diagonally opposite goals and defends the two other goals. A goal is scored by shooting into one of the two goals from inside the shooting zone or by dribbling the ball over one of the two goal-lines.

VARIATION

The coach and his assistant (or player), both behind each end-line, suddenly and simultaneously change the colour of the cone goals and act accordingly so that one team always attacks two of the four goals. A goal can be scored only by dribbling the ball across the coloured cone goal-line marked during the flow of the game. Modifying the colour of the goals during the development of the game helps to improve the player's perceptive skills, since their field of vision is an area of 360 degrees.

 **EFFECTIVE QUESTIONING**

Which of the two goals is the best one to attack? The players should attack the goal that is defended by only one defender. To do so, they should create a 2v1 situation and exploit this successfully to score.

How should the attack be carried out (by running with the ball or passing)?

- Passes make the game faster and enable free space to be used more effectively.
- Frequent changes of direction when running with the ball may create more space and cause the defender to make a wrong decision or a positional error.

How can the attacker create a situation in which his or her team has a numerical advantage? By changing direction when running with the ball and then switching the play.

9. Choose Any of the Four Goals

The three attackers always attack the goal that they consider to be less defended. The coach can specify whether a goal has to be scored by shooting from inside the shooting zone or by dribbling the ball across any goal-line (6 metres wide).

6 m.

6 m.

12 m.

VARIATIONS

- A goal only counts if the nearest defender is at least 5 metres away when the ball is dribbled across the goal-line.

- A team of three players has 10 ball possessions with the other team defending the four goals. An attack ends when a goal is scored, or the ball goes out of play or when a defender touches the ball. Each attack starts in the middle of the field. The defenders have to position themselves intelligently to prevent the attackers from scoring. The objective of the game is to teach the attackers to use the space with intelligence and to play so securely that they are able to score 10 times with 10 ball possessions.

- The four goals can be positioned anywhere on the end-lines or side-lines.

EFFECTIVE QUESTIONING

How can I disguise the direction of my attack? First of all by running in another direction to fool your opponent. You can then accelerate and change direction to leave your opponent behind or take the ball past him.

What does the attacker with the ball have to pay attention to? He needs to take his eyes off the ball (head up, peripheral vision) so that he can see what the defenders are doing in front of the goals and what his two team-mates are doing so that he can employ the right tactics.

10. Giving Width When Attacking

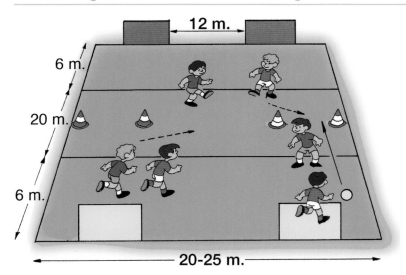

This variation on mini-football encourages the players to build up attacks by playing down the flanks and to give width to their attacks. Two 6-metre-wide goals are formed by placing cones near the side-lines, about half way down the field. The attackers must not start the buildup in the centre (danger of counterattack if possession is lost) but must attack using the wings. A goal is only valid if the attack has started with a dribble or pass of the ball through one of the two cone goals in the centre of the field.

VARIATION

Both goals in the centre are set up parallel to the side-lines instead of the end-lines. The attackers may only enter the opposing team's half of the field when the ball has been played through one of the two goals.

11. Mini-Football With One Outlet-Player on Each Side-Line

A mini-football team is now formed by five players, three playing inside the field and one additional one is offering him- or herself for a pass, moving on each side-line. Once they receive the ball (preferably from the opposite part of the field) being on the side-line they may enter the field while the passing player has to move out and replace the receiver.

12. Channelling Attacks

The official rules of mini-football without goal-keepers apply (see page 127). If a team scores in the goal on the right it is awarded three points, and if it scores in the goal on the left is it only awarded one point. In this way, the defenders learn how to close down the available space and channel attacks toward the side of the field where they are better prepared.

13. Controlling Through Passes Behind One of the Mini-Goals

Experienced players older than 12 are able to send a through pass from midfield through one of the two goals placed on the 6-metre line to a team-mate, who may not spend more than five seconds inside the opposing shooting zone behind the two goals. Once the player controls the through pass inside the shooting zone, he or she has to score in either of the two goals on the end-line.

What is the easiest way for a team to score? By playing the ball to a front runner who makes him- or herself available behind the two goals immediately after the team wins possession of the ball.

When should the striker run into position to receive the pass? When he or she sees that a midfielder has an opportunity to play a through pass and has made a visual agreement with him or her. The striker then sprints into the shooting zone.

Where should the striker run? A sudden diagonal sprint behind the defence is always promising. Good timing in running free, accurate passing and football intelligence are the crucial factors that determine whether a goal is scored.

3v3 Triathlon

Just like the 2v2 triathlon in level 1 (see page 81), the 3v3 triathlon should be included periodically as part of the training programme. The triathlon helps players learn to read situations and react to the moves of two other team-mates as well as to a maximum of three defenders.

The figure below illustrates the ideal organisation for the triathlon competition. In this example, teams representing Asia compete against teams representing North America until a winner is decided. The blank spaces next to each game are for coaches to use in recording scores.

Asia Versus North America

Teams	South Korea	China	Japan	Pakistan
Names of players				

Teams	El Salvador	Mexico	United States	Puerto Rico
Names of players				

First game scores: 3v3 with four intersecting goals (4 × 3 min).			Second game scores: 3v2 with counterattack (4 × 3 min.)			Third game scores: 3v3 with two wide goals (4 × 3 min.)		
KOR-SLV			KOR-MEX			PAK-MEX		
CHN-MEX			CHN-USA			JPN-SLVA		
JPN-USA			JPN-PRI			CHN-PRI		
PAK-PRI			PAK-SLV			KOR-USA		

Final result: Asia _____   North America _____   Technical delegate: _____

Note: During the triathlon, changing the composition of the team is not permitted.

I. 3v3 With Four Intersecting Goals

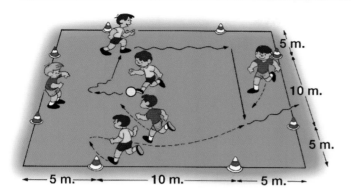

- Each team attacks the two wide goals assigned to them and defends the other two.
- Throw the ball to start the game.
- There are no throw-ins.
- Free kicks or dribbles should be taken no less than 3 metres from the goal-lines.
- To score, a player has to dribble the ball from a spot inside the pitch across one of the two opposing goal areas.
- Duration of the game: four periods each lasting three minutes, with one minute's rest between periods.

2. 3v2 With Counterattack

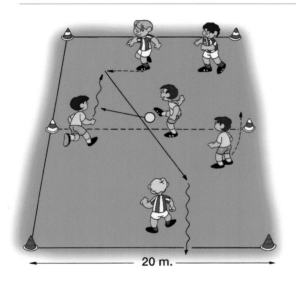

- During each period, one team alternately attacks the two 20-metre-wide goals.
- Two opponents defend the goal, while the third is placed in the opposite goal area waiting for a pass from his or her team-mates.
- After each attack, the defenders have to rotate: One of the two joins his or her team-mate in the opposite goal so that it is always 2v3.
- Once the ball has been lost by the attackers, these players should tackle back immediately—but never from behind the centre-line.
- A goal is scored with a dribble across the goal-line.
- Both teams may score.
- Change positions every period, switching between the attackers and defenders.
- Free kicks or dribbles should be from no less than 3 metres from the goal-line.
- Duration of the game: four periods each lasting three minutes.

3. 3v3 With Two Wide Goals

- Set the dimensions of the playing area as in the illustration (20 by 20 metres, with goals 20 metres wide).
- Use a ball toss to start the game.
- Free kicks and dribbles should be taken from no less than 3 metres to the goal-lines.
- To score, the ball must be dribbled across the opposing goal-line.
- Duration of the game: four periods each lasting three minutes.

Rules of 3v3 Mini-Football With Goal-Keepers

Mini-football with goal-keepers is considered the ideal team competition for 9-year-old players. It allows them to spend an entire season preparing for the greater demands of the 7v7 game, which they will play the following year. In mini-football, boys and girls may still play together on the same team.

Field

The size of the mini-football pitch is 22 by 32 metres. On each end-line, there are two goals measuring 2 by 1 metres. The goals are 12 metres apart. The penalty area or shooting zone is marked by a line parallel to and 6 metres from the end-line. A goal is only valid if it is scored from inside the shooting zone.

Teams

A mini-football team is made up of only five players, one substitute, four players allowed to play at the same time on the pitch, with one as goal-keeper. The keeper is not allowed to leave the shooting area. The competition should not be played with fewer than four players per team.

 After either team scores a goal, both teams must substitute one player. These players must enter at the centre-line, after their team-mates have left the field from the same spot. If this rule is broken, the other side will be awarded a penalty attack from the centre of the mini-football field against the opponent's goal-keeper. See 'Penalty' in the Rules section below for more information.

Duration

If only one match takes place for the 9-year-old players, the competition should last for three 10-minute periods, with five-minute breaks between the periods. If several matches are played on the same day (for instance, in a tournament or festival), the recommended duration of play is two 10-minute periods.

Technical Rules

A player may not play the ball with hands, be in an off-side position or use violence.

Free Kick—For any breach of rules in any part of the field (except for the defenders in their own defensive zone), a free kick is awarded for the other side. To put the ball into play, the player may choose either to pass the ball to a team-mate or to dribble it. All free kicks must be taken at a distance of no less than 3 metres away from the shooting zone, with the defenders also more than 3 metres off the ball.

Penalty—There is no simple penalty kick on goal for an intentional breach of the rules inside a team's own 5.8-metre zone, but the opponent will be awarded a penalty attack, which starts from the centre of the field. In a penalty attack, all the players (except the goal-keepers) must remain 5 metres behind the attacker in possession of the ball. After the referee has given permission for the attack, they all may interfere in defence as well as in support. The goal-keeper starts his or her defence from the end-line. In case of an infringement of the rules by any defender, the free attack is repeated.

Corners—Mini-football with goal-keepers has no corners.

Kick-Ins and Side-Outs—The ball is brought into play with a free kick from the side-line or from the 5.8-metre line.

Start and Restart of the Game—Always start or restart the game with a ball toss in the centre of the field.

Equipment

Ball: A No. 4 ball should be used.

Clothing: All the players of a team wear vests of the same colour.

Protection: All of the players should wear shin guards.

Referee

A referee is in charge of the game. There are no referee's assistants. In mini-football, referees should be under 18 years of age if possible. This ensures that new referees come up through the ranks.

Structuring an Internal Mini-Football League

Most of the FIFA member countries for decades have used the full 11v11 game as only youth competitions independent of the age of the young footballer. In fewer than 15 countries worldwide, the 7v7 game on a smaller pitch has replaced the 11v11 game on the full pitch. But experiences in the last decade of the past century have shown that the best results in the development of 8- and 9-year-old players are achieved when they play neither the full nor the 7v7 game. Rather, an internal mini-football league for these youngest players should be organised within the larger club.

To ensure the stimulation of game intelligence, the 8- and 9-year-old football players are exposed every month through a modification of rules to a different, more difficult and complex mini-game:

March

Mini-football: One defender is obliged to remain in the proper shooting zone.

April

Mini-football with official rules:

2nd weekend: A goal is valid only when everybody touches the ball after its recovery.

3rd weekend: A goal is valid only when none of the attackers puts the ball into the air.

4th weekend: A goal is valid only when all team members are inside the opposing half.

May

Carrying the ball through one of the two goals:

2nd weekend: An acrobatic skill has to be shown when crossing the goal-line with the ball.

3rd weekend: A goal is only valid when one team-mate remains in his or her own half for covering.

June

Mini-football on diagonally opposed goals:

1st and 2nd weekend: Scoring with a shot from inside the shooting zone.

3rd weekend: Scoring with carrying the ball across one of the two goal-lines (6 m. wide).

4th weekend: During the development of the game the position of the four goals is modified.

July

Mini-football: Attacking the ball has to be kept six seconds in possession with one player staying behind.

September

Mini-football on any of the four goals:

1st weekend: Scoring with a shot from inside the shooting zone.

2nd weekend: Scoring with carrying the ball across any goal.

(continued)

(continued)

3rd weekend: Scoring with carrying the ball through any goal with an opponent at more than 5 metres.
4th weekend: During the development of the game the position of the four goals is modified.

October

Mini-football with passes out of the midfield to a forward:
2nd weekend: When the ball arrives in the shooting zone, everybody can move up to support.
3rd weekend: Only aerial passes are allowed to the forward.
4th weekend: The forward is the only player who is not allowed to score.

November

Mini-football with long passes from the midfield through any of the two goals:
1st and 2nd weekend: A fourth player offers himself or herself behind the two goals to receive the long pass.
3rd and 4th weekend: A fourth player defends both goals from a position in front of them.

December
Mini-football: Using a goal-keeper and a substitute.

Taking Mini-Football Toward 7v7 Football

The transition from mini-football to 7v7 football should always proceed through a progressive series of games without any rush. To help the players develop a feel for the larger field, the coach initially sets up a mini-football pitch in the centre of a 7v7 football field. The players are asked to carry out more-complex tasks from game to game. The number of players and the size of the field are gradually increased until the players have learned to fulfill their functions in all seven positions.

Games for Mini-Football Field

1. 3v3 With and Without Goal-Keepers

The game is played on a 7v7 field. The mini-field is positioned exactly in the middle. Each team of three players has one player who has to remain in the shooting zones. A goal can only be scored by a player who gains possession of the ball inside the shooting zone.

VARIATIONS WITH GOAL-KEEPERS

- A goal-keeper is at each goal. A goal can only be scored from *inside* the shooting zone.
- A goal-keeper is at each goal. A goal can only be scored from *outside* the shooting zone.

VARIATIONS WITHOUT GOAL-KEEPERS

- The action radius of the third player is no longer limited to the shooting zone.
- A goal is scored only by dribbling the ball across one of the two goal-lines (cone goals).
- One player of each team must take up a position in the shooting zone to receive a through pass from the midfield.

Games for 7v7 Football Field

1. 3v3 Dribbling Through a Cone Goal

Once the ball has been dribbled across one of the two goal-lines (cone goals) of the mini-football field, a goal can be scored in the 7v7 football goal.

VARIATION

After the ball has been dribbled over the two goal-lines, all the players can leave the mini-field until a goal is scored or the ball goes out of play.

2. 3v3 Plus One Front Runner

Each team has one striker (front runner) who takes up a position behind one of the cone goals outside the mini-football field. The player tries to receive and control an accurate pass out of the midfield in a side position and then score within three seconds against a goal-keeper in the 7v7 football goal (6 by 2 metres).

At the start three players of each team contest the possession of the ball in the midfield, which they are not allowed to leave. When a team has possession, it tries to play an accurate pass to its striker. Practice takes place first without and then with goal-keepers.

3. 3v3 Plus Two Front Runners and One Defender

This is much the same as the previous game, except that there is now an additional striker behind the second cone goal and a defender in front of the two cone goals.

The defender tries to intercept the through passes from the midfielders in front of the cone goals. If he or she succeeds, the defender passes the ball to the three team-mates in the midfield. If the defender does not succeed and the ball reaches one of the strikers, he or she helps the goal-keeper defend the situation.

VARIATIONS

- The defender plays behind instead of in front of the two cone goals. Therefore we have a 2v1 situation behind the goals of the mini-field.

- The game is first played without, then with, off-side. Every five minutes the players swap roles and positions until each player has occupied every position once.

4. 7v7 With Restrictions

All four cone goals are removed so the strikers can move around freely but always outside of the mini-field.

VARIATIONS

- Once the ball has been passed outside the mini-football field to a striker, one or two midfield players may support the ball receiver (or the only defender) and move upfield (downfield) to offer themselves for a pass or for supporting the only defender.

- Now we are playing with one goal-keeper, one free defender, three midfielders and two strikers, 7v7 first without and later with the off-side rule. Every five minutes the players swap roles and positions until each player is familiar with every position and has gained important experience.

All activities proposed in levels 1 and 2 have as the objective that players under 10 years of age learn to enjoy and play mini-football successfully. All the games (for players of basic abilities as well as the simplified games) presented in this chapter together with their tailor-made competitions are seen as so many pieces forming a complete puzzle and the complete game of mini-football. As the youngsters play mini-football, your reviewing the games for basic abilities in level 1 and the more difficult and complex ones of level 2 (all of which should be considered as corrective exercises for mini-football) will help them improve and consolidate most of the football fundamentals. In addition, having the players practice the different variations of mini-football (including the mini-football pentathlon), thanks to the two goals to attack and to defend, further consolidates their basic skills. New experience in such important capacities as perception, anticipation and decision making are essential for the preparation of the 7v7 football game, which is explored further in the next chapter.

Games
for 7v7 Football

In football the brain counts a lot. All players have two legs,
two hands, two ears and two eyes but only one brain.

Understanding football involves comprehending how the game develops. The coach must teach players not only many individual and team skills but also thinking skills. Without understanding the most common situations that occur in the game, it is difficult to make correct decisions. Without mastering the playing skills, on the other hand, these decisions cannot be carried out. The most natural way to develop *reading* and *reacting* skills is to expose youngsters to many different simplified games, which teach the players how to be in the right place on the pitch at the right time. This is precisely what the simplified games in level 3 are meant to do.

Reading the game means observing and analysing the location of team-mates, opponents and the ball as well as the speed and direction of play. This ability allows players to react and to anticipate the next play.

Three Basic Game Situations

Everything that happens on the football pitch occurs in one of these three situations:

1. The ball is loose and neither team has it.
2. The team has the ball on offence.
3. The team is on defence, preventing the opponent from scoring.

These three conditions frequently change phases, but during each of them the player must constantly read and react. How to react depends on the player's position in relation to the ball and his or her proximity to the team's own goal. A golden rule or precondition of interpreting any game situation is that the player must face the play to see the situation; only then can he or she react. Turning one's back on the play (as many front runners do, for example, when they receive the ball) is a cardinal mistake.

Loose-Ball Game

The reaction of the player closest to the loose ball dictates whether the team will be on offence or defence. This player's first thought should be defensive until he or she can read the situation perfectly. Generally, the closest player's reaction to a loose ball is to become the ball carrier. While the face-off for the ball is occurring, all other players involved in the game situation (team-mates of the possible attacker and those of the possible defender) must know their roles in advance in case their team-mate wins, loses or draws in the loose-ball game. During the loose-ball game, does the player correctly recognise his or her proximity to the ball? Does he or she know how to assess the distance from it (in relation to that of the nearest opponent), taking into account the player's and the opponent's speed? When the situation is not clear, does the player recognise whether the distance from his or her own goal allows him or her to make an offensive or a defensive decision? *Statistics have shown that the team that wins the most loose balls usually also wins the game.* Therefore, to improve a win–loss record, the players should concentrate on winning those loose balls!

Offensive Game

While the player who is closest to the ball chooses between beating the opponent or passing the ball, he or she also considers the team-mates' positions farther away from

Playing a game of football without thinking is shooting without aiming.

the ball. Most of them should support the ball carrier and join the attack. The more support the ball carrier receives, the more options he or she has. The ball carrier should have at least three safe passes to his or her fellow players who, by running free, give width and depth to the attack and help spread the defence. The width of the attack is determined by how far apart the players position themselves in the outside lanes and by their occupying all attacking positions. It also depends on where they are in the centre lane, from which distribution or passing of the ball is the easiest. The depth of the attack is the distance between the players who are closest to and most distant from the ball. Whenever possible, there should be low, medium and high depths to the attack.

How quickly the transition takes place from defence to offence or vice versa is of great importance. Modern football is a game of quick transitions. The most dangerous attacking situations can be created after a successful tackle, when the new attack is launched literally within a second. Generally it takes more time for the defence to recognise that they have to change their roles. Attackers who make use of quick transitions from defence to offence generally attack an unorganised defence, whereas a slow transition might result in an attack's being against an already-organised defence.

The first player, who either beats his or her opponent and carries the ball up the pitch or passes it to the closest supporting player and their nearest supporting teammate are the key players. When an attacker without the ball creates passing options, the transition becomes much quicker than in the case when the ball carrier is forced to keep running with the ball in order to create space and time for himself or herself.

Knowing when not to move is as important as knowing what move to make.

Defensive Game

The player of the other team who was not as close to the ball in the loose-ball situation then becomes the defender. This person is the key player on defence: After all, his or her quickness and kinds of movements determine how his or her team-mates have to defend. If the player is aggressive, his or her team-mates defend by close 1v1 coverage. But if the first opponent is passive, his or her team-mates only cover the zone.

The player should quickly put pressure on the ball carrier, at the same time receiving immediate support from the closest team-mate and the rest of the defending players. The role of these defenders depends on their distance from the ball also and whether they are the second-, third-, fourth-, or fifth-closest player to the checking defender. While facing the ball and personal opponent simultaneously, with the head swiveling at all times, the defender may decide to switch opponents without forgetting to choose a correct position between the attacker and his or her own goal. Does the closest checking player take the space away from the ball carrier? Does he or she get immediate support by team-mate defenders? Does the whole defensive unit still give immediate support to the checking player after it seems obvious that the opponent will win the loose ball? The ball carrier who is being checked by the closest defender often is not the most dangerous player—someone among the potential pass receivers is.

It is part of a coach's functions to watch how his or her defenders perform in these four types of play or roles:

1. An opponent with the ball
2. A player checking the ball carrier
3. Opponents who are supporting the ball carrier
4. Players who are covering the checking defender or the area away from the ball

The more a young football player understands the game, the better he or she will be able to see, read and react to all game situations.

Organising the Training Session

Here are a few recommendations for structuring a training session for players aged 10 to 12 years:

1. Instead of starting with a warm-up (which is not mandatory for children up to 12 years), the session should always begin with a simplified game in which the coach presents specific game-related problems to the few players of each team.

2. During a 10-minute game, observe and analyse the technical and tactical playing performance of the players. After the game, assign and carry out a series of corrective exercises to ameliorate the problem situations you have discovered. The choice of these corrective exercises depends on the technical-tactical aspects that have lowered the quality of play (for example, you might work on tackling at the right moment, not too late and not too early).

3. After isolated skill practice (always seen as a function of performance in the simplified game), the game resumes. See whether the weaknesses you had previously noticed have been overcome with the help of the corrective exercises or whether other aspects of the game still need improvement. Through systematic questioning from you

as coach, players can become aware of the importance of specific football knowledge; ask them to work out the correct patterns.

Other training tips:

➤ To facilitate the observation, analysis, decision making, and motor response of the young players, no more than seven youngsters per team should participate in the official competition.

➤ The space in which the simplified game takes place should initially be rather wide and deep to give the players enough time to decide their moves and enough space to carry them out. The coach should reduce the time and space only when the level of technique is high enough to allow the players to draw their attention to other aspects inherent in the football game . Gradually, then, both these parameters become similar to those of the official competition.

➤ Learning and perfecting basic abilities and capacities must be considered an important part of each training session. The more game-like the situation you present to the players in training, the more they are able to transfer the experience to the game.

➤ It should be obvious that you alternate exercises and games of high intensity with those of low intensity.

➤ As the capacity of play improves, the multi-lateral games are introduced less often in the training sessions. Multi-lateral games, apart from being used to contribute to the intensity, variety and fun of the training, ensure the indispensable development of basic abilities.

➤ The training of coordination skills and physical capacities (such as various kinds of resistance, speed and strength) should be an integral part of the practice session.

➤ Thanks to players' improved perception and capacity of abstraction at this stage (level 3) coaches need provide only a demonstration of the sequence instead of explaining a determined skill or tactical move in detail. This is usually sufficient to allow players to reproduce the same pattern with ease.

➤ It is especially important for coaches to treat everyone the same way and for them not to show favouritism. Generally, prepubescent football players are pleased with their coaches if they are fair with everyone.

Simplified Games for 3v3

The simplified game is still an ideal framework for discovering, understanding and resolving specific game-related problems.

1st **Simplified Game**
Maintaining Ball Possession 3v1

Mark off two adjacent squares of 8 to 10 metres. In one, three attackers keep the ball against one defender. In the adjacent square, two of the defender's team-mates wait for a pass from their colleague if his or her defence in the 3v1 succeeds. Once they control the ball, the former defender joins the two team-mates to try to keep possession of the ball in another 3v1 situation.

8-10 m.

8-10 m.

A switch of play from one to the other playing area also occurs when one of the attackers infringes on the rules or the ball played by the attackers runs out of the limited zone. In both cases the defender kicks the ball from the side-line to one team-mate in the adjacent area, with the opponents staying at a distance of at least 3 metres. Immediately after the successful kick-in, the player joins his or her team members in the adjacent area. Here it is their turn to keep possession in the new 3v1 situation. If one defender runs out of energy, he or she may switch positions with a team-mate of the adjacent square. After a five-minute practice, organise a competition with one player of the adjacent area counting the seconds of ball possession.

Duration of the game: three periods of three minutes each. After nine minutes of play, the team that achieves the best time is winner. After every change of area (squares), a rotation takes place in the defending team.

VARIATIONS

- After passing to a team-mate, the attacker must move at least 5 metres out of his former position. Using this rule helps develop the players' orientation and perception.
- To stimulate ball control, the attackers must play aerial passes. Passes along the ground are not allowed.
- Keep track of the number of successive passes played exclusively with the less-skilled foot.
- Count the number of first-time passes during one ball possession.
- Have three attackers face one defender in both playing areas. The group that keeps the ball longer wins.

TRAINING OBJECTIVES

- Learn to avoid playing the ball into the opponent's range of action.
- Learn to pass the ball with precise timing, not too early and not too late.
- Learn when to pass and when to dribble.
- Learn to pass the ball accurately, quickly and without indicating its trajectory.
- After passing the ball, be prepared to receive it again; learn to support the ball carrier and consider the support given by the team-mates.
- As defender, learn to press the ball carrier and anticipate the opponent's play.

CORRECTIVE EXERCISES

Most of the Passing, Receiving and Shooting Games (beginning on page 55), as well as all of the 2v2 simplified games (begining on page 94), make good material for remedial work.

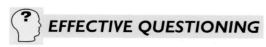 **EFFECTIVE QUESTIONING**

Where should the two team-mates of the defender ideally position themselves in the grid on either side? Explain why. The two team-mates should ideally offer themselves for a pass as far away as possible from the centre-line that separates the two grids. By doing so, they will have sufficient time to receive and control the ball (as the defenders are far away), as well as to decide upon the next move.

What are the tasks of the three attackers who should maintain possession of the ball as long as possible? Generally the ball should be passed only when the ball carrier is under pressure. In case both team-mates are supporting the ball carrier, the pass should be executed to the better-positioned player who is farther away from the only defender. But in case nobody is available for a pass, the ball carrier may dribble into an open space to gain some time for a pass or look out for better passing options.

When dribbling the ball, should the attacker shield it with his body, positioning himself or herself between the defender and the ball? Each pass should have sufficient speed, and its direction should not be indicated with the eyes or any body movement. After a successful pass, the passer should offer himself or herself for a return pass by immediately moving to an unoccupied space.

When should the attacker avoid a pass and instead keep the ball under close control? In case the attacker does not see any passing option, he or she should keep the ball in possession and dribble it into an unoccupied space where he or she might get new angles of passing.

How should a pressed attacker act in a 1v1 situation? The ball carrier should position his or her body between the defender and the ball, shielding it like that until he or she gets support from a team-mate.

What are the characteristics of a good pass?

- A good pass always reaches a team-mate who is not immediately put under pressure by a defender.
- A good pass is not executed too early or too late and allows a team-mate to play the ball in more favourable conditions.
- A good pass has sufficient speed and has been disguised so as to not allow the defenders to read the intention of the passer.
- A good pass is generally played along the ground where it can be controlled easier and more quickly than an aerial pass.

Why should aerial passes be avoided when the objective is to maintain possession of the ball? Passes played along the ground are quicker and easier to control than aerial passes.

When in this particular game does the ideal moment to pass the ball arise? When being put under full pressure by an opponent, the attacker had better pass the ball. That means that the pass is born of necessity.

What role should a player perform after he or she has successfully passed the ball? Immediately after his or her successful pass, the player should move out of position and offer himself or herself again in an area not controlled by any opponent.

When the team's objective is to maintain possession of the ball, should you pass the ball into the run of your team-mate or directly into his or her feet? To facilitate the team-mate's reception, the ball should be passed directly into his or her feet.

When do you have to play the oncoming ball directly (with one touch) and when do you decide to control it? In case an opponent presses the player at the moment of receiving the ball, the player passes the ball with the very first touch. In this situation he or she should choose not to control the ball with many touches as this involves risk of losing its possession.

In case an attacker loses possession of the ball, what should we expect him or her to do? The attacker (as well as all his or her team-mates) should switch immediately to defensive functions without creating a pause between attack and defence.

What should an intelligent defender who intends to repossess the ball from three attackers (1v3 situation) do? The player approaches the ball carrier diagonally in such a way that it obliges him or her to do what the defender anticipated: passing the ball to an opponent, whom the defender intentionally left unmarked.

2nd   Simplified Game
Fast Attack

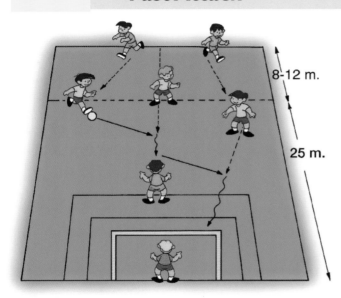

8-12 m.

25 m.

Set up a 7v7 football pitch. Divide the youngsters into three attackers and three defenders, with an additional goal-keeper. The three attackers start with the ball from the centre-line of the field and try to beat a defender (the 'sweeper') situated in front of the penalty zone. The attackers may only score goals from inside the zone. When the attackers first touch the ball on the centre-line, the two defenders, situated 8 to 12 metres behind them, begin pursuit. Their job is to try to help the sweeper, who is doing everything possible to delay the attack.

The attack ends

- when a goal is scored,
- when the attackers commit a rules infringement,
- when the ball is played outside of the mini-football field, or
- when the defenders can touch the ball three consecutive times or pass it once between them.

When the defenders commit an infringement of the rules inside the penalty area, a penalty kick from 9 metres against a neutral goal-keeper is awarded. After five fast attacks, both teams switch positions and functions until each team has defended and attacked 10 times. After each attack the 'sweeper' rotates. In the second series of attacks, the players in attack as well as in defence must assume different playing positions. The defenders who support the sweeper should now also start from different positions on both side-lines.

After the competition, use probing, open questions to work out with your players what the most effective fast attack would be, considering aspects of the dribble, of passing, of controlling the ball and of shooting.

VARIATIONS

- After a successful tackle or interception, the defenders must pass the ball across the centre-line or through one of the two goals, which should be established on the centre-line in the wing positions.
- The attackers may not pass the ball more than three times (or you can specify twice).

- Three attackers play against two defenders, with one tackling from behind. (This variation is for more-advanced players.)

TRAINING OBJECTIVES

- Consolidate the execution of the basic skills of dribbling, passing, receiving and scoring at high speed.
- Create correct habits for counterattacking: For instance, initially pass the ball from the depth of the pitch directly into the path of the team-mate, receive the ball on the run, use longer direct passes instead of many short passes and control the ball before making a pass.
- Learn to read the game: Know when to pass or not pass the ball, always considering the actions of the three defenders who condition the attacking play.
- Learn to look out for an effective attack. Three offensive actions are better than four. After carrying the ball to the third defender, make a diagonal pass into the run of one of the supporting players to either side. If this player then shoots from a safe distance, he or she is likely to assure a successful conclusion of the fast attack.
- Learn to cooperate in defence and to systematically delay the counterattack when there are too few supporting players.

 **EFFECTIVE QUESTIONING**

Which of the three attackers should have the ball at the initiation of the fast attack? This depends on the position of the three defenders in front and behind the attackers. Generally the centre forward should have the ball, since he or she has the shortest distance to score and the best passing options.

How should the centre forward initiate the fast attack, with a pass to one of the wings or with a quick dribble? A pass to one of the wings would slow down the attack and give the two defenders coming from behind an opportunity to interfere. But when the centre forward is carrying the ball quickly to a space on the left or right side of the central defender, he or she obliges the defender to move out of the central position. Then the pass has to be executed into the opposite direction into the run of the other wing. This player in the meantime has taken over a more central position in front of the goalpost closest to him or her. This allows the wing an optimal shooting angle.

What is the best moment for executing a pass? When the central defender is about to tackle, the pass should be played into the run of one supporting team-mate. Good timing of the pass (not too late and not too early) as well as its direction will not allow any defender to prevent the attacker from carrying out a shot on goal in this 2v1 situation.

Which factors does the centre forward have to consider before passing the ball? The pass depends not only on the position of the central defender (Is the defender in a frontal or side-on position?) but also from the behaviour and proximity of the two defenders who are tackling back from behind the three attackers. The pass also depends upon the availability of the two supporting wingers (Who has a better shooting angle? Who runs into an off-side position?).

What is the ideal position of the centre forward when one of the wings is in possession of the ball? In case the central defender tackles the winger in possession of the ball, the centre forward should fall back or run into the space behind the defender (attention with the off-side rule) to offer himself or herself for a through pass. The third attacker always adapts to what his or her other two team-mates do.

What are the tasks of the two attackers without the ball? They have to support the ball carrier, always remaining behind the ball (off-side). They must also position themselves sufficiently far away from the defender to not be pressed by him or her when they look out for a shot at goal from a position, ideally in front of the nearest goalpost. This allows an optimal shooting angle.

When passing the ball, which other remarks would you like to add? When the attacker passes the ball, the player should

- never indicate its direction and mislead the defender through dummies, fakes and feints or through just looking into another direction.
- direct the ball into the run of the team-mate to allow him or her to receive the ball level with the defender.
- immediately offer himself or herself in front or behind the ball receiver to allow the attack to flow.
- do it with preference to the opposite direction of his or her attacking move. When the attacker takes the opponent with him or her, it allows the receiver of the pass on the opposite side more time to think and to act because the defender is farther away.

In case there is an unmarked space in front of him or her, what should the attacker do with the ball? He or she should penetrate by dribbling with the ball and look out for a shot on goal.

Tell me something about the tasks of the other two attackers when the third one looks out for a shot on goal. First, they should make themselves available to receive the ball without being in an off-side position. In case the third attacker took the shot, they should look out to occupy an optimal position in front of the goal for taking the rebound. In doing so, they should not disturb each other and should not come too close to the goal-keeper.

How do you resolve a game situation in which you have a numerical superiority of 3v1?

- No time should be lost to conclude the attack before the only defender receives support from the recovering defenders. That is why as few passes as possible should be played to overcome the defender.
- A second aspect is to play as simply as possible to avoid unnecessary risks and mistakes. That happens when the ball carrier passes the ball at the correct time (when the defender tackles him or her), which means not allowing the defender any time to tackle the receiving left or right winger again while he or she prepares to shoot at goal.

What can a single defender do when he or she faces three attackers? The defender has two opportunities:

- Delay the attackers through retreating slowly back toward the goal and thus gaining some time for the midfielders to support him or her. By doing so, the numerical inferiority of 1v3 could be turned into a situation of equal numbers (3v3).
- He or she should force the ball carrier in the centre to pass the ball as early as possible or as far away as possible from the goal to a winger who, generally,

has fewer passing options than a centre forward and therefore could be more easily channelled by the defender. Causing the three attackers to execute two or more passes will slow down the attack and allow the recovering midfielders to join in defence. While delaying the attack and retreating in the field, the single defender should change his or her attitude in case he or she notices that the ball is out of control of the ball carrier.

How does the presence of the two midfield players behind the three attackers influence their play? Before the fast attack is initiated by the ball carrier, he or she should analyse the game situation (particularly the position of the opponents). Depending upon their position, the ball should always be passed, at the moment the central defenders show intent to tackle, into the run of a team-mate who is farthest away from the midfielders' tracking back.

Should the two recovering defenders try to tackle the player in possession of the ball or try to intercept the passes between them? While the central defender tries to delay the individual attack from the centre forward, the other two defenders may gain some time to assume positions up the field, which will allow them to intercept the pass to any wing. Either way, the three defenders should work out a plan to stop the three attackers from scoring.

CORRECTIVE EXERCISES

The following corrective exercises should be included in the training programme as needed.

1. Dribbling and Tag Games

Review the Dribbling Games beginning on page 40—particularly Tag Game on page 50.

2. Tackling From Behind

This practice is done with two players in part of a mini-football or a playing field. One attacker starts with a ball from the centre-line. A defender stands 3 metres behind this attacker and follows him or her, trying to execute a successful tackle before the attacker can control the ball in the penalty area.

To attack with success the forward must

- move quickly,
- invade the path of the defender who nears him or her (to avoid a collision and an infringement of the rules, the defender must slow down running speed), or
- feint a stop of the ball; while the defender reacts to this new situation and prepares a tackle, the attacker can suddenly change speed and escape.

After three attacks, the defender and attacker switch roles. Make sure that both players have a similar running speed.

3. Delaying the Opponents' Attack

This practice uses six players. After the coach's visual signal, an attacker in the centre of the mini-football pitch dribbles the ball toward one of the two opposing goals defended by an opponent who starts from the end-line. This defender closes down on the attacker and channels him or her to one side of the field.

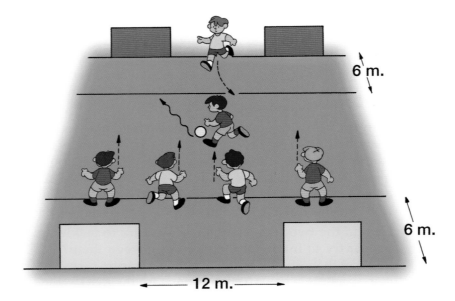

Meanwhile, after the initiation of the attack, four other players (two attackers and two defenders) run from the opposite shooting zone onto the field to support the single attacker or to tackle or intercept the pass.

A goal can be scored only from inside the shooting zone. The attack of the three (one plus two) finishes, when

- one of the attackers scores,
- the attackers lose the ball to the defenders,
- an attacker infringes on the rules, or
- when the ball runs out of play.

The players rotate positions on the second and third attacks, and the teams switch functions after each full rotation. The team that manages to score the highest number of goals in six attacks wins. In case of a foul by one of the defenders, the attack has to be repeated. As a variation, the two supporting defenders and the two supporting attackers may start from the line of the shooting zone, thus putting more pressure on the attackers.

3rd Simplified Game
3v1 Plus a Defender Who Covers

The game, which involves six players, is played between the centre-line and one line of the penalty area of a 7v7 football field. Set up cones to establish two 15-metre-wide goal areas on the penalty area and centre-line (see illustration). Three players are in possession of the ball and start their attack from the centre-line, aiming to alternately control the ball in a goal set up on the edge of the penalty box. This goal, as well as the one established on the centre-line, is defended by a single defender who must always remain on the same line without entering the field. One additional midfield player must always tackle first. After the conclusion of the first attack, with or without success, the three attackers turn around to attack the opposite wide goal, again tackled by the same midfield player and a third defender who covers him or her.

An attack finishes

- when a goal is scored with a dribble across one of the two goals,
- when the ball runs out of play, or
- when one of the two defenders wins the ball and manages to execute a pass to one of his or her two team-mates.

15-20 m.

15 m.

Duration of the match: three periods of two minutes until every defender has played once in each position. The forwards are also asked to switch their positions every two minutes.

 ## EFFECTIVE QUESTIONING

Which tasks does a ball carrier have to fulfill before he or she plays the ball? First the ball carrier has to analyse the position of the closest defender, the distance in relation to him or her and the position of the two team-mates. But before the ball carrier comes to a decision about the next move, he or she also has to perceive the position and attitude of the covering opponents behind him or her. Only after having processed all this valuable information is the player able to choose the best possible attacking move. The ideal solution would be to dribble the ball diagonally toward the defender in front and oblige him or her to move slightly out of the centre. Then the carrier can pass the ball into the run of the team-mate on the opposite side.

Which mistakes do the three attackers make frequently?

- Instead of playing in a triangle, which allows more passing options, they remain all on the same level.
- The wings come too close to the ball carrier instead of giving sufficient width to their attack.
- The 'last' pass before controlling the ball on the goal-line has not been directed into the run of a wing.
- The ball carrier does not hide his or her intentions and through gestures gives the covering player an opportunity to anticipate where he or she is going to play the ball.

VARIATIONS

- When the midfield player wins the ball, the other two defenders may leave their positions on the end-lines and move to receive a pass. If they manage to pass the ball twice, they now attack, while the former three attackers have to take over the defending positions and functions.
- After dribbling the ball across the goal-line, the attackers have to score from a distance of 11 metres into a goal defended by a neutral goal-keeper.

TRAINING OBJECTIVES

See the first simplified game on page 153, which has the same objectives.

CORRECTIVE EXERCISES

Choose from earlier simplified games for keeping possession of the ball in 2v1 or a 3v1 situation.

4th   Simplified Game
3v3 With Four Intersecting Goals

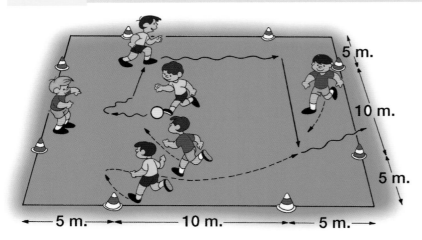

Teams of three players simultaneously defend two opposite goal areas (which should be 10 metres wide) and attack the other two. The illustration shows the setup and field dimensions.

The game is started by a ball toss into the centre of the square. When the ball runs across any side-line, there is a kick-in from where the ball left the playing area. During a free kick or kick-in, the opponents must be at least 5 metres away from the ball. To score, a player has to dribble the ball through one of two opposing goals.

Duration of the game: four periods of three minutes.

VARIATION

- Use the same variations as for the game 2v2 With Four Intersecting Goals on page 80.

TRAINING OBJECTIVES

- Practice and consolidate the technical and tactical objectives of the game 2v2 With Four Intersecting Goals from page 80 and of the previous simplified games.
- Learn to delay the tackle to gain time for receiving the support of a team-mate.
- Learn to always attack the goal that is less defended.
- Learn to channel the opponent's play into the desired direction (for instance, into a team-mate's tackling area or away from the goal).
- Ensure width and depth coverage.
- In defence, learn to pressure the ball carrier to force him or her to commit mistakes.
- Defending in 1 on 2, learn to delay the tackle to avoid getting outplayed before the support of a team-mate arrives.
- Learn to always attack in a triangular formation, while the defence must assure width and depth (cover) and be able to pressure the ball carrier to force him or her to commit mistakes.
- In attack, learn to watch for a 2v1 situation—and to avoid a 1v1 situation when possible.

- Be able to suddenly change the direction and rhythm of the attack without dribbling the ball too close to a defender.

CORRECTIVE EXERCISES

See the simplified game 2v2 With Four Goals on page 102.

EFFECTIVE QUESTIONING

Which of the two cone goals should be attacked? When in possession of the ball, the three attackers have to watch for which of the two cone goals is less defended. This depends particularly on the position of the central defender and his or her distance to either of the two goals.

How can the attackers systematically create an outnumbered situation (2v1) in front of one of the opponent's goals? When the ball carrier directs the attack toward one goal, he or she obliges the central defender to support the team-mate in the attacked goal. In case the ball carrier suddenly changes his or her direction and speed and carries the ball toward the opposite goal, he or she creates a 2v1 situation with support from the other team-mate.

5th Simplified Game
3v2 With Counterattack

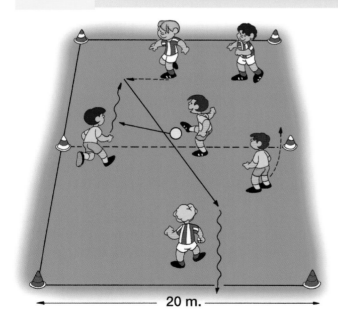

20 m.

Use a football field with two 20-metre-wide goals established on the centre-line and the penalty-area line. In each half, station one team of three players that is to alternately attack the two goals. Two of the three opponents always defend the goal that is being attacked to prevent the attackers from dribbling the ball across their goal-line. Meanwhile, their third opponent remains in the opposite goal, ready to receive a pass from one of his or her team's two other defenders, should they manage to win the ball from the attackers. After receiving the ball, the third defender scores with a dribble across his or her own goal-line without any tackle back from the attackers (they may tackle only in the upper part of the pitch).

An attack ends

- when the attackers score a goal,
- when the ball runs out of the playing area (across one of the end-lines), or
- when the defence scores, after having recovered the ball and passed it across the imaginary centre-line to the third defender.

After the conclusion of each attack, one of the two defenders must quickly run toward the opposite goal to re-establish (with the third defender) the 'three attackers on two defenders'. In case of an infringement of the rules by an attacker, a free kick is awarded to the defenders—still with the attackers being allowed to defend only in the upper part of the field and never beyond the centre-line. During a free kick for the attackers (taken no closer than 3 metres from the goal-line), the defenders, too, must remain at least 3 metres away from the ball.

Duration of the game: 10 attacks for each team or, for more advanced players, four periods of three minutes each.

EFFECTIVE QUESTIONING

In a 3v2 situation, which one of the three attackers should become the ball carrier? Consult the Effective Questioning section for Fast Attack on page 157.

Should the ball-carrying player in the centre pass or dribble the ball? Consult the Effective Questioning section for Fast Attack on page 157.

When should you pass and when should you dribble the ball in a 3v2 situation? Consult the Effective Questioning section for Fast Attack on page 157.

On which criteria does it depend that you pass the ball toward the left or right side? The direction of the pass not only depends on the position and distance of the defender in relation to the supporting attackers but also on the way both defenders have decided to stop the attack in numerical superiority (they may defend on the same level, retreat or one defender positions him- or herself slightly in front of the other one who then covers).

In which direction should the ball be passed in a 2v1 situation? The ball should be passed diagonally into the run of the team-mate after having committed a defender to a tackle. The receiving player should always receive the ball levelled or slightly in front of the defender (for the possibility of an off-side position) but always far outside of the range of action.

What is the most efficient way to resolve a 3v2 situation? While approaching the two defenders, the ball carrier should suddenly run straight to the one who encourages this defender to tackle. At the same moment, the team-mate from the same side has to move farther away from the defender to establish a 2v1 situation.

What can the two defenders do to avoid the success of the three attackers? First, they should do everything to encourage the attackers to pass the ball to one wing. When this happens, the wing is pressed and channelled to the side-line with the second defender covering.

In case the centre forward has the ball, both defenders should delay their attack and retreat in the field in order to gain some time. While retreating, body feints should be executed to induce the attackers to commit mistakes or to play more than two passes that would slow down their attack.

What are the most frequent mistakes committed by defenders in a 2v3 situation? Besides rushing to the attacker who controls the ball close to his or her feet, another serious mistake is when both defenders are playing in line on the same level, because then nobody is able to cover the tackling player. During the retreat, patience is needed to wait for the most suitable moment to tackle.

VARIATIONS

- The three defenders don't have to switch positions. Therefore, the attackers practice the 3v1 attack at one goal-line and the 3v2 attack at the other goal.

- Instead of using two 20-metre-wide goals, the game is played using four 6-metre-wide goals (as a type of mini-football).
- Behind each end-line, a football goal is established at a distance of 11 metres. Immediately after controlling the ball on the end-line, the ball carrier practices shooting at a goal defended by a neutral goal-keeper.

TRAINING OBJECTIVES

- Practice and consolidate the technical and tactical objectives of the previous simplified games.
- Learn to systematically create the 2v1 situation in attack and to achieve a high percentage of success.
- Learn to tackle back immediately after losing possession of the ball.
- As defenders, acquire the patience to wait for the best moment for tackling or intercepting the ball.
- As defenders, learn to force the attacker to play the ball into the desired direction.
- As defenders, learn to counterattack quickly.
- As defenders, think continuously about what to do next, not forgetting to switch positions after an attack is concluded.

CORRECTIVE EXERCISES

Use the first four of the 2v2 simplified games (beginning on page 94).

6th Simplified Game
Three Teams on Two Wide Goals

Use a football field between the two off-side lines. One team of three players is in the centre of the pitch and alternately attacks one of the two wide goals established on the off-side lines. This goal and the opposite one are each defended by (a) two opponents (from the two other teams) who play midfield well in front of the off-side line, and (b) a third one who covers them without being allowed to tackle, being away from the line.

The attackers have 10 attacks (five against each goal) in which to try to dribble the ball as often as possible across this line (to get one point) and score in a goal area

30-40 m.

6 metres by 2 metres without (or later with) a goal-keeper for two points. After every three attacks, the cover defender changes with one of the other defenders on the team who is in front of him or her.

An attack finishes when

- a goal is scored,
- the ball runs across one off-side line or a goal-line,
- a defender gets possession of the ball and passes it to a team-mate, or
- the attackers commit an infringement of the rules.

The winning team is the one that gets the most points in 10 attacks.

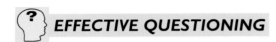

EFFECTIVE QUESTIONING

Please consult the questions and answers from the previous simplified games.

VARIATIONS

- Each 3v3 team has two minutes to score a maximum number of goals. The faster they develop their attacks, the more chances exist to score.
- The teams change, depending on the outcome of the attack. When the defenders manage to win the ball and also execute at least two passes on their team, they become attackers of the opposite goal. While launching their attack, the former attackers defend the goal where their attack failed. If the attackers score with a dribble, they continue to attack.
- The attackers can only play a maximum of four passes and work to find the most effective attack.
- To simplify the attack and practice goal scoring, three players form the defence. They either have one defender in front of the off-side line, one defender who covers playing on the off-side line and a goal-keeper; two defenders playing on the off-side line only and a goal-keeper; or two defenders in front of the off-side line and a goal-keeper.

TRAINING OBJECTIVES

- Attackers should learn that before passing the ball, they must consider not only the positions and actions of the defenders but also the movement of the covering defender on the off-side line.
- Understand how essential it is that the attacker in the centre is the one who should be in possession of the ball—either when the defenders are close or when one defender is going to execute a tackle.
- Consolidate the skills learned in the previous simplified games, and especially the principles of assuring width and depth in attack.

CORRECTIVE EXERCISES

Use the first five of the 2v2 simplified games (beginning on page 94).

7th

Simplified Game
Maintaining Ball Possession 3v2

12-15 m.

12-15 m.

See the rules for the ninth simplified game beginning on page 112 for teams formed by two players. The main differences are that the number of players per team has increased here from two to three and the dimensions of the pitch are increased (to a square with sides measuring 12 to 15 metres). The attacking three players have six possessions of the ball and aim to keep the ball for as long as possible. When the ball runs out or is pushed out of the playing area by the defenders, one of the two attackers should be replaced by the third one who up to now has been waiting outside the area. Keep track of the seconds the three attackers keep possession of the ball. If you have more than three teams, you can organise a tournament to establish the best team.

EFFECTIVE QUESTIONING

What are the main tasks of the player in possession of the ball? The player has to play in an upright position that allows him or her to perceive the game situation at all times, telling him or her when and where to pass the ball or dribble it in an unoccupied zone of the grid. When the player decides to pass the ball, he or she should not indicate its position or its direction in any movement the opponent may anticipate. After a successful pass, the player should move immediately into an unoccupied zone, communicating constantly with his or her two team-mates.

What should the attackers without the ball do? First, they should make the playing field as big as possible. They achieve this by running away from the ball carrier and occupying positions in which they are not marked by any defender. In case they receive a ball when being under pressure, they should look out for a first-time pass. They should always be on the move and communicate with the team-mate in possession of the ball.

What should the two defenders do to gain possession of the ball? They have to apply pressure to the attacker by doubling up so one defender can support the other, especially when the defender is in a corner of the grid. While one defender is tackling the attacker and covering the space on his or her left side, the second defender is anticipating a pass to the right side. Dedication and aggressiveness are necessary to make the playing field as small as possible for the attackers. Last but not least, executing dummies while tackling is another way to force the three attackers to make mistakes.

TRAINING OBJECTIVES

- Learn to consider and then make use of the space available in the depth of the pitch.
- As an attacker, avoid positioning yourself in a straight line with team-mates. As a ball carrier, learn to always position yourself in a triangular formation to ensure two options for passing.

- Be able to disguise the direction of your pass.
- Develop sufficient speed of the ball when passing.
- Know when to pass and when not to pass.
- Learn to systematically look out for the 2v1 situation.
- Remember to lift the head while dribbling the ball.
- After a successful pass, learn to run in to a space unoccupied by a defender.
- If there is a pressing defence, learn to use direct or wall passes.
- As defenders, learn to constantly reduce the space and time available to the three attackers and to anticipate their play, especially in the depth of the field.

CORRECTIVE EXERCISES

Use the ninth simplified game for 2v2 (see page 112), the first six simplified games in this chapter for 3v3 (beginning on page 153), and the Passing, Receiving and Shooting Games (see page 55).

VARIATION

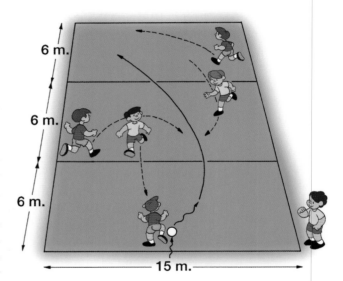

- This variation applies to more-advanced players. Mark off a playing area 15 metres wide and 18 metres deep, separated into three zones of 6 metres each. The players are three attackers, two defenders, and one substitute for a defender. (For more experienced players a smaller playing area can be used.) One zone is assigned to each of the three attackers. Without being allowed to leave their assigned area, they try to keep possession against the two defenders, who may play in any of the three areas. Initially, none of the defenders is situated in the first attacker's zone. But immediately after the attacker touches the ball, both defenders may press him or her. When one of the defenders tackles successfully and manages to touch the ball three consecutive times, or when the ball runs out of play, the substitute (who should track the time with a stopwatch) moves into the playing area and replaces one of the defenders. With every attempt, the three attackers should try to keep the ball for 10 (or, later, for 15) seconds. The winning team is the one that keeps the ball the most times for 10 (15) seconds within 10 attempts. If only five players are available, the successful defender changes position and function with the attacker who failed.

8th Simplified Game
Through Passes With Three Teams

The game is played by three teams of three players in one half of the 7v7 football field between the centre-line and one end-line. A central zone with a depth of 10 metres and a width of 35 metres is flanked by two zones, which are only 8 metres deep (limited by the end-line or centre-line) and again with a width of the 7v7 football field (35 metres). In each of

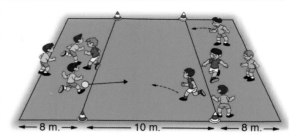

these two lateral zones a team of three players faces one defender. In the first zone, the players maintain the possession of the ball against one defender. Their objective is to pass the ball as often as possible to the opposite zone where one of the three team-mates should manage to receive and control the pass through the midfield. Three defenders, one in the first zone, a second in the midfield and a third in the zone of reception, do their very best to force the six attackers to commit mistakes.

None of the nine players is allowed to leave the zone assigned to him or her in order to fulfill offensive or defensive functions. Only the defender in the field of reception is allowed to do so in order to anticipate the pass played to one of his three opponents. Rotate the role of defence between the three teams after every five ball possessions for each of the two attacking teams (10 attacks in total). The winning team is the one that manages to play more through passes to a front runner.

EFFECTIVE QUESTIONING

What is required to play a successful through pass? Before a through pass is delivered, the ball carrier has to analyse the game situation in order to identify the availability of a zone in which the ball can be delivered. Then the passer should agree visually with the potential receiver through eye contact to find out whether he or she can communicate. Finally with a cue that the opponent is not aware of, such as a head or hand movement, the potential receiver should indicate to the passer where he or she should serve the ball with a correct direction and sufficient speed.

The ball carrier has the choice between three different attacking moves. Which one should he or she choose in which situation? The first option is a through pass to an unmarked front runner. In case this is not possible, the player looks for a second option that is a pass to a better-positioned team-mate in the same zone. A third option is that he or she carries the ball out of the range of action of the defender, shielding it with his or her body to gain some time or receive different passing angles.

Which position should a front runner or midfield player assume when receiving long passes out of the defence? A side-on position allows him or her to see the passer as well as the defender (and the goal) behind him or her. Furthermore, the side-on position allows the player to continue the attacking move much quicker (may be a shot at goal) without being obliged to lose time for his or her turn.

When does an ideal opportunity arise in a game to play a through pass? This happens immediately after having recovered the ball from the opponent. A through pass is then more successful since most of the opponents are still having an offensive attitude and therefore none of our attackers is marked.

What are the functions of the three defenders who have to play in three different zones?

- The defender in the initial zone should reduce the time and space of the ball carrier by not allowing him or her to play a precise through pass to a front runner in the opposite field. With this aggressive attitude, he or she should force the player with the ball to dribble.
- The defender in the central zone chooses a position more downfield to get more time to intercept passes that don't have sufficient speed or miss accuracy. He or she communicates with the third defender, who is some metres behind in the zone of reception.
- This defender, as well as the one in the central zone, has to read the game and anticipate the trajectory of the long passes in putting him- or herself in the position of a receiving player. There are many cues between the passer and the receiver that the second and third defender will learn to interpret to their advantage.

As a receiver, would you prefer to receive an aerial pass or a pass played along the ground? Whenever possible, flat passes should be played to a front runner. Aerial passes are difficult to control and also time consuming, especially when a defender is close to the receiver.

VARIATIONS

- The defender in the central zone may play in any of the three zones.
- Instead of passing the ball along the ground, the attackers are obliged to execute aerial passes that develop the skill of receiving and controlling aerial balls.
- In case 12 players are available, four attackers play against one defender in the grids outside, and two defenders act in the centre zone intercepting passes.

TRAINING OBJECTIVES

- Learn to analyse the game situation and depth of the playing area, using peripheral vision, before executing the through pass.
- As a passer, learn to communicate and establish visual agreement with the receiver; pass the ball exactly when the receiver is ready.
- Be able to disguise the direction of your pass.
- As defender, don't allow the attacker sufficient time to think and prepare his or her play.
- Learn to anticipate or read the opponent's play.

CORRECTIVE EXERCISES

Use the fifth, ninth, and tenth simplified games for two-player teams (pages 108, 112, and 114) as well as test three of the decathlon (see page 76) to improve the reach of defenders and teach the attackers to disguise the direction of the pass.

9th

3v3 With Two Wide Goals

Players use one half of a field, playing between one end-line and the centre-line. Set up goals on both lines (see illustration for the dimensions and placement). To score, an attacker must dribble the ball under control across the opponent's goal-line, which is the width of the pitch.

Duration of the game: four periods of three minutes each.

40 m.

20 m.

EFFECTIVE QUESTIONING

How do the three attackers control the ball on the opposing goal-line defended by three opponents? The three attackers have to form a triangle, always ensuring sufficient width and depth to their attack. This way, they are creating sufficient space in between the defenders that could be used to their advantage. The attackers should always look out for creating 2v1 situations and avoid 1v1 situations that may give the opponents the opportunity to counterattack.

Which is the most efficient pass for the ball carrier? To encourage the ball carrier to look out for through passes, one of the team-mates should offer him- or herself behind the defence to receive the ball and score. In this simplified game, there is no off-side unlike in the 7v7 football game, where off-side starts from a 13-metre line.

How should a front runner receive the ball? The player should preferably assume a side-on position that allows him or her a quick continuation of the attack. It must also give him or her a much better vision, especially at the very end of the playing field where goals are scored.

What does a player have to consider when executing a free kick? The player should execute it as quickly as possible (especially when one team-mate is unmarked) to surprise the opponent's defence, or the player does it very slowly to carefully study all possible passing options.

When do we have to accelerate and when do we have to slow down our attack? An increase in the pace of attack is always indicated when playing with numerical superiority (for instance 3v2) or when a gap appears in front of the ball carrier. Slowing down the attack is a necessity when one team-mate is in an off-side position, when none of the team-mates offer an optimal passing option or when most of the attackers are exhausted.

Where, generally, is attacking space available on the field? Generally there is some space available on the opposite side to where the ball is currently being played. This space should be used systematically with long, flat and speedy passes into the run of a team-mate, 'switching the play'.

What are the key points for successfully executing a throw-in? No risks should be taken with a throw-in. If possible, a throw-in should be taken quickly, before the opponent has had time to mark all of the attacking players. When playing a 7v7 game, the attackers and defenders should know that the off-side rule does not apply when a throw-in is used to restart play. This can be considered as an advantage for the attacking team.

How should a defender mark a personal opponent who does not have ball possession? The defender should always position him- or herself between the opponent and the goal but slightly more inside and closer to the goal than the opponent. From this position, the defender should perceive the ball and the opponent at the same time.

How should a defender position him- or herself in relation to a ball-carrying attacker? The defender should never face the attacker straight on since this gives the attacker the opportunity to beat him or her with a dribble to either side. It is better that the defender meets the attacker in a side-on position. This allows the defender to accompany the attacker as well as to channel him or her into a desired direction (for instance toward a side-line or toward a team-mate who covers him or her).

Are there any other considerations for the defender to take into account when he or she faces 1v1 situations? The defender should always initiate a tackle from a tiptoe position (on the balls of the feet), keeping the weight of the body equally distributed between both legs. To maintain balance, the player should not separate both legs more than shoulders' width and should put one foot in front of the other. He or she should bend the knees slightly to be ready to tackle at any second when the ball may be too far away from the feet of the attacker. The tackle, must be executed very quickly and with surprise without putting all the weight of the body to the front leg. This would prevent the player from executing a second tackle in case of a miss. While carefully observing the ball (not the legs of the opponent), the player should have in sight the other opponents and also the team-mates closest to the ball. In case the tackle is successful, the player should switch as quickly as possible from a defensive pattern to an offensive one.

What should a defender who is closest to a team-mate's 1v1 situation do? Without losing attention for his or her personal opponent, the defender should anticipate a possible failure by the team-mate and cover the space behind the first defender that could be exploited by the attacker.

When should a defender mark the opponent and when should he or she mark the space? The way of marking depends on the distance between the defender and the attacker. When the ball is close (perhaps less than 15 metres), the defender should mark the opponent very closely, being closer to the goal than the attacker. The marking is less tight in case the ball is farther away. This allows the defender to intercept passes in the space as well as passes directed into the feet of the opponent.

VARIATIONS

- After controlling the ball across the opposing goal-line, the attackers have to conclude their attack with an immediate shot on a football goal 11 metres behind it and defended by a neutral goal-keeper.

- The same game can be played with four goals (each 5 metres wide), two of them placed on each goal-line separated by a distance of 10 metres (see illustration). To score, the attackers have to either dribble or shoot the ball into one of the opposing goals.

TRAINING OBJECTIVES

In attacking, players work toward these goals.

- To know what to do when you are not in possession of the ball; that is, make yourself available for a pass in an area that is not controlled by the defending side. This way, the player in possession of the ball has the choice to either penetrate in the space that the attacker has created or pass.
- To attack in a triangular formation, ensuring width and depth.
- While dribbling the ball, to observe the behaviour of both opponents and team-mates in order to be able to make good decisions.
- To avoid revealing the next move.
- To take responsibility for each attacking move; any mistake may result in a goal for the opponents.

In defending, players work toward these goals.

- No player rests on the defence; on the contrary, they all participate fully in attack as well as in defence so that three defenders are always active.
- To ensure width in the defence, covering the whole width of the goal.
- To make sure that cover is always provided to the player who is tackling a ball carrier by defending in a triangular formation.
- To channel the attack into the direction you want and then keep the ball in this area, also crowding it with your team's other defenders.
- To delay tackling as necessary until being sure of receiving support from a team-mate.
- After each conclusion of the opposing attack, remembering to complete the defence at the opposite side (concentrate on your task).
- To be able to take free kicks quickly and before the opponent defenders can set up a 'wall' in front of one end-line.
- To initiate a counterattack quickly, with or without the help of the other defenders, by executing an accurate and fast pass to the third player in the opposite goal.
- To disguise the direction of this long pass as well as of any pass in the attacking 3v2 situation.

CORRECTIVE EXERCISES

Choose from any of the earlier simplified games.

<table>
<tr><td>**10th**</td><td>Simplified Game
3v3 With Passes Through Any of Four Goals</td></tr>
</table>

Use half of the football pitch, placing four goals (each 2 metres wide) 5 metres inside the field (see illustration). After a ball toss into the centre of the pitch, the players of both teams try to pass the ball to another team-mate *through one of the four goals*. Any reception of the ball behind a goal but still inside of the playing area is considered good for a point. Scoring twice in a row in the same goal is not allowed. All free kicks must be taken from a distance of at least 5 metres away from the nearest goal. After every two goals scored, all players rest for two minutes; during the rest they discuss their positive and negative actions of play.

 EFFECTIVE QUESTIONING

What attributes do you expect from the players in a winning team?
- To be successful, we have to cultivate our play without the ball. The first aim is always to maintain possession of the ball and the second is to pass the ball through any of the four cone goals to a team-mate.
- To get away from an opponent, our players should often change the speed and direction of their runs.
- A team should communicate well, in attack as well as in defence.
- Besides a high level of physical abilities (speed, endurance and dexterity) also visual, cognitive and motor capacities (perception, decision making and execution of actions) should be well developed to win this simplified game.

VARIATIONS

- A neutral player plays with whatever team is in possession of the ball.
- Play the same game with teams formed by four players each.
- Instead of passing, dribble the ball through any of the four goals.

The game can also be played on a mini-football pitch with the objective to pass to a team-mate from any area in the centre of the field through any of the four goals.

TRAINING OBJECTIVES

- Improve play without the ball and cooperate with team-mates, adjusting to their behaviours.
- Be able to frequently change the speed and direction of your run (with the ball as well as without it) to gain some time and space for the next move.
- Run into the space behind the defenders and look out for the less-defended goal (it is imperative to change position after a successful pass).
- Reduce dribbling with the ball to a minimum, and move the ball quickly between team members with hard passes.
- Play direct or wall passes as required.

CORRECTIVE EXERCISES

See the corrective exercises given under the third simplified game for teams formed by two players (2v2 with Four Goals, page 102).

Simplified Game
Centring the Ball

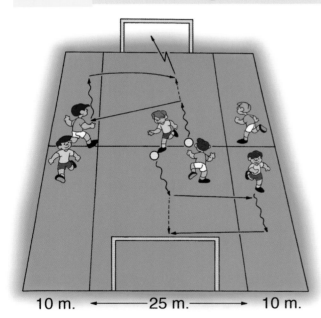

10 m. ← 25 m. → 10 m.

Divide a football field into three corridors, the two lateral ones 10 metres wide and the central one about 25 metres wide. Each team attacks one goal; one of the team's players should be in the right wing and another in the left wing position, while the third player enters the central corridor. Both centre forwards pass the ball to one of their wings, who must receive it within his or her zone. After having controlled the ball, the wing advances without any opposition until he or she arrives more or less level with the penalty area. There, he or she centres the ball to the centre forward, who followed in the central corridor, or to the opposite wing. This wing, being level with the penalty-box line, leaves the corridor to position him- or herself for executing a header from in front of the second goal-post. The centre forward, however, occupies the zone in front of the first goalpost. Both teams practice in the same attacking formation for at least three minutes. Then places are switched until everybody has played in all three positions. As a next step, hold a competition in which the team scoring more goals—with a header—out of 10 attacks wins. The competition is over when all players have performed 10 times in the centre forward position.

? EFFECTIVE QUESTIONING

What are the tasks of the player who centres the ball?

- The wings should be capable of executing well-timed centres with accuracy that should be directed 8 to 10 metres in front of the goal, making the task of the goal-keeper more difficult.
- Centres with a low trajectory and high speed are more dangerous than soft ones that have a high trajectory and take more time to reach the centre forward and can therefore be more easily intercepted.

Which aspects have to be considered by players who score with headers? Before scoring with a header, the player has to 'read' the speed of the ball, its spin, the height of the aerial pass, its trajectory and its possible point of landing. Any mistake in the optical-motor assessment may result in a wrong decision and bad execution of the header.

Whenever possible, the attacker should run toward the oncoming ball in order to give the header more speed. Know how to gain an optimal position in front of the goal and how to apply correct heading technique.

VARIATIONS

- Players use gymnastic balls or No. 3 balls to facilitate the execution of accurate centres and headers.
- The coach permits the wing to centre the ball when stationary before centring with the ball on the run.
- A goal-keeper is included in the game but may play only from (remaining on) the goal-line.
- The goal-keeper plays with no special restrictions imposed.
- More-experienced players practice this game with a defender who marks one of the other two attackers. The wing must therefore decide to which attacker he or she should centre the ball: to the centre forward or the wing of the opposite side.

TRAINING OBJECTIVES

- Learn to centre the ball.
- Gain experience in the header.
- Learn to assume an optimal position in front of the goal before executing the header.
- Learn to run toward the oncoming ball before executing a header.

CORRECTIVE EXERCISES

See the first two variations above, which are helpful remedial activities.

Level 3 Competitions

The 4v4 triathlon and 7v7 football further develop the innate potential of players 10 years and older.

4v4 Triathlon

Include the triathlon periodically in the training programme to enhance players' abilities to read and react to more-complex situations and to an increased number of players. The figure below shows how a triathlon competition can be organised. In this example teams representing Asia and Australia compete against teams representing Europe until a winner is decided. The blank spaces next to each game are for coaches to use in recording scores.

Asia and Australia Versus Europe

Teams	South Korea	Australia	Uzbekistan
Names of players			

Teams	France	Netherlands	Ireland
Names of players			

First game scores: Dribble across the opponent's end-line (3 × 3 min).			Second game scores: Long passes out of the midfield (3 × 3 min.)			Third game scores: Score, defend and counterattack (4 × 3 min.)		
KOR-FRA			KOR-NLD			KOR-IRL		
AUS-NLD			AUS-IRL			AUS-FRA		
UZB-IRL			UZB-FRA			UZB-NLD		

Final result: Asia/Australia _____   Europe _____   Technical delegate: _____

Note: During the triathlon, changing the composition of the team is not permitted.

1. Dribble Across the Opponent's End-Line

Two teams of four players each use one half of a football pitch, playing between the end-line and the centre-line. Both teams try to control the ball to any spot of the opponent's end-line. The game starts with a ball toss to the centre. Players must be positioned at least 4.5 metres from the end-line for free kicks and throw-ins.

Duration of the game: three periods of five minutes each.

2. Long Passes Out of the Midfield

This game is also played on a football pitch between one off-side line and the centre-line. On each end-line of this field you should use cones to mark off a 3-metre-wide goal, set 13 metres from each goalpost (see illustration). Two teams play in the midfield. Start the play with a ball toss. Without leaving the area of the midfield, each team tries to pass the ball through one of the opponent's two goals. It's a good idea to have plenty of reserve balls to ensure effective practice.

Duration of the game: three periods of three minutes each.

3. Score, Defend and Counterattack

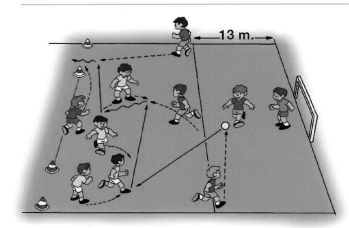

Again, use just one half of the 7v7 football field, setting up two extra goal areas with cones set in the wing positions on the centre-line. Start the play with a ball toss in the centre. One team attacks the regular goal; the other team defends it and attacks the two goals in the wing positions on the centre-line. The defenders score with a long pass through one of these two goals.

For all other rules, please consult and use the football rules given in the next section of this chapter. It works best to use a neutral goal-keeper in the regular goal area (see illustration). Every three minutes the attackers and defenders should switch positions and functions.

Duration of the game: four periods of three minutes each.

Rules of 7v7 Football

These are the rules that apply to the 7v7 game. If a rule is not specified here for a situation you and your players face in the game, the official rules of the game of football should apply.

Field

The 7v7 pitch is a rectangle measuring 50 to 65 metres in length and 30 to 45 metres in width. This size allows you to fit three of these fields into one regular-sized football pitch. All other measurements are given in the diagram.

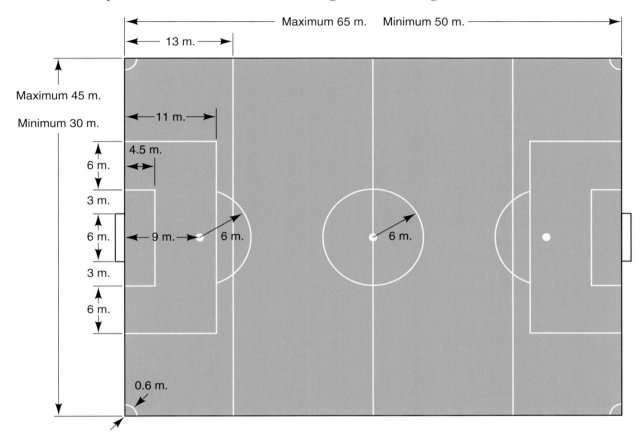

The field's dimensions are adapted to the physiological characteristics of young football players. In fact, the measurements take into account all aspects of the game including these:

1. Physical Preparation
   * Most of the playing workout is aerobic.
   * Frequent, short runs are characteristic, either with or without changes of direction and rhythm, jumps and sudden stops.
   * More demands are made on the young players' coordination abilities.
2. Technical Preparation
   * The players have frequent contact with the ball, which benefits their developing basic skills.
   * Because players are exposed to less-complex game situations, their self-confidence grows, which results in their taking more initiative and using their innate capacity for imagination and creativity.
   * This version of football includes frequent occurrences of the basic and standard game situations, such as shooting a goal from any distance or angle, or the systematic use of the 2v1 situation in attack.

3. Tactical Preparation
   - In defence, it is easier for players to cover the attackers because of the shorter spaces the attacking players occupy.
   - In offence, players frequently change the front of the attack, use more wall or first-time passes, and attack more from the second line.
   - The shorter distances allow players to gain valuable experiences in such standard situations as corners, throw-ins, free kicks and penalties.
   - Communication skills and cooperation are acquired under ideal conditions.

Young goal-keepers benefit more than any other players from the ideally sized goals in the 7v7 competition. When they defend a goal measuring 7.32 by 2.44 metres, goal-keepers often worry about any shot at goal. Only very rarely can they show their real talent because of the enormous size of the goal. However, by defending the smaller goal areas (6 by 2 metres) better adapted to the heights of young players, they are more confident of saving the shot. This confidence enhances their performances and overall enjoyment of the game.

Teams

The competition is played by two teams composed of nine (minimum) or 10 (maximum) players. Only seven members of one team, however, may play at the same time on the pitch, one of them defending the goal.

At least five players per team must be present to start the game. After the initiation of the match, the other players can join in. The two or three reserve players may substitute at any time for a player who is on the pitch, provided the official rules for substitution of players are put into practice. The only exception is the rule that a substituted player may return to the playing field as often as his or her coach considers it convenient. If one team for any circumstances during a match should remain with fewer than five players, including expulsions by the referee, the referee concludes the match and declares the team with too few players as 0-3 losers.

Duration

Two periods of 25 minutes, with five minutes of halftime. If you hold a tournament in which several matches are played on the same day, reduce the duration of the matches to two periods of 20 minutes each.

Technical Rules

In addition to the official rules of off-side, in a 7v7 football game a player has to be inside the 13-metre zone of the opposing team to be considered in an off-side position. All other criteria for an off-side stated in the official rules remain valid. All infringements of the rules are penalised with direct free kicks.

Equipment

Players must use a No. 4 ball in the 7v7 game. Its circumference must measure between 63.5 (minimum) and 66 (maximum) centimetres. The ball's weight at the start of the game should be between 340 and 390 grams.

Using a ball adapted in size and weight to the heights and physical capacities of young players is imperative for learning to manoeuver the ball well for these reasons:

- It facilitates the pass and the shot at goal because the size and weight of the ball are adapted to the smaller foot and lesser power of younger players.

- Young players need not lift their foot excessively as they do to dribble or receive the full-size ball; therefore, they can remain in balance.

- In beating an opponent or executing dummies, youngsters are encouraged (by the smaller size of the ball) to move the foot above the ball or to pass it between the legs of the opponent.

- They avoid developing some bad habits caused by using the traditional football. With the official ball, young players generally use the foot tip to 'toe poke' long clearances or shots at goal, many of them thereby falling into a bad habit that will be difficult to eradicate later.

- Using a No. 4 ball encourages young players to use headers ('kick' the ball with their heads) more frequently. The use of this ball also drastically improves technique, because players aren't afraid and usually do not close their eyes at the moment of impact.

Referee

To encourage interest in becoming referees among youngsters, it is helpful to use only referees who are younger than 20 years of age for 7v7 football matches. This referee applies the rules previously stated and must be quite familiar with them.

Advantages of 7v7 Football

In most of the FIFA member countries, the 7v7 football game is hardly known. Information is therefore given here about the many reasons that have motivated some countries to move away from tradition and introduce 10- and 11-year-old players to a competition that is perfectly tailored to their physical and mental capacities: 7v7 football.

1. All players have more frequent contact with the ball and therefore learn the skills of passing, dribbling, receiving, beating a man, shooting and tackling better.

2. There are more corner kicks and 9-metre penalties, allowing the young players to gain more experiences in these standard situations.

3. Fewer players on the pitch (14 instead of 22) facilitate the understanding of the game by each player since less information has to be processed before coming to a correct decision. Because the ball can reach any player at any moment, all have to focus their attention on the next move.

4. The orientation and positioning of each player in the limited space inside the pitch are easier because fewer players form a team. This stimulates communication and cooperation skills within one team. The integration of a player into the team is therefore made easier.

5. As the distances between the front runners and the rest of their team-mates is much shorter than when playing the full game on the full pitch, an interchange of positions between defenders or midfielders with a front runner can be seen quite frequently. This avoids a premature specialisation in one particular playing position. 7v7 football demands more versatility than 11v11 football.

6. When playing with only seven players, the ball is cleared few times with a wild kick upfield. Instead, players treat the ball better and play with it more than against it as happens frequently in the chaotic situations of an 11v11 game.

7. Learning to dominate the important parameters of space and time is much easier than in the full game.

8. In 7v7 football, each player is more capable of mentally preparing for the game, reading the field, making decisions and executing action because there are fewer players and a smaller field to contend with.

9. As the 7v7 game has less-complex game situations, the 10- and 11-year-old players don't have to necessarily rely on the feedback of their coach. They are able to correct their mistakes themselves. A player at this age becomes coach-dependent when playing the full game because of its complex game situation.

10. 7v7 football makes spotting talents very easy because a coach can see the deficiencies and virtues of a player relatively clearly.

11. The contribution of a less-skillful player becomes more important the longer a game lasts because his or her participation in the initial part of the game is still fresh. Weaker players progress more when competing in 7v7 and not in 11v11 football, where they are condemned to be almost a spectator.

12. The goal-keepers also progress more because they participate more frequently in the game.

13. The tasks of coaches inexperienced in managing teams are much easier to accomplish with a smaller group of players than would be the case in 11v11 football.

14. 7v7 football could become a good school for referees under the age of 20; a game with fewer rules and with only 14 players on a restricted field is less complex and therefore easier to control than the full game.

Besides the important lessons learned by young players with the various activities proposed in this chapter, there is still something missing for any team to achieve a good performance in the 7v7 football game: the development of young goal-keepers (see chapter 8).

8

Developing Young Goal-Keepers

'Tomorrow's success is founded on today's preparation.'

Sir William Osler

Because few coaches have played as goal-keepers, their knowledge of how to train them is somewhat limited. Relatively few coaches give sufficient attention to the training of this important player—even though everybody knows that winning or losing a match can depend on the goal-keeper's performance. Whereas other team members can compensate for the errors of a field player, a goal-keeper's mistake usually results in a goal.

Although modern football demands good all-around skills from all players, the goal-keeper must be treated as the only *specialist* on the team. In contrast to other team members, the goal-keeper covers a very limited territory and is the only player allowed to play the ball with the hands. Because of the goal-keeper's specific function and importance, special attention should be given to his or her development.

Profile of a Goal-Keeper

The great influence a goal-keeper's performance has on the result of the game often puts the player in the centre of decisive game situations. After a fine performance, everybody congratulates the goal-keeper, but if the performance wasn't satisfactory, the goal-keeper can receive severe reprimands. That is why a goal-keeper must be a calm person. The player should be confident about his or her abilities, building constantly on this self-confidence through positive self-talk and frequent training.

A goal-keeper should express or radiate calmness and confidence to other team members, thus positively influencing their performance level. On the other hand, the goal-keeper's strong personality and confidence can negatively affect opponents who focus too much attention on the play of the goal-keeper when shooting.

When the goal-keeper is insecure, shows nerves or is slow to make decisions, these poor qualities undoubtedly influence outfield players negatively. The team's defenders, as well as its attackers, will likely take fewer risks in offence and be afraid to attack, worried about the security of their own goal. Just these few comments explain why any average team with an excellent goal-keeper can win or at least tie the match against a much stronger team with a less-skillful goalie. It is therefore important to examine the essential qualities of goal-keepers.

Speed

The most important physical capacity for a goal-keeper is speed—reaction speed, acceleration, power and quick limb movements. These qualities of speed allow the player to stop balls shot at more than 130 kilometres per hour or to close down an attacker approaching the goal with the ball under control. However, speed is not the only physical capacity to take into consideration. It should be combined with excellent coordination and flexibility, along with the other qualities described in this chapter.

Accurate Decisions

To be able to benefit from the qualities of speed, it's imperative that the goal-keeper effectively use whatever information is available before the opponent's shot on goal. In other words, the goal-keeper must anticipate the eventual outcome of an attack from the opponent's early moves. The goal-keeper must base perceptions on an excellent knowledge and understanding of what is going on in the game. How a goal-keeper

Qualities of a Successful Goal-Keeper

Physical Capacities

- Ability to diminish reaction time
- Ability to execute movements quickly
- Quick power

Coordination Capacities

- Balance
- Ability to combine various movements
- Good sense of direction
- Good rhythm
- Sense of space and time

Emotional Capacities

- Concentration
- Aggressiveness (with respect for the rules)
- Courage
- Ability to maintain calmness and confidence in stressful situations
- Rationality
- Leadership

Perceptual Capacities

- Visual acuity
- Ocular dominance
- Depth and distance perception
- Peripheral vision
- Visual reaction time
- Anticipation
- Ability to recognise, interpret and anticipate situations close to the goal with the ball at the centre of attention
- Visual memory
- Optical-motor assessment

'We are what we repeatedly do.'

—*Dr. Ric Charlesworth*

© davidsandersphotos.com

can read the game determines how he or she can act. The more experience and knowledge goal-keepers have, the more they are able to focus on the most relevant sources of information. Expert keepers have developed a better visual search strategy than less-experienced keepers, who usually watch only the ball and are less aware of the position and movements of the players off the ball. Therefore, as a coach, you play an important role, directing the learner's attention to relevant sources of information.

Considering that more than half of the job of a keeper is mental conditioning and judgment (which both come from experience), it's understandable that most of the errors among young players are caused not by their technique but by weak decision making. Technically well-prepared and physically fit goal-keepers still must be trained to become excellent decision makers. Errors in decision making are caused by poor attention, poor perception, a lack of determination or a lack of knowledge (from poor coaching sessions). It's fundamental that young players learn to quickly process all relevant information and select the best motor response to execute after developing a high level of physical fitness.

For goal-keepers, tactical training has to be considered as important as technical preparation. The older the goal-keeper, the more that tactical training should replace technical work (in which no decision making is required initially). Goal-keepers aged 14 and up should be systematically exposed to a great variety of problems included in simplified games specifically designed to improve their performance. Through these games they learn to choose the most effective response among several possibilities.

Courage

Other aspects of the goal-keeper's performance, besides staying calm and being suitably aggressive, are having courage and determination. Being courageous is imperative, especially during 1v1 situations, shots executed from short distances and during corners. The goal-keeper's capacity to control arousal level will minimise errors. Studies have demonstrated that performance deteriorates under high levels of arousal; this is especially true of cognitive performance, which includes problem solving and decision making. Every goal-keeper is exposed to high levels of stress 15 to 25 times during a game. At such times, the player is aware that any small mistake can dramatically change the outcome of the competition. In other words, everyone expects him or her to be a perfect player, and the goalie has to live with this expectation. To overcome the challenge of expectation, the goalie should be a master of the inner game of football, which involves positive self-talk (for example, 'Today's my day!' 'I'm the greatest!' 'Nobody can score against me!'). When the ball is far away, the goal-keeper should execute some fundamental technical or warm-up drills that keep him or her physically and mentally ready for the next decisive action.

Tips for Training Goal-Keepers

To optimise performance, goal-keepers should play other positions during training sessions. This will help them develop psychologically and physically and improve performance. Furthermore, playing outfield, goal-keepers experience the sort of tension and difficulties attackers feel when trying to overcome the last player of the opponent's defence. The experiences gained when playing as defender or as attacker allow goal-keepers to perform with greater success. Goal-keepers who have played mini-football in their first six years (with two goals to be defended simultaneously) have a higher level of perception and greater knowledge than traditionally trained goal-keepers. And thanks to the logical progression of their active involvement in competitions, they become quicker mentally and can anticipate the opponent's play better than those who have had a traditional training program based mainly on acquiring technical skills.

Ideally, a goal-keeper's specific training is directed and supervised by a specialist goal-keeper coach, usually a former, experienced goal-keeper. However, in most cases, the goal-keeping coach doesn't know how to link the coaching of the goal-keeper with that of the defenders—an important task with the increasing integration of goalies with the whole of the defence.

When a specialist coach trains a player, through a variety of exercises and games in which the young goal-keeper must solve the common problems of competitions, the youngster acquires a broad knowledge and experience that allows him or her to select the most appropriate technique in a given situation. The young player also learns to execute skills correctly with requisite speed, flexibility of the muscles and mobility in the joints. Furthermore, such training creates goal-keepers who have learned to command and lead team-mates with an authoritative voice. Goal-keepers must develop clarity and brevity in their instructions ('It's mine!' 'Leave it!' 'Out!'). This is imperative for creating effective commands. Finally, the aspiring goalie learns to encourage team-mates with positive comments.

Unfortunately it's not unusual to see many young players who are limited in their performance outside of the goal to suddenly decide to become goal-keepers. Coaches should encourage players to become goalies only when they display a certain natural talent for this particular position. Unless players bring to the position a certain basic level of the desired capacities, those players will not make good goal-keepers.

'No practice wastes talent.'

—*Leonardo da Vinci*

Goal-Keeper Development Model

The development model for goal-keepers consists of four levels. The diagram on page 188 illustrates each level and its divisions.

Basic Stance

The basic stance is the ready position that goal-keepers adopt before their dynamic interventions in the game. The following tips will help increase young goal-keepers' success:

➤ Always initiate the movement from the tiptoe (on the balls of feet) position.

➤ Maintain balance. The feet should be positioned shoulder-width apart with the arms and hands raised at about waist level.

➤ Keep the weight of the body equally distributed between both legs to avoid finding yourself wrong footed.

➤ Keep the knees over the toes.

➤ Bend the knees slightly to be ready to spring (the upper leg and lower leg should form an angle of 110 to 120 degrees).

➤ Maintain good balance with the trunk inclined slightly forward.

➤ Draw the attention mainly to the ball, but also stay aware of the positions of team-mates and opponents.

➤ Relax when the ball is being played more than 40 metres away from the goal, assuming the basic position just immediately before a shot can be made.

Level 1
Exercises and games with or without one attacker (Learning of fundamental skills in foreseen situations)

Stance and positional play	Saves (catch, interception and deflection)	Clearances (punch, throw or kick)	Playing out of goal

Decathlon
(Execution of skills and decision making in foreseen and unforeseen situations)

Level 2
Exercises and games with two or more attackers (Consolidation of skills and decision making in modified situations)

Stance and positional play	Saves (catch, interception and deflection)	Clearances (punch, throw or kick)	Playing out of goal

Level 3
Exercises and games with attackers and help of one or two defenders
(Improvement of skills and decision making in foreseen and unforeseen situations)

Stance and positional play	Saves (catch, interception and deflection)	Clearances (punch, throw or kick)	Playing out of goal

Level 4
Simplified games that frequently involve the goal-keeper
(Mastery, execution and correct decision making in unforeseen situations)

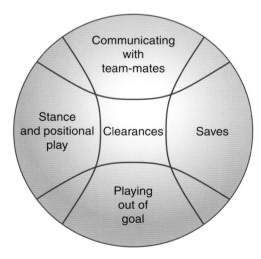

The development model for goal-keepers.

Position Play

A vital skill for goal-keepers to develop is the ability to position themselves in such a way that allows the interception of the ball with a minimum of movement. Finding the best possible position in relation to both the attacker with the ball and the goalposts helps goalies cut down the number of desperate saves and last-second moves. When good goal-keepers play, it seems as though the balls always come straight to them. Each of their saves looks easy. Goal-keepers who frequently execute acrobatic dives are not the best ones because their positional play is at fault. On the contrary, experienced keepers, conditioned by their fine positional play, hardly need to dive or leap.

Many goal-keepers feel most comfortable standing on, or very close to, the goal-line. However, increasing situations in today's games oblige goal-keepers to master the game away from the goal-line and sometimes to act as sweeper. In general, a goal-keeper moves to intercept a ball along an imaginary line from the middle of the goal to the ball. When moving forward on this imaginary line toward the attacker with the ball, the goal-keeper will reach a point at which he or she can cover the attacker's whole shooting angle without having to execute a dynamic save using a large range of motion. The closer the goal-keeper gets to the opponent, the less time and the smaller the angle available for the attacker to score. But the more the goalie moves away from the imaginary line from the goal to the ball, the less his intervention is likely to succeed.

Exercises for Stance and Position Play

1. This first exercise helps inexperienced goal-keepers visualise the triangle made by the goalposts and the attacker with the ball. As coach, position yourself anywhere on the 11-metre line (on a 7v7 football field) or the 16.5-metre line (on a full regulation field). Two cords (long pieces of rope) should be tied to the goalposts, one on each, and then both tied to your right ankle. Depending on how the coach moves along the 16.5-metre line, the goal-keeper modifies his or her position. The keeper tries to remain on the imaginary line bisecting the shooting angle and must come far enough forward to easily reach the right rope with the right foot and the left rope with the left foot. At the same time, the hands should reach out to control the space to both sides. If the keeper cannot reach both ropes with the feet, the keeper knows that he or she is badly positioned, which would allow the attacker enough of a gap to score.

2. One player dribbles the ball along the lines of the penalty area, frequently changing direction. The goal-keeper, meanwhile, assumes a ready position about 3 metres outside the goal and always positioned on the line that bisects the shooting angle, also moving according to the direction and speed of the attacker. The goal-keeper's coach should position behind the net to carefully observe and analyse the positional play of the goalie and correct this playing position whenever necessary.

3. Set out five balls no farther than 2 metres inside the penalty area (see illustration). One player strikes them all, one after another, into the goal. To allow the goalie sufficient time to choose a correct basic position and location from which to make a save, the attacker, after every shot at goal, has to run out of the penalty area before returning to shoot the next ball.

Variation

Assign the same exercise with a second attacker positioned close (about 5 to 6 metres) to the goal-keeper. The second attacker's primary function is to pick up the rebounds from the goalie or from the posts, but from a position in front of the goal he or she may also deflect the shot at goal directly into the net.

4. Two attackers at the edge of the penalty area pass the ball to each other across distances of between 8 and 12 metres. Meanwhile, the goal-keeper has to adapt position in the goal to the changing position of the ball. One of the two attackers should try to surprise the keeper with a shot before he or she can assume an optimal position to save the ball.

5. Four players work with the goal-keeper in this activity. One attacker on either side of the goal passes the ball from the end-line to one of his team-mates on the line of the penalty area. The player who receives the ball may score with a first-time shot or may instead pass it, either back to the end-line or to a team-mate at one side, at least 5 metres from the passer. The idea is for any attacker to surprise the goal-keeper with a shot. The aim of the goal-keeper in all phases of this exercise, however, is to demonstrate correct positional play, allowing him or her to narrow the angle for any shot at goal.

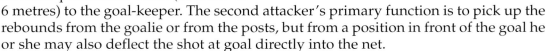

6. As coach, you should stay behind the goal to observe the play. Give a visual signal to start the exercise. Six players, situated in different attacking positions on the 11-metre (or 16.5-metre) line, then try to score quickly with a shot. Give the goal-keeper feedback on any problems in positional play that you observe from your post behind the goal. The goalie's aim is, at the instant of the shot, to always position himself or

herself on the line bisecting the shooting angle. This task becomes easier when all attackers face the centre-line. So after the coach calls a player's name, that attacker turns around and shoots so quickly at goal that the goal-keeper has hardly any time to adopt a correct position in the goal area or to assume an optimal, basic ready position. As a goalie improves, you can diminish the goal-keeper's time further by calling out the attackers' names at shorter intervals.

7. Five players are situated around the centre circle of the football field with a diameter of 18.3 metres. Their aim is to manage to pass the ball from outside the circle through any of the three 5-metre gates established in the centre of the circle in the form of a triangle (see illustration). A goal-keeper defends all three goals at the same time, moving from one goal cone to the other according to the position of the ball. Work with the goalie to always take small steps while continuing to watch the ball's trajectory; this technique allows the player to transfer his or her body weight easily from one leg to the other. The result should be an optimal positional play,  preventing the five attackers from scoring goals. Clearly, the goal-keeper would not be able to adapt quickly enough to the demands of this game by using long strides.

8. A right wing (or left wing) penetrates deeply into the opponent's half. After having dribbled the ball through a pair of cones (the goal) placed outside the penalty area and about 3 metres away from the end-line, the wing may strike or pass the ball either to the centre forward or to the other winger who moves to be in front of the second post. Whoever receives the pass tries to score with a first-time shot or header. In this exercise the goal-keeper must continually demonstrate an optimal level of positional work without coming fully out of the goal. When the goalie covers the angle of the wing's shot close to the nearby goalpost, his inside foot is already placed in such a way that he or she can quickly cover the goal in case of a centre. The wing never lets the goal-keeper know whether he or she will try to score, execute a dummy shot or centre the ball. Only when the goal-keeper learns to quickly switch positions can he or she face both forward players and prevent a goal from being scored.

Exercises to Improve Reaction Speed

To improve the goal-keeper's speed of reaction, lighter balls should be used, especially the No. 4 ball, with these exercises.

1. Two attackers stand on the line of the goal-keeper area, at both sides of the penalty point. Their objective is to deflect the shots that a third player executes from the edge of the penalty area into the goal. To surprise the goal-keeper, the third attacker may also shoot directly—without having his or her team-mates divert the ball.

2. The coach shoots the ball at different speeds and heights into the goal, defended by a goal-keeper turned so that his or her *back* is facing the attacker (see illustration). Only when the coach calls the goalie may the player then turn around to fix the ball, save it or clear it out of the area.

3. From a position behind the goal, you, as coach, visually signal one of three attackers, all in possession of a ball and all situated inside the penalty area at different distances from the goal. While the signalled player executes a shot, the goalie assumes an optimal, correct ready position to prevent the ball from going into the goal. Give the goalie feedback as necessary.

4. Stand behind the goal, ready to visually signal two attackers. The two players, each with a ball and situated about 35 metres from the goal, dribble with the same speed toward the penalty area. They should stay separated by at least 8 metres. When they come within about 20 metres of the goal, which is defended by a goal-keeper, let them know through a signal (which should be invisible to the goalie) to carry out the shot at goal. One attacker shoots, while the other one goes for the rebound.

5. Use a 7v7 football goal, and position the goalie on the ground just outside a post. One attacker dribbles the ball from 6 metres outside the penalty area, aiming to score from inside the area. When the player starts the individual attack, the goal-keeper gets up from the ground to adopt a position in the goal and assumes a basic ready position; he or she tries to carry out the save. The attacker (who could be another goal-

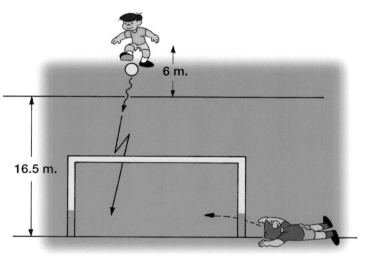

keeper) has four attempts to score without ever entering more than 2 metres into the penalty area. The goal-keeper should start twice from each goalpost.

Saves

In football matches the intervention that goal-keepers carry out most frequently is a catch. However, goal-keepers can also save the ball with an interception or deflection. In general, a goal-keeper can reduce the ball's speed entirely with a catch (of either high or low incoming balls). The goal-keeper not only uses the hands but also places an added barrier beyond the ball with the body and legs.

There are three golden rules for catching the ball in the air or on the ground:

1. Get the body behind the ball whenever possible.
2. Get the ball to the chest as it is caught.
3. Cushion the ball softly.

After a catch, with or without a leap, the ball remains in the possession of the goal-keeper who continues play with an offensive action, for instance with an accurate throw or kick of the ball to one of his team-mates.

After a successful save, the goal-keeper can choose to throw or kick it to a team-mate. If there isn't time to reach the ball with both hands, the goal-keeper intercepts the shot without controlling it. The techniques of deflecting the ball over the bar or around the post are probably the most difficult ones for the goalie to master. Before the ball arrives level with the goal-keeper's body, the hand closest to the oncoming ball should meet it, with the leg of the same side bent, regardless of whether the goalie intercepts or deflects the shot with a dive on the ground or in the air. Young goal-keepers often err by trying to stop low shots directed toward a corner of the goal with the opposite (upper) hand. This mistake reduces the diving goal-keeper's reach considerably, and the player must then stretch out completely to intercept or deflect the ball around the post.

Unfortunately, many goal-keepers are trained in diving and catching low or high balls without the presence of team-mates who might affect their play or even players who might be potential goal scorers. It's important to know that the performance of the goal-keeper and attackers improves little when stationary balls or balls in movement are simply shot at goal. To learn how to anticipate the best possible interventions, the goalie needs to be exposed to real game situations during training. The practice of game situations, in the presence of defenders and attackers and with the speed of competition, improves any goal-keeper's performance. The goal-keeper learns to read the game, decide what technique to use and decide when to interfere.

Consequently, exercises and games whose objective is to improve the technical aspects of saves (such as catching, intercepting, or deflecting the ball with or without a leap; being upright or obliged to dive) should not give the goalie advance knowledge of when, from where, or how the shot will be taken. By training in this more realistic way, the goal-keeper is forced at the instant of the opponent's attack to find the best possible solution. After making the decision, he or she then acts accordingly, without any loss of time.

During practice, the coach must carefully observe how well the young goalie executes different goal-keeper techniques and tactical plays, evaluating performance and also noting whether the goalie and last defender demonstrate optimal communication and cooperation. To ensure effective learning, the mistakes should be corrected *immediately* after their occurrences. During the process of the youngsters' learning from mistakes, the coach should remember also to praise the players.

Exercises to Improve Reception

1. Shot With Opponent (1v1)
See Scoring Against One Defender on page 64.

Variations
- Use two defenders instead of one. The first closes down the attacker with the ball, and the second covers.
- Use a goalie, defender and two attackers. Play the game as 2v1, starting with a pass from one attacker at the end-line to a team-mate who is situated on the 16.5-metre line. After the initial pass, the defender and the goal-keeper (both starting from the end-line) try to prevent the shot's scoring. (Review Scoring in a 2v1 Scenario on page 64.)

2. Quick Shot (1v2)

The coach stands inside the penalty area to start the game. The coach quickly passes the ball from inside the penalty area to one of three players who are expecting it in different positions at the edge of the penalty area. All three players should be at least 5 metres away from each other. The one who receives the ball played by the coach tries to score a goal while the remaining two do everything they can to prevent his or her scoring.

3. Goal-Keeper Plus 2v1

Two attackers, situated 8 metres outside the penalty area, try to overcome a defender and score in less than eight seconds. The attack finishes

- when the ball leaves the field of play,
- with an infringement by the attackers or the defenders (penalty),
- with an off-side, or
- after eight seconds.

The goal-keeper learns when to leave the goal-line and when to remain in goal. As players improve, shorten the allotted time to five seconds.

Variation

Three players start their attack from 25 metres in front of the goal, with two defenders waiting for them at the edge of the penalty area. The goal-keeper, besides showing a correct stance and good positional play at the instant of the shot, must decide whether to stay in goal or to run out of it. Subsequently, the keeper has to select and execute the most effective defensive action to avoid a goal's being scored with the first or second shot (rebound).

4. Goal-Keeper Plus 4v2

This game involves four forwards against two defenders, as well as the goalie, on a 7v7 football field (see illustration). The attack is initiated with a free kick on the centre-line. The four forwards must score within five seconds (you can instead specify 8 seconds), trying to avoid playing all in line and running into an off-side position. Due to the numerical superiority of the attackers in relation to the defenders, the goal-keeper is frequently involved and, therefore, improves quickly.

25 m.

Clearances (Punch, Kick or Throw)

If the close presence of one or more opponents prevents the goal-keeper from catching a high-flying ball with both arms, protecting it with his trunk, he or she should clear the ball with one or both fists. Sometimes external conditions, such as rain during the match or a wet field, should suggest that the goalie not try to catch the slippery ball. When a ball is too difficult to catch because of its height or speed, or the presence of opponents, it's better to either punch it with one or both fists or clear the ball with a deflection over the bar or around the post.

In punching with the fists, bending and extending the arms quickly in the moment of impact, the goal-keeper's accuracy and power can clear the ball out of the reach of the opponents. The distance of the clearance depends on the power developed by the goal-keeper—as well as on the speed of the oncoming ball. The goalie first learns to punch the ball with both fists held together. Care should be taken that the thumbs are held outside the fists; otherwise a broken thumb could occur.

Initially the goal-keeper is trained to punch the ball back into the same direction from which it came. Subsequently, the goalie learns to confront high-flying balls that come from either side. In this situation the player should always use the fist farther away from the oncoming ball to clear it. For example, the goal-keeper should use his or her right fist when the centre comes from the left but use the left fist when the ball is centred from his or her right side.

Within a split second the goal-keeper must perceive the spot from where the ball is kicked, correctly assess its trajectory, spin and speed and determine whether to catch it, deflect it or punch it. In this game situation, the goal-keeper's attention focuses mainly on the ball. The goalie modifies the position in the small area, following the ball's trajectory, making sure that he or she decides to rush out of goal only when there's a good chance of catching or clearing the ball before anybody else can play it.

It is imperative for playing outside the goal that the goal-keeper feel the precise moment to rush out of the goal. Any mistake the goalie makes in assessing the ball's speed, height or trajectory, or the opponent's running speed could result in a goal.

Exercises for Evaluating the Trajectory of the Ball

17 Exercises With a Partner

1. One player throws the ball into the air while the other player claps until the descending ball is caught.

2. Use the same drill, but throw the ball with one hand above the head into the other hand.

3. One player throws the ball into the air, and, at the moment that the ball reaches the ground, both players clap their hands to verify that both perceive the situation the same way.

4. Both players, each with a ball, face each other at a distance of 10 metres. Player A throws the ball to B. To catch the thrown ball, player B lobs his or her ball into the air high enough so that he or she is able to catch and return the ball to A before collecting his or her own lobbed ball. A and B should try to achieve 20 passes (10 both ways) without committing any mistakes.

5. Use the same drill, but both players alternate passing the ball to each other and lobbing the ball in the air to themselves.

6. Use the same drill, but after each throw the players have to change their position. Additional instructions could include gradually shortening the distance between both players. Count the times both players are capable of switching position and catching the ball thrown by the partner into the air.

7. Throw the ball above the head to your partner, who collects it with both hands close to his or her shoulder.

8. One player throws the ball with one hand (left or right) or kicks it with any foot up in the air. When the trajectory of the ball reaches its highest point (the ball does not rise or descend), the player and partner have to clap their hands or turn a somersault. The partner continues the process by collecting the ball with a jump into the air and then repeating the exercise.

9. One player kicks the ball into the air while the partner evaluates the possible landing point and approaches it. The partner assumes a prone posture, hoping that the ball will touch his or her body. The exercise can be performed between both players competitively.

10. Each player kicks a ball into the air and is responsible for collecting it in a sitting position, in a supine position, after a jump in the air or after turning a somersault.

11. One goal-keeper kicks the ball as high as possible into the air. Before it can touch the ground, the keeper has to run twice across the path the falling ball would have on the ground. Who can run under the ball twice more before it bounces for the second time? The same exercise is carried out with a partner. One kicks the ball into the air and the other runs.

12. One goal-keeper kicks the ball into the air. At the moment the ball hits the ground, the same goal-keeper should jump over it without being touched at all by the bouncing ball. The objective is to avoid being hit by the bouncing ball three times.

13. One goal-keeper kicks the ball into the air while his or her partner on the side calculates the time and location of its landing. The partner then approaches the location and receives and controls the ball with the chest, thigh or instep or by forming a roof above the ball with the interior of the right or left foot in such a way that the ball bounces only once. Before the partner controls the ball, the first goal-keeper tells him or her which technique to apply.

14. Both goal-keepers are situated inside the penalty box. One keeper kicks a ball into the air (its direction and its height depend on the capacity of the opponent) while the other one tries to prevent the ball from touching the ground anywhere inside the penalty box, collecting it when possible with outstretched arms above his or her head after a jump (2 points).

15. While one attacker, positioned 25 metres in front of the goal, runs 5 metres toward the ball, the goal-keeper inside the goal turns a somersault and quickly assumes an optimal basic stance to save the oncoming ball. The attacker takes shots from various distances and various angles using various techniques (frontal or lateral, volleys and drop-kicks).

16. One attacker shoots at goal from different distances and angles. The goal-keeper, situated with closed eyes in front of the goal, opens his or her eyes upon hearing the impact between the attacker's foot and the ball. The goal-keeper uses this sound to allow him or her to evaluate the trajectory of the oncoming ball and to save the shot.

17. One goal-keeper kicks the ball into the air. When the ball reaches its highest point, the goal-keeper advises the partner, then closes his or her eyes and anticipates the exact time the ball needs to touch the ground. The player tells the partner when the ball will hit the ground. In the following practice both players change functions. The goal-keeper who judges the moment the ball bounces correctly on two occasions becomes the winner.

Exercise Between Three Players

Two attackers, each with a ball, try to score from 20 metres at the same time. The goal-keeper has to concentrate only on the first ball.

Exercises for Intercepting High Centres

1. Prevent the ball from landing inside the penalty box. Various goal-keepers clear the ball with a volley shot (frontal and lateral) or drop-kick into the penalty box. The lobs arrive initially from the centre of the field and later are played from various angles so as to simulate all possible game situations until high balls are being centred from the wing positions. Finally, the distance between the passer and the goal-keeper should be shortened to give him or her less time to evaluate the oncoming ball's movement. The aim of the goal-keeper is to evaluate the trajectory, speed, height, length and spin of the ball to prevent it from touching the ground inside the penalty area.

2. The same exercise is practiced with an active centre forward participating. The centre forward tries to intercept the ball and score with a header or a deflection. The goal-keeper defends the goal but also tries to prevent the ball from touching the ground inside the penalty area.

3. See Challenge in the Air on page 213 and Dribble Across the Opponent's End-Line on page 205.

4. Reception or interception of centres. A right wing and a left wing, both some 30 metres away from the goal, alternately centre the ball in front of a goal with a goal-keeper. The keeper starts 2 metres out of the goal, in line with the ball and a little bit closer to the nearest post, and then moves to intercept the crosses from the flanks. Once the keeper manages to receive the ball in the air, he or she throws it along the ground to the wing of the opposite side.

Variation

Corner kicks should be taken alternately from both sides toward a centre forward, who contests for the ball with the goal-keeper.

5. Reception of centres in the presence of two or more opponents. Three attackers position themselves in front of the goal, one in front of the goal-keeper and one in front of each goalpost.

6. 3v3 (or 4v4, 5v5, 6v6) game with two 7v7 football goals in one half of the 7v7 football field. Double the size of the penalty area and play with one outlet player in each team (right wing or left wing), who is positioned in a 5-metre-wide channel established at the side-lines. Only the wing is allowed to play in this channel. A goal is valid only when it is scored after a cross from the wing.

Variation

Each team has two outlet players, one in each channel. Before a goal can be scored, the three or four players in the midfield have to pass the ball into the channel and to their winger. The winger then progresses without any opposition and centres the ball with accuracy to a team-mate. The goal-keeper has to intercept this centre or defend the consequent shot.

Receptions and Clearances in the Air

Following a study of Claudio Filippi (1994), goal-keepers these days have to dominate and control the whole penalty area. They have to practice how to receive and clear aerial balls more than ever before as well as receive balls that remain on the ground. Statistics from the FIFA World Championships between 1994 and 1998 prove that coming out of goal to block or clear the ball has increased by 70 per cent in only four years.

To make fewer mistakes when coming from the goal-line to conquer the loose ball, goal-keepers in their training sessions should do the following:

➤ Assume an optimal position in front of the goal at the moment of the centre.

➤ Modify their position in the area after having studied the flight characteristics of the ball and the position and movements of the attacker and defenders.

➤ Know how to best use their explosive strength to jump for the ball.

➤ Evaluate the trajectory of the centred ball in the air. This means to take into consideration the ball's starting place, its speed, its spin, its highest point, its bounce and its possible point of landing. Knowing how to process all this information from the oncoming ball allows the goal-keeper (but also the defenders and attackers) to anticipate where to go for the ball, to catch it, to clear it with one or two fists or deflect it. The keeper furthermore should recognise the ball's spin and speed and whether an attacker has bent the trajectory of the ball to make it concave or convex. All this information is necessary to arrive at correct decisions and prepare the most efficient technique to intercept the ball.

To be able to clear aerial balls that he or she was unable to block, the goal-keeper should choose to clear the ball with only one fist or with two fists, always looking out to clear the ball to zones that are not controlled by opponents.

Aerial balls that come to a goal-keeper from a frontal position should always be cleared with two fists as this allows more distance and more accuracy than doing it with one fist. But when aerial balls come in from any side, a clearance with only one fist, generally with the external one, should be used. That means that balls from centres that arrive from the left side (seen from the goal-keeper) have to be cleared in the presence of several attackers to the right lateral zone with the right fist.

The capacity to clear aerial balls with one or two fists can be acquired with practice. A suitable practice situation, interception from aerial centres, is contained within the progressive series of exercises. For goal-keepers who do not have any restrictions in their play, the 11th simplified game, Centring the Ball, on page 175, will provide additional training.

When a ball is centred in front of a goal, the goal-keeper rushes out to play it only when he or she is 100 per cent sure of being able to touch the ball before anybody else could. It is very important to choose the precise moment for going out of goal to meet the oncoming ball. That is why committing any mistake in calculating speed, height, spin and trajectory of the ball as well as taking in consideration the play of the attackers means that the opponent will probably gain a good opportunity to score.

Dominating and controlling the whole penalty requires more than just tall, strong and explosive goal-keepers. These characteristics obviously help, but there are other requirements:

➤ Speed in perceiving and analysing the game situation
➤ Experience in handling high oncoming balls
➤ Ability to rapidly choose the most efficient technique to resolve the problem
➤ Speed and determination in approaching the oncoming ball and speed in executing the chosen motor skill

Clearance Exercises

Practicing game situations frequently can improve and train the goal-keeper's capacity to punch the ball with one or two fists, dive for it, catch it or deflect it. A good example of a true game situation is test 6 of the goal-keeper decathlon, Defend the Goal-Keeper's Area, found on page 212. Also, on page 237, the 10th simplified game, 4v2 With Headers, provides realistic training. Practicing corners from either side (progressively increasing the number of attackers and defenders) is also helpful.

1. Long Clearances

The coach or an attacker plays balls at different speeds and heights from outside the penalty area to the goal. Depending on the characteristics of the shot at goal, the keeper saves and then clears the balls into a designated area of the field.

2. Clearance to the Side-Lines

After having saved a shot at goal, the goal-keeper clears the ball as quickly as possible through one of two goals set up with cones on the side-lines of the penalty area on the left and right sides. The direction selected for the clearance depends on the play of the attacker, who, after the shot at goal from 16 metres, goes on to defend one of the goal areas.

Variation

After the save, the keeper has to clear the ball within three seconds through one of three goals set up (with cones) inside the penalty area. Two attackers (one at 16 metres and the other 11 metres away) try to prevent his or her scoring through one of the three goals, using any clearance technique.

3. Accurate Clearances With Five Attackers

Four attackers position themselves around the penalty area. A fifth one has possession of the ball and dribbles it close to the edge of the penalty area until he or she decides to execute a shot at goal through a gap created by the four team-mates. While the goal-keeper interferes, all attackers go for a possible rebound, which must be taken within three seconds after the goal-keeper's first intervention. None of the attackers is allowed to deflect the initial shot at goal. Depending on the distance of the nearest attacker at the instant of the save, the goal-keeper decides which technique to use. It is important for the goalie to clear the ball to spaces that the five attackers are not covering. For every clearance of the ball out of the penalty area, the keeper wins one point; the attackers can gain two points only with rebound goals and one point only with a direct goal. For any infringement committed by the keeper, a penalty is awarded to the attackers. All five attackers may shoot the moving ball from the edge of the area as long as they do not miss the goal. If an attacker fails, however, she or he is replaced by another player. The game is over once all five players have been replaced.

Variations

- The coach does not allow the goal-keeper to block the shots at goal.
- Two defenders assist the keeper, looking for defensive rebounds. They interfere from a position close to both goalposts immediately after the shot on goal, clearing the ball out of the danger zone.

4. Clearances Against Three Attackers

Three players stand 30 metres in front of one goal, serving as attackers. Once they penetrate slightly into the penalty area (but not more than 2 metres), one of them shoots and the other two do everything they can to pick up the rebound. The goal-keeper, who may not block the ball, should clear it through a zone the attackers leave uncovered.

Variations

- The three attackers must face a defender in addition to the goal-keeper.
- Two defenders stand next to the goalposts and assist the goal-keeper in clearing the ball from the penalty area (defensive rebound).

Playing Out of Goal

Game statistics show that a goal-keeper interferes not more than once in three minutes. Most of the interventions take place outside of the goal area, especially at centres, when one attacker manages to control the ball in his or her area without any defender being able to interfere before the shot at goal, when the ball is played back to the goalie. Often an intervention occurs when the ball is loose in the penalty area as a result of a rebound from the post or any player's body, or to a loss in the control of the ball by one of the defenders or an attacker.

In all these cases, the goal-keeper must decide in only a split second whether to rush out of goal or to remain close to the goal-line. If even the slightest possibility exists that another team defender could still prevent the attacker from taking a shot, the goal-keeper should stay in goal. Once a keeper decides to run out to confront the situation one on one, however, he or she should do it aggressively and not modify the play half way.

In a 1v1 situation the goal-keeper must be prepared to find the correct response to the attacker's two possible actions: dribbling or shooting. The goal-keeper should narrow the shooting angle as well as possible through the run-out, but the player must also learn to hold back patiently, forcing the opponent into hurried actions or mistakes. In this response, the keeper should keep upright as long as possible, with arms stretched wide to reduce the ball carrier's vision and distract him or her. With this behaviour the goal-keeper can easily adapt to the attacker's offensive actions and, by executing a dummy, even oblige the opponent into doing what he or she wants.

After having sharply assessed the time and space parameters when an attacker tries to play the ball around him or her, the goal-keeper may dive with determination to block or, even better, collect the rolling ball. But if the ball is out of the keeper's range of action, he or she should try to cover the shooting angle with a fine positional play.

During the run-out, the goalie should accelerate as much as possible during the first metres but then must slow down the running speed as he or she nears the attacker. Only in this way can the keeper react successfully in the basic ready position.

The farther the goal-keeper finds himself or herself outside of goal, the more possibilities exist for the attacker to beat him or her. This is especially true if the keeper goes down too early, allowing the attacker to lift the ball over the goalie's outstretched body.

In playing the position, the goal-keeper must follow the same basic rule that guides other defence players for the team. Facing an opponent one on one, the goalie must reduce the space and time available to the attacker as much as possible to force the opponent to speed up (and often, therefore, to commit errors). The less time and space available for the attacker, the better the chances for the goal-keeper to win the duel.

Exercises for Playing Out of Goal

1. Running, Lying Down and Stretching Out in Front of the Ball

The goal-keeper rushes out with speed and aggressiveness. The aim is to lie down just in front of the stationary ball placed in various spots in front of the goal at a distance of 6 to 8 metres. While lying down and stretching out, the goal-keeper collects the ball with both hands. From this position behind the goal, the coach evaluates the

goal-keeper's technique of running out and getting down, looking for these aspects:

- A quick approach in a straight line up to the stationary ball

- Getting down quickly from a vertical into a horizontal position so that an attacker would not be able to pass the ball below the keeper's body as he or she was lying down

- Good positioning of the hands when collecting the ball on the ground

2. Challenge With a Stationary Ball

Set a ball down on the ground in front of the penalty area, as in the illustration. One attacker gets on the edge of the penalty area, facing a goal-keeper positioned in the centre of the goal. Give the players a visible signal for them to start. Both try to reach the ball first and then play it, but they have different objectives: One intends to score and the other one wants to clear the ball out of the penalty area. Depending on the attacker's and the goal-keeper's speed, the goal-keeper has to decide whether to kick the ball first or to hold back, covering the shooting angle of the attacker by placing his or her body close to the ball and thus forcing the attacker to try dribbling. If the attacker has been forced to a dribble, the goalie should get down, stretch out and grip the moving ball as the opponent runs into range. It is useful if you, as coach, modify the ball's position inside the area—as well as the distances between the competitors—to give the players more experience in optical-motor assessment.

3. Challenge With a Moving Ball

An attacker pushes the ball from the edge of the penalty area some 6 to 8 metres into the area. The player then tries to control it again before the goal-keeper can do so. After assessing the speed of the ball, the distance from the attacker and the speed of the opponent, the goal-keeper decides what to do. Remaining in goal is certainly a mistake. That is why the keeper should choose between running out to block the shot or the dribble of the attacker and trying to clear the loose ball before the opponent can. By practicing this situation frequently, the goal-keeper can gain valuable experience in coping with loose balls in the penalty area.

4. Challenge in a Real 1 v 1

Situate an attacker on the edge of the penalty area and the goal-keeper on the goal-line. At your signal, the attacker has four seconds in which to beat the goal-keeper with a dribble and score from any spot inside the goal-keeper's area.

Variations

- A wing passes the ball across the penalty area to another team-mate, the attacker, situated on the edge of the box. While the ball is on its way and the attacker is controlling it, the goal-keeper rushes out, trying to do whatever is possible to avoid a goal being scored with a shot or successful dribbling. The goal must be scored within five seconds of the initial pass to count as a point.

- A midfielder passes the ball from different positions outside of the penalty area into a wide space between an attacker at the edge of the penalty box and the goal-keeper standing on the goal-line. Both assess the situation with the intention to win the challenge.

5. The Sweat Box

Use cones to mark off a square that measures 6 metres on each side, and call on four attackers plus one keeper. The goal-keeper plays inside the square against an attacker who starts from a position 8 metres outside. To collect a point, the goalie must prevent the attacker from running with the ball under control across the square. If the attacker loses control of the ball or happens to play it across one of the side-lines, the goal-keeper wins the match. After the first player has attacked, the second, third and fourth launch their individual attacks. The competition ends after 12 attacks, with every opponent player having attacked three times. Generally the goal-keeper should win more points than the attackers. The purpose of this exercise is to train the goalie to condition the opponent's play through the application of body feint. Convincing someone of a feint works only when the manoeuvre is executed in time and when the attacker is about 3 to 4 metres in front of the goalie.

6. Twice 2v1

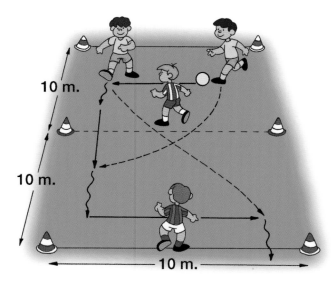

Designate the playing area with cones as shown in the illustration, and use two attackers, one defender, and one goalie. The attackers first face the defender at the 10-metre line. After having played out the first defender and controlled the ball in the first wide goal, the two attackers take on the second defender, who is the goal-keeper. He or she defends the second goal, set 10 metres behind the first one, but should move out of goal only after the ball has been controlled in the first one. To beat the goal-keeper and score a valid goal, one of the two attackers must control the ball on the second goal-line without having been in an off-side position during the development of the attack.

7. Dribble Across the Opponent's End-Line

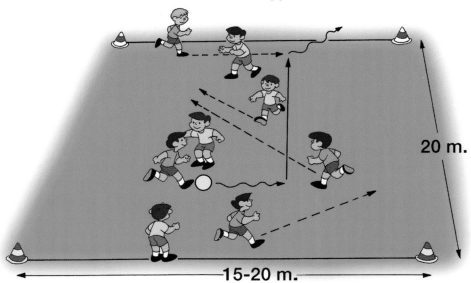

20 m.

15-20 m.

This is a variant of the first simplified game for the 4v4 triathlon (see page 177), so you should use its rules and setup with the players. Consult the illustration here as well for setting up the pitch and play. In this variation one field player of each team becomes a goal-keeper. The goalies may play in any part of the field and may use their hands.

Common Mistakes Made in Playing Out of Goal

Most young goal-keepers make the same common mistakes, and these are the most frequently encountered errors in playing outside of the goal area:

- Remaining on the goal-line instead of running out aggressively to encounter the attacker in possession of the ball.
- Speeding the exit too much because of thinking a team-mate still can interfere before the shot at goal is to be taken.
- Not establishing good communication and cooperation with other defenders, resulting in a poor synchronisation of actions between the goal-keeper and defenders.
- Approaching the attacker with too much speed, instead of slowing down when the goalie is about 5 metres from the attacker. When the keeper reaches an attacker who is still on the run, the attacker has no problem in beating or passing him or her with ease.
- Clearing the ball but without accuracy (perhaps even to an opponent) and without power (not sending it far enough away from the goal so that the ball may return in a few seconds).
- Going down on the ground too frequently, almost like a habit, instead of remaining upright and in a balanced position.
- Going down into a sitting position instead of down toward one side.
- Tackling the attacker feet first while going down.
- Losing contact with the goal when rushing out to one side to an attacker who has a narrow shooting angle—instead of remaining in goal, covering the shooting angle and preparing for a possible shot at goal after a back pass.

Attacking Play

Today the goal-keeper has to be considered as the first attacker of the team because his or her tasks are not limited to prevent the opponents from scoring. Numerous examples demonstrate that intelligent goal-keepers are capable of long and precise passes, given in the most appropriate moment, to create goal opportunities. On the other hand they may give the ball and perhaps a goal away to the opponents for not reading the game situation correctly, for making a wrong decision or badly executing the technique chosen for a pass.

Considering that two-thirds of all the keeper's interventions have offensive characteristics (Filippi 1994), it is logical that there is an increasing need for goal-keepers to practice their offensive play daily. In this way, keepers gain important experience in such an important yet underestimated section of their performance.

Like all other players on the pitch who gain possession of the ball, goal-keepers also have to perceive and analyse the game situation, then come to a correct decision about the most efficient technique to use to resolve the problem. Finally, they must restart the game with a well-executed pass to the best positioned team-mate in the right moment and without indicating the ball's direction.

To select a technique for initiating an attack, the goal-keeper has various options:

➤ An aerial pass or a pass along the ground
➤ A kick or a throw
➤ A kick with the left or the right foot
➤ A kick with the ball stationary or moving
➤ Frontal or lateral volley in which the keeper rotates the body or does a drop-kick to allow the ball receiver to continue the attack as quickly as possible

The goal-keeper's decision about what technique to apply depends on the following:

➤ The availability of the potential receiver (establishing a visual agreement with him or her before the pass is played)
➤ The marking of the team-mate (Is he or she without any marking or does somebody mark the player from a side or from behind?)
➤ The distance between the passer and the potential receiver
➤ The positioning of the opponent's defence
➤ The actual game's score in order to risk or play with maximum security; whether to pass the ball as quickly as possible or to delay it, taking into consideration the rule that the goal-keeper has to release the ball within six seconds

Generally goal-keepers should start their attacks with throws to team-mates who are positioned in the goal-keeper's half, using the player who is considered the distributing player. But in case the goal-keeper collects the ball from an opposing attack finishing on the right side, he or she should initiate the next attack on the opposite side where fewer defenders are around to stop the progression of the new attack. Because there are front runners who anticipate the goal-keeper's first pass, the goal-keeper should pass the ball to his or her team-mate only after having carefully studied the game situation.

It is fundamental that goal-keepers do everything to facilitate team-mates' reception and control of the ball. That is why the keeper looks to pass the ball with speed along the ground into a team-mate's run. The goalie should never pass it backward, obliging the receiver to turn around and be surprised by an opponent. For passing the ball to a front runner in the opposing half, as happens with counterattacks, the keeper uses long kicks into the open space, which cover sufficient distance but often don't have accuracy.

The goal-keeper's offensive play becomes particularly important when he or she signals to team-mates the need to counterattack through his or her first precise pass into space. Once the goalie has decided to initiate a counterattack, he or she quickly executes an accurate kick into the run of a team-mate in the midfield. Besides being precise, the pass should have a low trajectory to give the opponent's defence less time to intercept it. That is why in the training of all goal-keepers, care should be taken to increase not only the distance but also the accuracy of their initial long pass, avoiding its high trajectory.

There are occasions when the goal-keeper is not able to play constructively as he or she is pressed by an opponent. Then the goalie is forced to clear the ball toward the side-lines and never toward the centre: The cleared ball may hit and rebound from the body of the pressing opponent.

Today most goal-keepers reinitiate play with a kick of the stationary ball once it runs across the end-line. In the past this task was carried out by a defender who now offers himself or herself to present another option for the goal-keeper to pass the ball to.

Exercises to Improve the Attacking Play of the Goal-Keeper

1. A wing defender passes the ball back to the goal-keeper, who approaches the ball to receive it with the external foot (paying attention to the surface of the pitch). Without stopping it, let it rebound diagonally into the direction in which the following low and hard pass is directed: to the opposite side to the other wing defender.

Variations

- The same exercise with two front runners as opponents. The one who is closer to the ball approaches the goal-keeper in a straight line when the latter receives it in order to gain experience passing the ball under pressure.

- The same exercise with two front runners, but the one closer to the ball approaches the goal-keeper in different ways so that the goal-keeper learns to decide which wing defender should receive the ball. The direction of the pass depends on the way the attacker approaches the goal-keeper.

- The same exercise with two front runners, who both press the goal-keeper, avoiding passing the ball to either of the two wing defenders. The goal-keeper then orientates the oncoming ball toward the centre and clears it into a marked square of 10 metres close to the centre-line in a left or right wing position. But in case one of the front runners comes too close to the goal-keeper, the alternative is a direct clearance to the side-lines without controlling the ball beforehand.

  Before receiving a back pass the goal-keeper should read the game and react to what the front runners are doing. The first rule for the goal-keeper is to not take any risks.

- As in the previous drill, except the goal-keeper may pass the ball to one of the wing defenders or to one of the two midfield players at a 25-metre distance who are shadowed by one opponent only. Once the goal-keeper receives the back pass, he or she should pass the ball without taking any risk to one of the four team-mates.

2. See Precise Ball Throwing on page 211.

3. See Precise Attacking Kicks on page 213.

4. Long passes to one of two front runners after an aerial reception of the ball. The goal-keeper collects a high back pass and then feeds a front runner positioned close to the centre-line on one side or to another team-mate farther up the pitch on the opposite side. The goal-keeper practices various techniques to find out which one is most successful.

Variation

The same exercise with one defender, who positions him- or herself between the two front runners. Needless to say, the goal-keeper always passes the ball to the less-marked attacker.

5. Long passes to one of three front runners marked by two defenders after an aerial reception of the ball. The number of goals should be counted with 10 initial passes by the goal-keeper.

6. Double the size of the penalty area and play 3v3 on two goals that are each defended by one goal-keeper (technically making this exercise 4v4). The second goal is placed opposite the first one on the 33-metre line. In addition to improving goal-keepers' attacking play, this game exposes them to all situations that can happen in the real game.

Variations

• Each team positions an outlet player, who is allowed to play only one touch close to each goalpost. This outlet player should be served frequently with throws or kicks in case other team-mates are less well positioned.

• At both flanks channels of 5 metres wide are marked with cones. Both teams position one wing in each channel. Before a goal can be scored, the ball has to be passed to one of the two wingers. The attacking goal-keeper agrees to learn a set-play with the marked winger. When the winger runs away from the goal-keeper followed by the opponent, he or she suddenly turns, faces the goal-keeper and receives the pass.

The Goal-Keeper Decathlon

The majority of coaches, especially those of young football players, find it difficult to combine their training of the field players with a simultaneous coaching of goal-keepers. This is where knowing the 10 tests of the goal-keeper decathlon comes in handy. The coach may encourage the goal-keepers to practice on their own for short periods of time, assigning them one or two tests while coaching the rest of the team. This way, the goal-keepers occupy their time efficiently until the coach can again involve them in the training and learning processes of the entire team.

The decathlon can be used as a competition between any number of goal-keepers. If a club or a regional federation decides to organise a decathlon for a specific age group, setting aside two days usually works well. Participation in this two-day competition (each of the days includes five tests against five different goal-keepers) generally motivates the contestants to improve in a great variety of abilities, such as positional play, techniques for saving shots, running out of goal, blocking shots while lying down and different clearance techniques. A goal-keeper has the opportunity to analyse his or her level of playing and compare the performance with peers and opponents. In turn, the youngster may feel inspired or encouraged to improve by undertaking a series of corrective exercises for whatever deficiencies are observed in his or her skills.

The goal-keeper decathlon is also useful as a test to evaluate the level of performance among goal-keepers. Not only can you evaluate the mastery of the specific keepers' skills, but you can scrutinise other necessary aspects of an optimal performance: attention, anticipation, visual-motor perception, vision, split-second decision making, will power and pluck, and physical capacities. Thanks to the goal-keeper decathlon, you have an ideal selection of evaluation criteria.

Note: Have goal-keepers between the ages of 10 and 14 years trained using No. 4 balls and defending 7v7 football goals (in other words, with dimensions of 6 metres by 2 metres) with penalty areas and goal-keeper areas for 7v7 football.

1. Save Twice

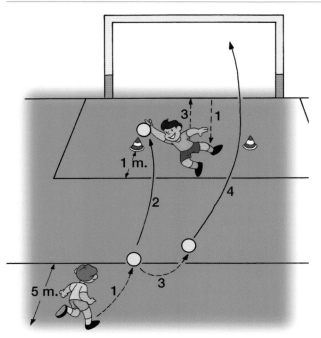

When using an 11v11 field, set up a pair of cones marking an extra goal at 4.5 metres in front of the regular goal area (3.5 metres when a 7v7 football goal is used). At the moment the attacking goal-keeper starts 5 metres outside the penalty area, the defending keeper rushes out of his or her goal to occupy the second one marked off by cones.

The attacking goal-keeper kicks his or her first ball from the edge of the area, allowing the defending one little time to reach the second goal-line, assume an optimal, basic ready position, and make a save.

Immediately after the save (preferably managed in an upright position) or an inaccurate shot, a second stationary ball is kicked from 10 (for a 7v7 football goal) or 15 metres over the defender's head toward the official goal. To be able to save the second shot directed to the goal, the goal-keeper runs backward and executes a second defensive action. Each goal-keeper has three double kicks from three attacking positions. After six shots, the goal-keeper who concedes fewer goals is the winner.

TRAINING OBJECTIVES

- Improve coordination through running both forward and backward, making sudden stops, assuming a correct ready position and correct execution of different skills (catch, punch, deflection, save-clear and dive), and even, when necessary, an acrobatic style.
- Develop power in the leg muscles.
- Demonstrate good positional play, always remaining on the imaginary line bisecting the shooting angle formed by the position of the ball and the two goalposts.
- Perfect the sense of balance, awareness and orientation when running backward.
- Quickly determine the most effective technique for avoiding the opponent's goals.

2. One Against One

A goal-keeper passes the ball into the feet of an opponent, situated anywhere on the 16.5-metre or 11-metre line that limits the penalty area. Immediately after this strong pass, the keeper may leave the goal-line to face the opponent. The task of the attacking goal-keeper is to score within five seconds.

The challenge ends with a goal, the ball out of the penalty area, a successful play by the defending goal-keeper or after five seconds. After the first challenge there are four more with the attacking goal-keeper starting from a different position in relation to the goal. Once five attacks have been carried out, both keepers switch their positions and functions. The goal-keeper who allows fewer goals to be scored with five attacks is considered the winner of this test.

TRAINING OBJECTIVES

- Limit the shooting angle of the attacker with a correct line of approach.
- Try to assume a correct basic position and ensure balance in the moment of the shot at goal.

3. Positioning in the Goal-Keeper's Area

The attacking goalie disposes of six shots, executing two each from a side of the penalty box and two more from beyond the 16.5-metre line but in front of the goal. The attacker's aim is to score a goal with either a free kick or get the ball to touch the ground in any part of the goal-keeper's area (4.5 by 12 metres). In either case the defending keeper would get a negative point. By using intelligent positional play, anticipation and acrobatic moves, however, the defending goal-keeper tries to prevent the ball's entering the goal or landing in the small area. After the first six shots both goal-keepers switch positions and functions. The goal-keeper who has fewer negative points is the winner.

5 m.

TRAINING OBJECTIVES

- Develop the capacity to quickly make correct decisions after carefully observing the ball's trajectory and speed.
- Execute defensive actions (catch, dive, deflection or punch) at maximum speed.
- Affect the attacker's shots by means of the positional play.
- Assume an optimal, basic ready position.
- Demonstrate will and nerve (even audacity).
- Improve visual-motor assessment.
- Oblige the attacking goal-keeper to do what you want him or her to do.

4. Precise Ball Throwing

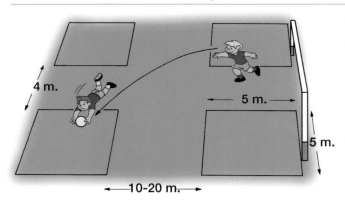

4 m.

5 m.

5 m.

10-20 m.

Set up four squares measuring between 4 and 5 metres per side, two in one zone and two in the opposite zone. A neutral zone, whose distance (10 to 20 metres) depends on the goal-keepers' level of power, separates the squares. Two keepers face each other, taking a central position between their two squares, which are only 2 or 3 metres apart. One throws the ball with the intention of having it land inside one of the two opponent's squares.

The defending keeper, by intelligently reading and reacting, does whatever he or she can to move out of the initial central position and catch or clear the ball before its landing in either square. The winner is the goal-keeper who manages to have the ball land five times inside one square of the opponent's zones.

TRAINING OBJECTIVES

- As defending goal-keeper, assume an optimal stance (tiptoe position with the legs slightly bent) and position in space to intercept all throws with vision skills.
- Improve throwing technique (as in discus throwing), accuracy and power.
- Learn to disguise the direction of the throw.

5. Defence of 10 Consecutive Shots

Both goal-keepers, each in possession of a stationary ball, face each other at a distance of 11 or 16.5 metres in their respective goals (7v7 or 11v11 goal). After an initial signal, both have to score within three seconds and at the same time observe and save the ball shot by his or her opponent. The goal-keeper who concedes fewer goals after 10 consecutive shots (two shots with the stationary ball placed on the ground, two drop-kicks, two frontal volley shots, two high throws and two passes along the ground with one hand) wins.

TRAINING OBJECTIVES

- Be creative and split your attention between your goal shot and the oncoming ball passed by the opponent. While keeping one eye on your ball you should observe and react to the opponent's shot at goal. This demands the abilities of perception and extremely short reaction time.
- Use different techniques for initiating the attack, disguising your shot as often as possible.

6. Defend the Goal-Keeper's Area

The attacking keeper has four attacks (set out four balls) to dribble the ball from various points outside the penalty area into the goal-keeper's area. When he or she touches the ball, the defending goal-keeper comes out to prevent the attacker's penetrating with the ball into the small area. A goal can be scored only from inside the small area. An attack ends when the ball is out of the penalty area, a goal is scored or the attacker commits an infringement. A penalty is awarded for an infringement of the defending goal-keeper. The winning goal-keeper is the player who concedes the fewer goals in four attacks.

TRAINING OBJECTIVES

- Learn to rush out of goal, cover the shooting angle and get down to collect the ball from an attacker.
- Condition (or influence) the offensive play of the attacker by executing dummy movements.

- Be aggressive when necessary and act with determination.
- Select the precise moment for getting down, stretching out, and collecting the ball from the attacker.

7. Challenge in the Air

Both goal-keepers position themselves in front of the goal, one beside the other, in order to clear the ball that a third player is throwing or kicking from any side into the air. Both goal-keepers try to gain their optimal position, jump up to catch the oncoming ball with both hands or try to clear it with one or two fists or even with one foot out of the penalty area.

The neutral player plays two centres each from outside the penalty box and throws two balls from the 16.5-metre line high into the air. The goal-keeper who wins most of the six challenges is declared the winner of this test.

TRAINING OBJECTIVES

- As goal-keeper, get used to an active opponent who will be physically close and perhaps in contact during battles for the ball.
- Assess the speed, trajectory, spin and height of the oncoming ball and then gain your ideal position to play the ball.
- Use your explosive strength at the right moment and put your body between the ball and the opponent.

8. Precise Attacking Kicks

Mark off two goal squares of 10 metres, setting them not more than 15 metres apart from one another; their size will depend on the age of the goal-keepers. From a distance of 20 to 25 metres, the attacking goal-keeper kicks the ball (not too strongly) to the goal. Within three seconds, the defending keeper collects the ball and clears it toward one of the two indicated squares on the right and left sides of his or her centre midfield position. In the first two clearances the goal-keeper must use the drop-kick and volley techniques in the third and fourth. The objective is to get the ball to land in one of the two squares. In the fifth and sixth clearances the goalie uses a kick to

simulate a restart of the game, with a stationary ball placed on the 4.5-metre line. The attacking goal-keeper tries everything possible to ensure that none of the six clearances touches the ground in one of his or her two squares. The keeper who executes more correct clearances is the winner.

TRAINING OBJECTIVES

- Kick the ball with accuracy and power.
- Disguise the direction of the clearance.
- Reduce the time between the ball catch and the clearance.
- Gain insight on which technique is the most efficient in various game situations.

VARIATION

The goal-keeper collects passes from one side-line and then clears it in two squares established at a distance of 25 to 50 metres on the opposite side.

9. Intercepting Rebounds

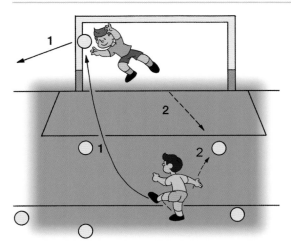

The younger of the two goal-keepers strikes a stationary ball from outside the penalty area to the goal, defended by the older player. This younger goalie has four shots from four attacking positions: two with a stationary ball and two with a moving one. Immediately after any powerful shot at goal, the attacker watches for a possible rebound, because the goal-keeper may *not catch the ball*. Instead he or she may only deflect or deviate it from a path toward goal to clear it.

The attacking goal-keeper should try to attack any rebounded balls, but, if the first ball misses the goal, enters or rebounds out of reach of the attacker, the attacking goalie runs to either of the two balls placed 3 metres outside the goal-keeper area as shown in the illustration. Both players dispute this second ball. While the keeper tries to clear it out of the penalty area or shorten the shooting angle, the attacker tries to score within less than four seconds after having executed the first shot. The player who concedes fewer goals after eight shots (four from outside and four from inside the penalty box) wins the match.

TRAINING OBJECTIVES

- Be prepared for a second defensive action after a first save.
- Improve perception and decision making.
- Improve coordination.

10. Penalty Shoot-Out

The younger of the two goal-keepers initiates the competition with a pass from the goal-line toward the second goal-keeper, who receives and controls the ball on the 9-metre or 11-metre point. Both goal-keepers then have to switch functions and positions. While the former defending goal-keeper runs to take a penalty kick, the other one rushes into the empty goal to save the penalty shot. This lasts until one or both have scored five times. The official rules of football are applied for the penalty shoot-out. The winner is the goal-keeper who does not concede five goals.

TRAINING OBJECTIVES

- Be mentally prepared to save a penalty kick.
- Concentrate only on the ball and do not let yourself be influenced by any move from the attacker.
- Wait for a mistake by the attacker and only save shots taken without accuracy.
- Don't wait for the ball to come to you. Go for it.

Alternate Test for the Goal-Keeper Decathlon

11. Sprint to Clear the Ball

Two goal-keepers play against each other. The coach or a neutral player bounces one ball from 9 metres in front of the goal. Both keepers, starting from the same goal-line, fight to clear the ball. The winning player is the one who manages to gain its possession or to clear the ball out of the penalty area.

The players continue with four more trials. For the second and third trials they start from a sitting position; for the fourth and fifth, they start from a prone (lying down) position. The overall winner is the goal-keeper with the better result out of five clearances.

TRAINING OBJECTIVES

- Improve reaction time.
- Improve the ability to accelerate.
- Improve the ability to make good, quick decisions.
- Improve the ability to anticipate.
- Improve willpower.

The goal-keeper is considered the most important player on the team (any mistake this player makes could result in a goal against the team), and special attention should be given to his or her development. Because most goal-keeper errors are caused less by technique than by poor decision making, it is fundamental to train young keepers not only in the technical but also the tactical aspects of play specific to the position. All young goal-keepers should be exposed regularly to a variety of exercises and games in which they learn not only to save balls but also to consider both their opponents and team-mates in their play.

9

Games for 8v8 Football

'Training is a process
of development
through gradually
increasing demands.'

Laurence Morehouse

The step-by-step approach is one of the keys to success in the Football Development Model, which uses the brain's innate ability to form memory-building connections. In the first three levels, all-important, basic game situations are broken down into series of small steps. These levels gradually and methodically lead to the final goal of youth football: to enjoy and successfully play the 8v8 game. The Football Development Model serves as an ideal bridge leading young athletes to play the full football game for the first time with two years of practice.

Complete Football Test

The Complete Football Test (see table below) should be used twice in the season—at its beginning and end—to get a comparison between the players' performance levels early and late in the season. Through this comparison you will gain a clear picture of their grade of improvement.

This is a simple test among different groups of six players. It assesses the players' technical, tactical and physical capacities in a global context. It also evaluates other essential aspects of their performance in football, such as vision skills, anticipating action, understanding or communicating with team-mates, decision making and stress management.

Complete Football Test

Order	Test	Confrontation between
1	2v1 With Counterattack, pages 79, 99	Pair 1/6v2/5, 3/4v1/6, 2/5v3/4
2	1st test of the decathlon, page 75	1v6, 2v5, 3v4
3	2nd test of the decathlon, page 75	1v5, 2v4, 3v6
4	2v2 With Four Intersecting Goals, page 80	Pair 1/4v2/6, 3/5v1/4, 2/6v3/5
5	3rd test of the decathlon, page 76	1v4, 2v3, 5v6
6	4th test of the decathlon, page 76	1v3, 2v6, 4v5
7	2v2 With Two Wide Goals, page 80	Pair 1/5v2/6, 3/4v2/6, 1/5v3/4
8	5th test of the decathlon, page 76	1v2, 3v5, 4v6
9	6th test of the decathlon, page 77	1v6, 2v5, 3v4
10	3v3 With Four Intersecting Goals, pages 141, 162	Team 1/2/3v4/5/6
11	7th test of the decathlon, page 78	1v5, 2v4, 3v6
12	8th test of the decathlon, page 78	1v4, 2v3, 5v6
13	3v2 With Counterattack, pages 141, 163	Team 1/2/4v3/5/6
14	9th test of the decathlon, page 78	1v3, 2v6, 4v5
15	10th test of the decathlon, page 79	1v2, 3v5, 4v6
16	3v3 With Two Wide Goals, pages 142, 170	Team 1/3/6v2/4/5

Scoring for the Decathlon. The player who wins the most tests in the decathlon gets six points; the second best, five; the third, four; the fourth, three; the fifth, two; and the sixth, only one point.

Scoring for the 2v2 Triathlon. For a victory in each game, both players of the winning team get two points.

Scoring for the 3v3 Triathlon. For a victory in each game, the three players of the winning team get three points.

Final Scoring. The player who wins the most points in the 16 tests is considered to be the all-around winning player out of the six participants. If two players have the same score in the final classification, event 10 of the decathlon serves as the tiebreaker.

The two players who are classified best of one group may challenge other winning players of two other groups, as may the third- and fourth-best or the fifth- and sixth-best. (The top two players of groups A, B and C play a new tournament, as do the third- and fourth-ranked players of each group and the fifth- and sixth-ranked players.)

Simplified Games for 4v4

These games are a logical continuation of the simplified games for fewer players in earlier chapters. They build on the skills the young players have already learned, and in turn prepare them realistically for the 8v8 game and, eventually, for regular 11v11 competition.

1st Simplified Game
4v2 in Adjacent Squares

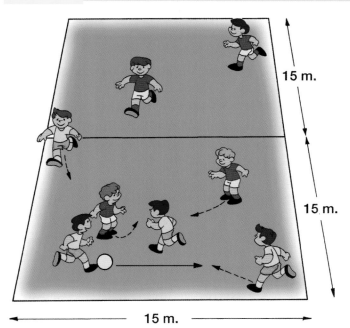

15 m.

15 m.

15 m.

Set up two 15-metre squares, as in the illustration, and form two teams of four players each. The team with the youngest players places its four players in one area, but the second team distributes its players between both areas: two in the first and two in the adjacent square. The four players of the first team try to pass the ball as often as possible among their team. Their objective is also to prevent the ball's running across the sides of the square or losing it to the two defenders, who are trying meanwhile to gain possession of the ball. If the second team's members do get possession, the defenders must pass the ball quickly to their team-mates in the neighbouring field. Immediately after the pass, they join their team-mates in the adjacent square, followed by two former attackers who now defend in that new area. To be able to play a pressing defence against the four attackers, it is advisable that after every change of possession of the ball, the two freshest or closest defenders run quickly into the other area.

When the ball played by any of the four attackers leaves the playing area, a kick-in is awarded to the two defenders, taken by one of their team-mates in the adjacent square, with the defender a distance of at least 5 metres away. To help motivate the players, call out every pass loudly. Each team tries to complete first 15 and later 21 passes to win the first set. The winning team is the one that attains the established number of passes in two sets.

EFFECTIVE QUESTIONING

Where should the team-mates of the two defenders ideally position themselves in the neighbouring grid? Explain why. It would be ideal for the two team-mates to offer themselves for a pass as far away as possible from the centre-line that separates the two grids. Doing so means they will have sufficient time to receive and control the ball (since the defenders are far away) as well as to decide upon the next move.

What are the characteristics of a good pass?

- It always reaches a team-mate who is not immediately put under pressure by a defender.
- It is not executed too early or too late and allows a team-mate to play the ball in more favourable conditions.
- It has sufficient speed and has been disguised to prevent the defenders from reading the intention of the passer.
- It is generally played along the ground where it can be controlled more quickly and easily than an aerial pass.

Why should aerial passes be avoided when maintaining possession of the ball? Passes along the ground can be controlled with more ease and speed.

Tell me when the ideal moment to pass the ball in this particular game arises? When being put under full pressure by an opponent, the attacker should pass the ball. That means that the pass is borne of necessity.

Explain the next step for a player who has just passed the ball with success. Immediately after the successful pass, the player should move out of position and offer him- or herself again in an area not controlled by any opponent.

When the team's objective is to maintain possession of the ball, should you pass the ball into the path of your team-mate or directly into his or her feet? To facilitate the team-mate's reception, the ball should be passed directly into his or her feet.

When do you have to play the oncoming ball directly (with one touch), and when should you decide to control it? In case an opponent presses the player at the moment of receiving the ball, the player should make a first touch pass and deny controlling it since this involves risks of losing its possession.

In case an attacker loses possession of the ball, what should we expect him or her to do? The attacker (as well as all the team-mates) should switch immediately to defensive functions without creating a pause between attack and defence.

To maintain possession of the ball, when should the attackers pass the ball and when should they dribble it? At the moment a defender presses the ball carrier, the latter has to pass it to a better positioned team-mate who has no defender close to him or her. In case the ball carrier has no option to pass the ball at all, he or she keeps it and dribbles it toward an unoccupied zone from where he or she may make contact with any of the other three team-mates.

What should the two defenders do to get the ball away from the four attackers? Once the ball is in a corner of the playing field, one defender approaches the ball carrier in a diagonal line. This particular line of approach obliges the ball carrier to pass the ball into the open space exactly as the covering defender has anticipated. The defender is then able to press the receiving player while controlling the ball.

VARIATIONS

- Count only those passes that cover more than 5 metres.
- The attackers try to keep the ball in their possession for 15 (later for 20) seconds. (See also the ninth simplified game, Maintaining Ball Possession 2v1 on page 112).
- After a successful pass is executed, the player must immediately run at least 5 metres in any direction.
- Three teams of four players participate. In one square, the four team-mates of team 1 play against two of the players from team 2. In the adjacent square, the other two team-mates from team 2 defend against the four players of team 3. The team of four players that can keep possession the longest wins.

TRAINING OBJECTIVES

- Maintain a high level of concentration for at least two sets.
- Avoid a 1v1 situation, instead systematically looking out for 2v1.
- Avoid entering into the range of action of any defender when you have the ball and try to pass it as soon as you have committed the defender. Use direct or wall passes as often as possible.
- As an attacker, learn to time dummies precisely to gain space, time and self-confidence, especially when you are drawn into a corner of the pitch where fewer passing options exist.
- Learn to run away from the defenders and make yourself available for a pass in a zone that is not controlled by the defence and that is not too close to the ball carrier. Receiving the ball in a position far away from the defence allows you more time and space to control it and play it again.
- Make yourself available in a zone not already occupied by a team-mate.
- Pass the ball with speed and accuracy.
- Avoid indicating the direction of the intended pass to your opponents.
- Bend your legs and keep your centre of gravity as low as possible to the ground when defending.
- Invite the ball carrier, through a body movement, to play the ball in the direction you want him or her to pass.
- Be aggressive when you defend, be prepared to go full out to reduce the time and space at the disposal of the attackers.
- Consider the position of your defending team-mates before you go for the ball. The defence is generally more effective against attackers situated in a corner of the pitch.

CORRECTIVE GAMES

Four players place themselves around an 8-metre square without being allowed to enter it. They should pass the ball to each other in such a way that it always runs along the ground and crosses two sides of the square before being received and controlled. Two defenders inside the square try their best to prevent the four external players from executing the passes during two minutes of play. After two minutes, the two defenders switch roles and positions with two of the attackers. The game is over when every player has defended for two minutes.

Variations

- Only first-time passes (no control of the ball is allowed before it is passed) across two of the lines count.

- A fifth attacker is introduced and positioned inside the square to receive a pass from one of the four team-mates outside the square. They may choose between a pass across two lines to another external player (to score one point) or to the fifth player inside the square. Every control of the ball by the fifth player with a subsequent pass to a team-mate outside the square counts three points.

<table>
<tr><td>**2nd**</td><td>Simplified Game
Fast Attack 4v2 With Three Teams</td></tr>
</table>

The game is played with three teams, each having four players, on a 7v7 or 8v8 football pitch. To start play, give a visible signal to two of the teams, both on the centre-line and in possession of a ball. They attack their respective goals in opposite directions. Two players of the third team defend each of these goals (see illustration). The team that manages to score first wins. When the two defenders or neutral goal-keepers gain possession, they must clear the ball across the centre-line. After five attacks and a complete rest in between them, the three teams rotate until each team has defended five times and attacked 10 times.

VARIATIONS

- Once the attackers have started their offensive moves, the defenders leave their positions—on the end-line, 10 metres behind any side-line or even on the same centre-line—in order to pursue and stop them from scoring.

- The attack begins from a limited area (15 by 15 metres marked close to the centre-line, side-line or both), positioned in the left or right wing.

TRAINING OBJECTIVES

- Attack in a diamond formation, that is, with depth and width.
- Use long, direct passes rather than horizontal passes.
- Try as often as possible to make a first-time play.
- Gain experience in goal scoring.
- As defenders, learn to delay and channel the attack.

 ## EFFECTIVE QUESTIONING

Tell me how you execute your passes during a fast break. Preferably through balls or diagonal passes should be played into the run of a team-mate who collects the ball in a zone that at that moment has not been controlled by any opponent. Square passes as well as long runs with the ball give the opponent the possibility to regroup. Instead of receiving and then taking time to control the ball, look and then pass it as often as possible with one touch. In other words, combine the reception of the ball with a direct pass.

How should the ball be collected in a fast attack? Neither the ball nor the attacker should be stationary. Receiving the ball on the run without stopping it at all is a must. The technique of reception and control of the ball should be executed in such a way that no time is lost to start the next attacking move.

How should a shot at goal be taken to conclude a fast attack? Most of the shots at goal are direct ones (first touch) without a previous control of the ball.

What should the two defenders who play in a numerical inferiority (2v4 situation) do? Before they face the ball carrier and force him or her to pass the ball, they should quickly retreat to delay the fast attack. The defenders should try to accompany the ball carrier as long as possible and then force him or her to pass the ball to a wing, which should finally be channeled away from the goal.

CORRECTIVE GAMES

Consult Dribbling Games (page 40), the simplified games for 2v2 (page 94) and the simplified games for 3v3 (page 153) for some good choices of remedial games.

 Simplified Game
3rd Through Passes to a Shadowed Forward

Review the rules for the eighth simplified game on page 169. This game is played on a 7v7 football pitch by two teams. Each team has two midfield players (who play between the two penalty areas), one forward (always situated in the opposing penalty area), and a fourth player who defends while remaining in the narrow zone formed by the off-side line (at 13 metres) and the proper penalty area (at 11 metres). If there are no off-side lines, the defender should move only on the 11-metre line. The two midfield players in possession of the ball try to pass to their forward, sending the ball into the opposing penalty area once the forward becomes available for a through pass. After controlling the ball (in an *off-side position*), the outlet player attempts to score against a neutral goal-keeper. The defender in the zone between the 11-metre and 13-metre lines tries to cover the zone, defending against any potential pass to this outlet player behind him or her. None of the players may leave his or her assigned zone. Every five minutes the midfield players of each team change positions and functions with their team's forward and defender.

❓ EFFECTIVE QUESTIONING

What requirements are there to play a successful through pass to a forward? Before a through pass is delivered the ball carrier has to analyse the game situation in order to identify the availability of a zone in which the ball can be delivered. Then the passer should agree visually with the potential receiver to find out whether he or she is ready to communicate. Finally with a cue (head or hand movement), which the opponent is not aware of, the potential receiver should indicate to the passer where he or she wants to serve the ball with a correct direction and sufficient speed.

The midfield player with the ball has the choice between three different attacking moves. Which one should he or she choose in which situation? The midfielder's first option is a through pass to an unmarked forward. In case this is not possible, he or she looks for a second option, which is a pass to a better positioned team-mate in the same zone. A third option is to carry the ball out of the range of action of the defender, shielding it with his or her body to gain some time or receive different passing angles.

Which position should a forward assume when receiving long passes out of the midfield? A side-on position allows him or her to see the passer as well as the defender (and the goal) behind. Furthermore, the side-on position allows the forward to continue the attacking move much quicker (maybe a shot at goal) without being obliged to lose time for his or her turn.

When is an ideal opportunity to play a through pass? This happens immediately after having recovered the ball from the opponent. A through pass is then more successful since most of the opponents are still having an offensive attitude and therefore none of our attackers is marked.

What are the tasks of the two defending midfield players? They should both restrict as much space and time from the two attacking midfield players as they can. Thus the attacking midfielders are unable to communicate with their forward and serve a through pass to him or her with accuracy.

Which one of the two midfield players should support the forward after a successful through pass? This depends mainly on the distances between forward and midfielder but also from the place where the forward receives the ball. In case he or she receives the ball on the right side, the left midfielder supports, and vice versa.

VARIATIONS

- Once the ball has entered the shooting zone, any midfield player or the defender may run into the penalty area to support the outlet player or to defend. Any attacker may score now.
- To learn the attack from the second line, participants apply the rule that only one of the midfield players may score after having served the ball to the forward.
- Advanced players should practice the through pass to a forward, who is closely marked by a defender inside the penalty area. Also have the players review the seventh and eighth simplified games for teams of two players (pages 110, 111) to improve their ability at playing through passes and to work on the reception and control of the ball while being marked. This game variation works well on a mini-football pitch.

EFFECTIVE QUESTIONING

How does the way of marking a forward influence the direction of the through pass played to him or her? In case the attacker is marked closely from behind, he or she expects the ball to be served directly into the feet. When the attacker is marked from the side, he or she expects a through pass to always be directed into the space available to the opposite side where the defender arrives later. When collecting the ball in the space behind, the attacker prevents the defender (shielding the ball) to reach it first.

TRAINING OBJECTIVES

In attack these are the objectives:

- Maintain a high level of concentration during two periods of five minutes each.
- Show strong communication and cooperation skills. The player who wishes to receive the ball should establish a visual agreement with the ball carrier, always signaling him or her where to pass the ball.
- Look up while dribbling the ball; after having analysed the situation and using knowledge of the football game, select the most efficient pass.
- Give preference to a through pass over a square pass or dribble.
- Determine what to do next even before receiving the ball so that play will continue as fluently as possible.
- Switch quickly from attack to defence when the ball is lost.
- Once the forward receives the through pass, his or her reception technique should consider the next move and the presence of a defender to be able to score in less time. (See the last variation.)

In defence these are the objectives:

- Quickly switch from defence to attack when the ball is won.
- Make the through pass difficult for the attackers by systematically reducing their space and time.
- Cooperate in defence. Always consider team-mates' defensive positions before executing a tackle.
- Read the play of the attackers to anticipate their intentions in time.

CORRECTIVE GAMES

Use the eighth simplified game for 3v3 (see page 169).

 Simplified Game
4th Rescue of Prisoners

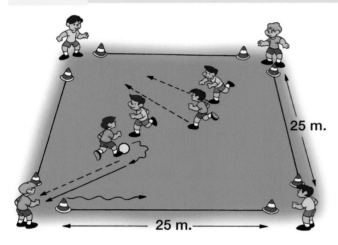

Mark off a square playing area that is 25 metres on each side, using a cone in each corner. Two players of one team compete against two players of the other team in this area. The teams' third and fourth players stand in diagonally opposite corners of the playing area (see illustration). The aim of the two attackers is to play 10 consecutive passes without letting the ball go out of the area's limits. The ball carrier may pass the ball to his or her team-mate, who tries to receive in the centre of the square, or to one of the two team-mates (prisoners) in the diagonally opposed corners (prisons). When the prisoner receives the ball at the respective prison goal, he or she is released from standing still, moves out of the prison and dribbles or passes the ball to any other team-mate. The former passer then assumes the position in prison.

Meanwhile, the two defenders in the centre do their best to prevent the team in possession of the ball from successfully passing. Every pass should be counted loudly enough to inform both the coach and opponents about the actual standing of the game. When the ball leaves the assigned playing area, a kick-in is awarded, with the defenders at a distance of at least 3 metres. The team that manages to play 10 consecutive passes three times or that keeps the ball in its possession longer is considered the winner.

 EFFECTIVE QUESTIONING

What are the characteristics of a good pass?
- It always reaches a team-mate who is not immediately put under pressure by a defender.
- It is not executed too early or too late and allows a team-mate to play the ball in more favourable conditions.
- It has sufficient speed and has been disguised for not allowing the defenders to read the intention of the passer.

- It is generally played along the ground where it can be controlled more easily and quickly than an aerial pass.

What are the main tasks of the player in possession of the ball? He or she has to play in an upright position that allows him or her to read the game situation constantly, showing when and where to pass the ball or dribble it in an unoccupied zone of the grid. When the player decides to pass the ball he or she should not indicate the moment or direction through any movement the opponent may anticipate. After a successful pass the player should move immediately into an unoccupied zone, communicating constantly with his or her two team-mates.

Why should aerial passes be avoided when the objective is to maintain possession of the ball? Passes played along the ground are quicker and easier to control than aerial passes.

Tell me, when is the ideal moment to pass the ball in this game? When an opponent under full pressure puts the attacker with the ball, the latter should pass it. That means that the pass is borne of necessity.

Explain what the job of a player who has passed the ball successfully is. Immediately after the successful pass, the player should move out of position and offer him- or herself again in an area not controlled by any opponent.

When the team's objective is to maintain possession of the ball, should you pass it into the run of your team-mate or directly into his or her feet? To facilitate the team-mate's reception, the ball should be passed directly into the feet.

When do you have to play the oncoming ball directly (with one touch) and when should you decide to control it? In case an opponent presses the player at the moment of receiving the ball, he or she should play a first touch pass and deny controlling it as this involves risks of losing its possession.

In case an attacker loses possession of the ball, what should we expect him to do? The attacker (as well as all the team-mates) should switch immediately to defensive functions without creating a pause between attack and defence.

When should the attacker decide to maintain possession of the ball and when should he or she pass it? In case there is no passing option, the attacker maintains possession of the ball and dribbles it. When the attacker is pressed by one or two defenders, he or she should deliver the ball to a better positioned team-mate.

VARIATIONS

Use these variations of the game in the following order:

1. Only long passes (more than 10 metres or from one part of the pitch to the other) count; draw a centre-line to split the square into two areas.
2. Only passes without a previous dribble count.
3. A player can be released from prison only when the pass is precise (that is, through the goal cones in his or her corner) or has been carried out with the less-skillful foot.
4. Instead of remaining in the small prisons, each of the four receivers chooses a position just behind one of the square's four side-lines from which to receive a pass from team-mates.
5. Only one receiver has to stay outside the square, being available to receive a pass anywhere outside the pitch (that is, 3v3 plus one outside player).

6. All four prisoners must constantly run, using different speeds and going in any direction around the playing field to be in position to receive a pass.

7. For improving first-time play, only first-time passes count.

8. To improve reception and control of the ball, the prisoners are released only after an aerial pass.

9. To improve header techniques, the prisoner may change positions with the passer only if he or she manages to return the ball to a team-mate with a header.

10. Practice these variations with five, six, seven and then eight players on each team; increase the dimensions of the playing area as the number of players increases.

 ## EFFECTIVE QUESTIONING

What does this game variation teach you? Before a defender attacks the ball, he or she should be aware of the position of fellow defenders nearby. The defender should also be aware of the position of his or her team-mates in attack and how they are marked in order to shift as quickly as possible from defence to offence.

TRAINING OBJECTIVES

- Be aware of all options before passing the ball to be able to select the most effective move (this is usually a pass to the player farthest away from the defenders).
- Make it simple and look for a high percentage of success in your passes; avoid getting into a 1v1 situation and keep the ball out of the range of action of any defender.
- Develop accuracy and speed with any pass, also trying to disguise its direction.
- Also see the objectives of the first simplified game in this chapter (page 219).

5th Simplified Game
Executing Consecutive Passes

30 m.

30 m.

Two teams of four players compete between the centre-line and the off-side line of a 7v7 football pitch (or in a square with 30 metres on an 8v8 football field), trying to keep possession of the ball and execute 10 consecutive passes from a distance of at least 10 metres. The official football rules apply. After one team manages to pass the ball 10 times in succession, there should be a two-minute rest interval before the game resumes. During the interval the players of both teams discuss their tactics for the next trial. The game is restarted with a ball toss. To win the game it is necessary to complete 10 consecutive passes three times.

? EFFECTIVE QUESTIONING

Please consult the questions and answers in the previous simplified game.

VARIATIONS

- The team that keeps the ball in its possession longer is the winner.
- Play the game in a smaller area (a square of 20-metre sides).
- Two players from each team remain on the border of the square at all times without entering it. These two players should constantly be in motion.

TRAINING OBJECTIVES

- Avoid a concentration of players close to the ball in order to make the defence more difficult.
- Read the game correctly to be able to select the most effective passing option.
- Learn to keep possession of the ball in critical situations, such as when opponents apply a pressing defence or when the ball carrier is drawn into a corner of the field.
- Know when to pass and when not to pass but dribble instead.
- Learn to shield the ball with the body.
- Add width and depth to the attack in order to stretch the opponent's defence; the attackers without the ball should constantly be ready to receive in those zones of the playing area that are under less control by the defenders.
- Before the execution of any pass, ensure that some visual agreement occurs between ball carrier and receiver.
- Play as a team and reduce individual play (especially 1v1) as much as possible.
- As defenders, place more players close to the ball than the attackers do; read the game to anticipate the next moves from the attacking side and to condition the opponent's play.

6th Simplified Game
Dribbling Across the Opponent's End-Line

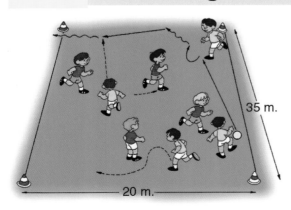

35 m.

20 m.

Use a 7v7 football pitch or an area 20 metres by 35 metres. Two teams of four players each compete between the centre-line and the off-side line, aiming to dribble the ball across the opposing end-line (that is, 35 metres away). The game starts with a toss of the ball. All free kicks must be taken from a spot at least 4.5 metres away from the respective end-line. There is no off-side. All other rules are the same as the official ones.

Duration of the game: three periods of three minutes each, with intervals of two minutes in which both teams should rest and elaborate on the tactics for the next three minutes' play.

EFFECTIVE QUESTIONING

What do the four attackers have to do to control the ball on the opposing goal-line defended by four opponents? When four attackers play together, they should do so in a diamond formation. Two are ensuring width, one on the right and the other one on the left side, while the other two ensure depth upfield and downfield. Maintaining this shape while constantly switching positions will make defending the four opponents very difficult. The attackers should always look out for creating 2v1 situations and avoid 1v1 situations that may give the opponents the opportunity to counterattack.

What is the most efficient pass for the ball carrier? To encourage the ball carrier to look out for through passes, one team-mate should offer him- or herself behind the defence where he or she can receive the ball and score. In this simplified game there is no off-side, as is the case in the 7v7 football game where off-side only starts from a 13-metre line.

How should a front runner receive the ball? He or she should preferably assume a side-on position that allows him or her a quick continuation of the attack. It will also give the forward a much better vision, especially at the very end of the playing field where goals are scored.

When do we have to accelerate and when do we have to slow down our attack? A change of pace is always indicated when playing in numerical superiority (for instance 4v3) or when a gap appears in front of the ball carrier. Slowing down the attack is a necessity when one team-mate is in an off-side position, when none of the team-mates had offered an optimal position or when most of the attackers are exhausted.

Where, generally, is there some space to be exploited on the pitch? Generally there is some space available on the opposite side where the ball is played. This space should be used systematically with long, flat and speedy passes into the run of a team-mate.

What should we do when the pressing defence of the opponent doesn't work? The ball carrier should anticipate the press of the opposing team and pass the ball backward to a retreated team-mate, who then clears the ball upfield to an unmarked forward or midfield player.

What are the key points for successfully executing a throw-in? No risks should be taken with a throw-in. Its execution should happen quickly and before the opponent has time to mark all the players. When playing a 7v7 game, the attackers and defenders should know that the off-side rule is out of force, which could be considered as an advantage for the attacking team.

What does a player have to consider when executing a free kick? He or she should execute it as quickly as possible (especially when one team-mate is unmarked) to surprise the opponent's defence, or he or she does it very slowly to study carefully all possible passing options.

In which way should a defender mark his or her personal opponent without the ball? The defender should always position him- or herself between the opponent and the goal but slightly more inside and closer to the goal than the opponent. From this position the defender should perceive the ball and the opponent at the same time.

When should a defender mark the opponent and when should he or she mark the space? The means of marking depends on the distance between the defender and the attacker. When the ball is close, perhaps less than 15 metres away, the defender should mark the opponent very closely, being more inside and closer to the goal than the attacker. In case the ball is farther away, the marking is less tight. This allows the defender to intercept passes in space as well as passes directed into the feet of the opponent.

How should a defender position him- or herself in relation to a ball-carrying attacker? The defender should never face the attacker in a frontal position since this gives the attacker the opportunity to beat him or her on either side. The defender meets the attacker better in a side-on position. This allows the defender to accompany the attacker as well as to channel him or her into the desired direction (for instance toward a side-line or toward a team-mate who covers the attacker).

Are there any other considerations for the defender to take into account when he or she faces 1v1 situations? The defender should always initiate a tackle from a tiptoe position (on the balls of the feet) and keep the weight of the body equally distributed between both legs. To maintain balance the defender should not separate both legs more than shoulder width or put one foot in front of the other. He or she should bend the knees slightly to be ready to tackle at any second when the ball may be too far away from the feet of the attacker. When executing the tackle, it must be a very quick and surprising one without putting all the weight of the body to the front leg since this prevents executing a second tackle in case of a miss. While carefully observing the ball (not the legs of the opponent), the defender should have in sight the other opponents and also the team-mates closest to the ball. In case the tackle was successful, he or she should switch as quickly as possible from a defensive pattern to an offensive one.

What should a defender do who is close to a 1v1 situation? Without losing attention to his or her personal opponent, the defender should anticipate a possible failure by the team-mate and cover the space at his or her shoulders to be explored by the attacker.

VARIATIONS

- Before playing this sixth game, youngsters should practice the following variation of it. Each team has five attacks, always starting from their proper end-line. When they touch the ball for the first time, their opponents initiate the defence from the opposite end-line. The attack finishes with either a goal or a loss of possession of the ball to the defenders. The defenders may not counterattack after having defended with success, however. The team that scores more goals in 10 attacks is the winner.

- More advanced players should practice in a smaller playing area (easier to defend) or in a much bigger area (to make the defence very difficult).

- This variant might be called 'Make It and Take It'. After scoring, the attackers *continue* to attack. They immediately turn around to attack the opposite goal, which should still be defended by the same opponents. The team that manages to score more goals in five minutes of play is the winner.

- Instead of attacking two wide goal areas, the attackers now try to score in either of two 4-metre-wide goals (alternatively, you can set up 6-metre-wide goals), situated in the wing positions on the two end-lines.

- Each team is in possession of one ball. To score, the team must control one ball on the opposing end-line and also be in possession of the other one.

TRAINING OBJECTIVES

In attacking these are the objectives:

- Play with a diamond formation and ensure width and depth in the attack.
- Lift the head while dribbling the ball to collect information that will allow you to pass the ball to the best situated team-mate.
- Know when to change the rhythm of the attack; learn to accelerate at the correct moment.
- Learn to be available as receiver in a part of the playing area that is not controlled by the defenders. This zone is usually farther away from the ball, at the opposite side of the pitch from where the ball is.
- Select the most effective passing option. Don't risk long passes when the likelihood of success is poor.
- Know what the correct option is for beating a pressing defence.
- Know how to execute free kicks and the kick-in successfully.
- Avoid getting into a 1v1 situation, which has little likelihood of success; instead aim to create 2v1 situations through systematic support of the ball carrier.

In defending these are the objectives:

- Position yourself between the opponent and the proper goal, staying closer to the centre of the field than is the opponent.
- Scan the game situation, observing in particular the ball but remembering to keep both the opponents and your team-mates in your field of vision.
- Ensure width and depth in your defence.
- Anticipate the ball carrier's intentions.
- Follow the game situation and practice a combined marking (marking closely in your assigned zone), a zonal marking or a player-to-player marking with constant communication among all four defenders.
- Use a side position to tackle an attacker in full control of the ball.
- Maintain a high level of concentration during the game.

7th Simplified Game
Long Passes Out of the Midfield

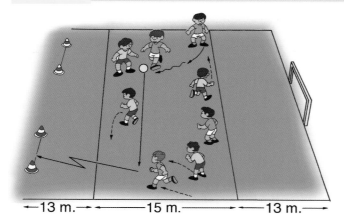

—13 m.— ——15 m.—— — 13 m.—

Two teams of four players only compete between the centre-line and the off-side line of a 7v7 football field. The game lasts for three periods of five minutes each. Start with a ball toss in the centre of the pitch. Each team then tries to gain possession of the ball and pass it, pressured by the defence of the opponents, through one of the two goal areas (marked by cones set 6 metres apart) established some 13 metres behind the opponent's end-line. No player may leave the assigned playing area. It helps the flow of play to place some reserve balls on each end-line in order to restart the game without delay after any long pass. While the attacking team does its best to create sufficient space and gain some time to prepare a long, precise pass, the opponents defend aggressively. Defenders try to always outnumber the attackers in the zone where the ball is being played. The young players will quickly learn that immediately after a successful tackle, there is an ideal opportunity to counterattack with a long pass.

EFFECTIVE QUESTIONING

When does an opportunity to play a through pass arise? Generally speaking, always immediately after having conquered the ball from an opponent. Before executing a tackle an intelligent defender has already analysed what is happening in front of him or her. In case the tackle was successful, the defender immediately plays a through pass to forwards or midfield players, who are now marked with less attention since their defenders had to support their attack.

Discuss reception and control of the ball. Before a ball is received the player should know what to do with it. Instead of controlling it in a stationary position the ball should remain on the move, being orientated in a determined direction in which the game is going to continue (orientated control).

What are the characteristics of a successful through pass? Most important is that the pass reaches its target (a team-mate). This demands perfect timing, accuracy, and speed and as little height as possible in order to facilitate control of the ball.

VARIATIONS

Have players try the variations in the progressive order listed here.

1. A neutral player supports whichever team is in possession of the ball.
2. At least three passes should be played in the centre of the pitch before a long pass can be executed.
3. A fifth attacker waits behind the two goal areas to receive the through pass and then control the ball in one of these goals between the cones. The coach may also ask this extra attacker to finish the attack with a shot into the 7v7 goal.
4. Instead of introducing an attacker as in the previous variation, a defender now stays close to each of the goals, trying to intercept the long pass to either of the goals. Once a goal is scored, the defender may change positions and roles with the attacker who made the long, precise and disguised pass.
5. Play the same game (variation 4, above) on a smaller pitch.
6. Two attackers, watched by one defender between them, are prepared to receive behind each of the goals. Their aim is to collect a long pass out of the midfield through one of the two pairs of cones, despite the defender's efforts to the contrary.
7. Remove the goals (cones) but station the two attackers more or less at the same place, about 13 metres behind the end-line. After receiving the long through pass, the attackers must score, despite the active presence of one defender and a goal-keeper.
8. Play as in variation 7, but include a second defender, who marks closely.
9. Play as in variation 8, but add a third defender, who acts as a free player.

TRAINING OBJECTIVES

- Fulfill the coaching objectives of the previous simplified games.
- Aim to execute a long pass immediately after recovery of the ball from the opponent.
- Learn to disguise the direction of the pass.
- Analyse the game situation before receiving the ball to find out whether a long pass is possible.
- Always look out for the long pass, but when its execution doesn't seem likely to lead to success, forget about it and instead choose a play that ensures your team's keeping possession of the ball.
- As defenders, try to reduce the space and time at the disposal of the ball carrier and his or her supporting players; after having recovered the ball, switch quickly to attack.

CORRECTIVE GAMES

Use the second, fifth or seventh simplified game for 2v2 (see pages 99, 108 and 110); the fifth, eighth or tenth simplified game for 3v3 (see pages 163, 169 and 174); and the third simplified game for 4v4 in this chapter (see page 223).

8th Simplified Game
Score, Defend and Counterattack

Form two teams of four players each who will compete in one half of the 7v7 or 8v8 football field. Use an official goal of 6 by 2 metres and add two 5-metre-wide goals marked by cones on the centre-line. It is also a good idea to add one neutral goal-keeper on each team. Start the game with a ball toss in the centre of the field. Both teams toss a coin to decide which will first attack the official goal and which will instead try to score by a pass from any distance through one of the two goals on the centre-line. For any infringement of the rules consult the 7v7 (page 178) or 8v8 (page 244) game rules, depending on the ages of the players.

Duration of the game: four periods of five minutes each; at each interval the teams change sides and goals.

 ### EFFECTIVE QUESTIONING

Which factors influence your decision whether to execute a shot at goal or a pass to a team-mate? There are many points to consider. For instance, the distance between the player with the ball and the goal, the shooting angle, the position, the number and the behaviour of team-mates close to the goal, and the position of the goal-keeper in and out of the goal are factors. Finally, the number, position and behaviour of the defenders close to the goal are factors to consider.

When a shot at goal is taken, what are the tasks of the other attackers and defenders close to that goal? Everyone should anticipate a possible rebound and try to position him- or herself in such a way that he or she is able to score or to clear the ball out of the penalty box. Coming too close to the ball is a frequent mistake carried out by the attackers, while defenders should always look to clear the ball toward any of the side-lines. Because of lack of time and many competing players around the oncoming ball, rebounds should be taken first time.

Why do the defending teams always achieve better scores than the attacking ones? This has something to do with a quick transition after losing possession of the ball. Generally attackers need more time to switch to defence than defenders do to switch to attack.

Which hints would you give your attackers in a corner kick?
- The ball should be directed to zones that the goal-keeper and the defender have difficulty controlling.
- The corner kick should have maximum speed, a low trajectory and a spin going away from the goal.
- The attackers should move in circles to get away from their markers and when the ball arrives, meet it with speed, aggressiveness and courage.

Which hints would you give to your defenders in a corner kick?
- Never hide behind an opponent. Position yourself on the same level with the attacker but closer to the goal (goal side).
- Always keep an eye on the opponent and also on the ball. Position yourself to see both at the same time.
- Never wait for the ball to come to you. Better to meet it as soon as you are sure about its speed, spin and trajectory. Anticipate or overtake your opponent.
- Don't forget to communicate with your defence.

Give me three basic rules for the throw-in.
1. The quicker the throw-in is taken, the less time the opponent has to build up his or her defence.
2. We never take risks when taking a throw-in within our own half. Therefore, it is advisable to pass the ball backward to unmarked team-mates.
3. In the opposing half we may take risks, especially when knowing that the off-side rule is out of force.

Which hints would you give to your defenders when the referee awards a free kick close to your goal?
- Immediately after the referee awards a free kick, ask one defender to position him- or herself behind the ball.
- This way the attackers cannot surprise us, and we will gain some time to organise our defence to mark the attackers. Always watch the ball and never turn away from it. The only exception is the player who communicates with the goal-keeper to prevent one part of the goal from not being covered.

What does a player have to consider when executing a free kick? He or she should execute it as quickly as possible (especially when one team-mate is unmarked) to surprise the opponent's defence. Alternatively, he or she does it very slowly to study carefully all possible passing options. Depending on the distance toward the goal, a shot at goal is taken or a pass to an unmarked player in a better position should be executed.

TRAINING OBJECTIVES

- Strive for the objectives of the previous simplified games for four-player teams.
- Know how to play effectively in the opposing shooting area.
- Watch systematically for the goal-keeper's rebound.
- Know how to execute free kicks well; gain experience in building up the defensive wall.
- Gain experience in the corners and the penalty area.
- Know how to defend without giving away a penalty.

CORRECTIVE GAMES

Review any of the previous simplified games as well as any of the games in chapter 4.

9th Simplified Game
Shooting Game With Four Goals

Form three teams that will use one half of an 8v8 football pitch. Ten metres inside the side- or end-lines of the half, you should add four goal areas with cones (6 metres wide). One team's four players defend the four open goals that you set out with cones. The other two teams attack or defend depending on which team has the ball. Their aim is to score in either goal from inside the playing area. After each goal, the goal-keeper clears the ball high into the air. The game continues when the ball runs behind any of the goals, but when it moves out of the marked area, one of several reserve balls close to each goal area should be brought into play by the goalkeeper of that goal. After every five minutes, the teams rotate so that the goals are defended by a different team. The team that scores more goals in 15 minutes of play is the winner.

A fourth team could take part with the role of collecting the balls shot out of the field and replacing them close to the nearest goal area.

? EFFECTIVE QUESTIONING

What information does the ball carrier have to consider when deciding whether to take a shot at goal or pass the ball to a team-mate instead? There are many points to consider, for instance:

- the distance between the player with the ball and the goal;
- the shooting angle;
- the position, number and behaviour of team-mates close to the goal;
- the position of the goal-keeper in or out of goal; and
- the position and behaviour of the defenders.

When is a shot on goal a must? A shot at goal is always taken when there is not a single defender between the ball and the goal and also when no better-positioned team-mate is available to pass the ball to. You always shoot when the distance toward the goal and the shooting angle are optimal and when you think that beating the goal-keeper with a dribble could be a risk.

When a shot at goal is taken, what are the tasks of the other attackers and defenders close to that goal? Everyone should anticipate a possible rebound and try to position him- or herself in such a way that he or she is able to score or to clear the ball out of the penalty box. Coming too close to the ball is a frequent mistake carried out by the attackers, while defenders should always look to clear the ball toward any of the side-lines. Because of lack of time or too many players around the oncoming ball, rebounds should be taken first time.

VARIATION

Only shots from a distance of more than 8 metres or kicks executed with the less-skillful foot count as a goal.

10th   Simplified Game
4v2 With Headers

Use the rules of the eleventh simplified game for 3v3 (see page 175) with two exceptions: The game is played by teams of four players and only one ball is used for both teams. Two players on each team start as wings, and two start in the centre of the pitch. The team that gains possession of the ball after the initial ball throw then passes the ball to one of its two wings, who is marked by the opposing wing. Once a wing manages to control the ball within his or her limited zone with three consecutive touches, he or she may advance without opposition. After the wing arrives level with the penalty area, he or she centres the ball to one of the two team-mates in the midfield. These team-mates should be supporting the wing during dribbling, with the aim to then score with a header. They are opposed, however, by two defenders playing in the central zone. Initially there are no goal-keepers, which makes scoring with a header much easier (see variation 6 for version with goal-keepers). After one of the defenders has recovered possession of the ball from the attackers, he or she should pass the ball to the wing (looking for one who is being marked less by the opponents) to direct the next attack toward the opposite goal. After each five-minute period, the four players of each team rotate until everybody has played in the three possible positions.

❓ EFFECTIVE QUESTIONING

What are the tasks of the player who centres the ball?
- The wings should be capable of executing well-timed centres, which have accuracy and should be directed eight to 10 metres in front of the goal. This makes the task of the goal-keeper more difficult.
- Centres with a low trajectory and high speed are more dangerous than soft ones, which have a high trajectory and therefore need more time.

Which aspects have to be considered by players who score with headers? Before scoring with a header the player has to read the speed of the ball, its spin, the height of the aerial pass, its trajectory and its possible point of landing. Any mistake in the optical-motor assessment may result in a wrong decision and bad execution of the header.

Whenever possible the attacker should run toward the oncoming ball in order to give the header more speed. Know how to gain an optimal position in front of the goal and how to apply correct techniques to the head kick.

VARIATIONS

Have players practice these variations in the order of progression given here.

1. The game is first played without defenders. Both teams attack, every one in possession of one ball (as described in the eleventh simplified game for 3v3 on page 175).
2. When the attackers manage to score frequently with a header, the game is made more complex and is played with one ball only. One of the two centre players of the opposing team is allowed to defend as a field player, while the other one remains on the centre-line.
3. Follow variation 2, except that the only defender has to play as goal-keeper; the goal-keeper can defend only with both feet on the goal-line.
4. There are no limitations for the two opposing defenders in the centre stripe, once they realise that their team is not going to attack. In general, one of them runs quickly into the goal to serve as goal-keeper, while the second one tries to intercept the centre.
5. Play using the original rules of the game (see previous page).
6. Play the original game with two neutral goal-keepers (see illustration on previous page).
7. The wings may choose between a centre and a shot toward the goal, which is defended by a goal-keeper.
8. The wing who is not in possession of the ball may join the two attackers in the centre stripe and participate in the goal scoring (making it 3v2).
9. Play as a free game, except that a goal may be scored only with a header.

TRAINING OBJECTIVES

Use the same objectives as for the eleventh simplified game for 3v3 (page 175).

CORRECTIVE GAMES

Use the eleventh simplified game for 3v3 (page 175).

Level 4 Competitions

Games for 5v5 (level 4) allow coaches to present their players with problems that are common in the 8v8 and 11v11 games.

Please review all the simplified games for 4v4 (games begin on page 219). Those games should be practiced with the same rules, including the same field dimensions and durations of the matches—simply add one more player on each team to make them 5v5. Even though 5v5 games are more difficult and complex, the training objectives and corrective exercises should remain the same as those given in the earlier 4v4 simplified games.

5v5 Triathlon

Three or four times during a season, a training session should be replaced with the 5v5 triathlon to give the 12- and 13-year-old players an opportunity to compete under more-stressful conditions in the most common situations of the 8v8 football game.

Successful performances in competitions like the 5v5 triathlon depend upon a number of variables, including the quality of the training programmes, coaches, referees and competitions. The figure on page 242 shows how the competition can be organised. In this example, teams representing Europe compete against teams representing South America until a winner is decided. The blank spaces next to each game are for coaches to use in recording scores.

1. 5v5 in Three Playing Areas

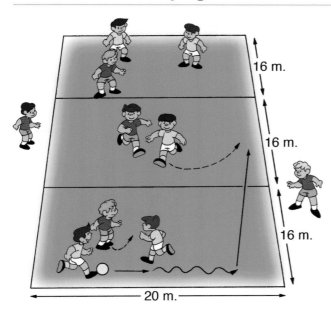

16 m.

16 m.

16 m.

20 m.

Divide the playing area into three equal parts, each measuring about 16 by 20 metres. One defender is in each third; two forwards are in the end areas, and one midfield player is in the middle area. The game is started in the first playing area from the 20-metre base-line. Two players try to keep possession of the ball there against one opponent. Without leaving the area assigned exclusively to them, the two should pass the ball either into the central zone to their midfield player or into the area farther away to one of their two forwards. The midfield player is closely marked by his or her opponent. The midfield player, as well as the two forwards in the opposite area, do their best to stay open for a pass, despite the active presence of a defender in each field. None of the players may leave the area assigned to him or her.

The five attacking players are given five ball possessions to achieve as many passes as possible, controlling the ball in all three areas. Their attack ends

- when one of the three defenders gains possession of the ball or kicks it out of the playing area,
- if the ball runs out of the pitch, or
- if an attacker commits an infringement.

After each attack the defenders of the first and third playing areas should be replaced by a fresh defender, who has been observing the game from a position outside the field (see illustration on previous page). When one team has had their five ball possessions, it is the defenders' turn to attack; the five former attackers now must defend (three times, with two substitutions).

VARIATIONS

- To help train the midfield player in receiving and controlling the ball, the players on the first pitch must pass the ball to him or her before he or she tries to continue the attack and distribute the ball to one of the two forwards in the third field. The aim of the five attackers becomes controlling the ball on the opposing end-line.
- To learn to use long passes, no player occupies the central area. With this game the attackers develop their ability to give accurate, hard and disguised passes after first establishing a visual agreement with one of their team-mates in the third area. On the other hand, the two single defenders learn to read the opponent's play, to control a relatively wide area and to tackle the two opponents.
- When more players take part in the game (for instance, twice the original 3v2), you should extend the width of the playing areas accordingly—until the official width of the football pitch is reached.

TRAINING OBJECTIVES

- Learn when to execute a short or a long pass, when to lift the ball into the air and when to play it along the ground.
- Select the correct occasion for a direct pass to the team-mate in the midfield or a long one to one of the forwards.
- Improve passing techniques (flat along the ground, with accuracy and power, without indicating the direction to the opponents).
- Learn to use cues or to establish visual agreements with the ball receiver.
- Improve play without the ball.
- Anticipate the opponent's play.
- Solve the situation of two attackers versus one defender with a high percentage of successes.

CORRECTIVE GAMES

Before having young players play the full version of this game, have them practice and experiment with these simpler formats:

- Use a free kick toward a marked attacker (a variant of the eighth simplified game 2v2, page 111) to learn to keep control of the ball in successive passes.

- Play to keep possession of the ball in the 2v1 situation (a variant of the ninth simplified game 2v2, page 112) to learn to create sufficient time and space for directing effective long passes to a team-mate.
- Play to keep possession of the ball in the 3v2 situation (a variant of the seventh simplified game 3v3, page 167).
- Use various activities from chapter 4—see section titled Passing, Receiving and Shooting Games (page 55).

2. 5v5 With Fast Attacks

Divide an 8v8 football pitch into three equal zones. The game is initiated in the central zone or area. There, four players from each team try to keep possession of the ball for five consecutive passes. After a team manages this or an even higher number of passes, its players must pass the ball to their forward, close to the opposing goal. Players (attackers as well as defenders) may not leave the midfield before the ball has been played into the attacking zone. After the reception and control of the long pass, the player stationed in the end zone must wait for the support of team-mates (who run out of the midfield after executing the through pass), not being allowed to score. The conclusion of the attack is hindered by a neutral goal-keeper and by the defenders, who should have also run from the midfield immediately after the long pass. The team that scores more goals after 10 ball throws in the centre of the midfield is the winner.

VARIATION

All five players on a team remain in the midfield. A team may leave the midfield and attack the goal only after having achieved three (later make it five) consecutive passes. All other rules are the same.

TRAINING OBJECTIVES

These are the same as for the eighth simplified game 3v3 (see page 169) and the third simplified game 4v4 (see page 223).

CORRECTIVE GAMES

These are also the same as for the eighth simplified game 3v3 (see page 169) and the third simplified game 4v4 (see page 223).

3. Score, Defend and Counterattack

See the eighth simplified game 4v4 earlier in this chapter. Use one half of an 8v8 football pitch, again adding cones to set up two 5-metre-wide goal areas on the centre-line across from the regular, 6-metre-wide goal (see illustration). It is a good idea to use a goal-keeper in the regular goal. Start with a ball toss in the centre of the pitch. One team attacks the regular goal. The other defends it and counterattacks with a pass through one of the two smaller goal areas.

Duration of the game: four periods of three minutes; after each three minutes, the teams switch positions and functions.

Europe Versus South America

Teams	Portugal	Scotland	Poland
Names of players			

Teams	Argentina	Brazil	Chile
Names of players			

First game scores: Dribble across the opponent's end-line (3 × 3 min).			Second game scores: Long passes out of the midfield (3 × 3 min.)			Third game scores: Score, defend and counterattack (4 × 3 min.)		
PRT-BRA			SCT-BRA			POL-BRA		
SCT-ARG			POL-ARG			PRT-ARG		
POL-CHL			PRT-CHL			SCT-CHL		

Final result: Europe _____ South America _____ Technical delegate: _____

Note: During the triathlon, changing the composition of the team is not permitted.

Understanding 8v8 Football

To a casual observer, football can sometimes appear complex. In fact, it is an exceedingly simple game once the basic concepts, skills and rules have been learned and understood.

The game has two distinct phases:

1. The attacking phase—when one's own team has the ball.
2. The defending phase—when the opposition has the ball.

The objectives (individual and team) for each phase are as follows:

1. Attacking phase
   - Keep possession.
   - Get the ball forward and penetrate the opposing defence at the earliest opportunity.
   - Create shooting and goal-scoring opportunities.
   - Score goals.
2. Defending phase
   - Regain possession of the ball at the earliest opportunity.
   - Prevent the ball from being played or carried forward, that is, penetrating one's own defence.
   - Deny the opposition's shooting and goal-scoring opportunities.
   - Avoid conceding goals (prevent goals from being scored).

The following capacities are required to achieve the objectives in each phase:

1. Attacking phase
   - Control of the ball and composure while on the ball.
   - Ability to run with the ball.
   - Ability to dribble the ball and dodge.
   - Ability to pass the ball.
   - Ability to receive and then control the oncoming ball.
   - Ability to create and convert goal-scoring opportunities.
2. Defending phase
   - Ability to mark.
   - Ability to delay, channel and close down opponents.
   - Ability to intercept and tackle.
   - Ability to prevent and deny shooting or goal-scoring opportunities.
   - Effective goal-keeping.

Each phase has its own required style of play:

1. The attacking phase is fluid, expansive and creative.
2. The defending phase is disciplined, organised and secure.

Similarly, these two phases determine the principles of play for the game.

1. In attack, go for possession, speed, support, penetration, concentration, width and mobility.
2. In defence, go for depth, delay, balance, concentration, organisation, security and speed.

To perform effectively in 8v8 football, players must understand the objectives, styles and principles of play required of them during the distinct phases of the game and in the different areas of the pitch. Most importantly, effective team play depends on individual players striving to master the basic techniques and skills and perform them well.

Rules of 8v8 Football

8v8 football is considered the ideal competition after youngsters have had two years' practice of the 7v7 game and until they reach the age of 14. It forms a bridge between the popular 7v7 game and the full game. The following rules apply only to 8v8 football. For any circumstance not covered in the following regulations, consult the rules of official football.

Field

8v8 football is played between the penalty areas of the official football field. The penalty areas are the zones between the 16.5-metre line of the official field (the end-line of the 8v8 pitch) and the centre-line. Goals from the 7v7 game are used and put in the centre of the 16.5-metre line of the official field. The penalty spot is situated at a distance of 9 metres from the goal mouth.

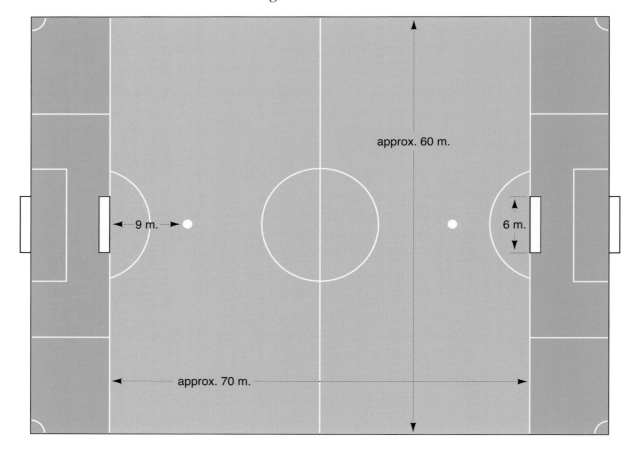

Teams

A team has a maximum of 11 players. Eight of them at a time are involved in the game. A substituted player may return at any time and as often as the coach decides. All 11 players must participate in the competition.

When intelligence, skill and will work together, we can expect a master-piece.

Duration

The competition lasts three periods of 25 minutes each, with five minutes' rest between them.

Technical Rules

For any infringement of a defender in his or her own half, the referee awards, depending on the severity, a free kick or a penalty (from 9 metres). In addition, the referee may card the player, adding a yellow card (temporary suspension up to 10 minutes) or a red card for a definite suspension.

Equipment

Continue to use a No. 4 ball for all competitions.

Referee

To promote young players' learning to officiate, the 8v8 football competition should be controlled by a referee (without assistants) under 21 years of age.

Advantages of 8v8 Football

8v8 football better matches 12- and 13-year-old players than the official 11v11 competition in several areas.

1. Each player touches the ball more often and is therefore more involved in the game. This more intensive participation not only enhances technical and tactical learning but also allows the youth coach to collect more precise information about the performance of each player as well as of his or her whole team as a unit.

2. Although the parameters of space and time are almost exactly the same (290 square metres per player or 300 square metres per player) as in the 11v11 game, the 8v8 game assures better learning (and facilitates a smooth transition to regular play) because there are only 16 players on the field. With fewer players on the pitch, the basic game situations appear more frequently, but they confront young players with less complex problems than in the full game. The players therefore can feel more capable, which results in self-confidence and, at the same time, greater motivation to learn even more.

3. Playing with the No. 4 ball size allows youngsters to reach any player on the pitch with a pass (something that is impossible to attain playing on the full field with the official ball). This aspect stimulates their visual perception. Besides, the size and weight of the ball are in perfect harmony with the level of speed and power of these players (especially true for girls). With the ball tailored to their

physical and mental capacities, better results occur in acquiring and consolidating the most important techniques.

The 8v8 competition therefore helps young players to develop correct habits for later use in the 11v11 game. There is no question that it is much easier to integrate a player successfully into the full game after he or she has been exposed to two years of the simpler problems in the 8v8 game.

4. All young goal-keepers between 12 and 14 years prefer to play 8v8 football instead of the full game. Why? Like their teammates, they, too, have the opportunity to play the ball more often because fewer players are involved in the game and because the ball approaches the vicinity of the goals more often. Therefore, they gain more experience in less time. And the size of the goal (6 by 6 metres) is perfectly tailored to their height.

5. With the ball more often played close to the goal, the forwards and defenders also gain valuable experience in the most decisive parts of the field—where any mistake or successful action can modify the result of the game. In 8v8 football they learn to deal with stressful situations and to take offensive and defensive rebounds.

6. With only eight players on a team, the game has fewer interruptions, with the ball in play for more time.

7. There is no physical overloading of any player, because the coach may change a player as frequently and as often as he or she considers wise. Rolling substitution improves team spirit and at the same time develops more versatile players who are capable of playing well in different positions. Because of the shorter distances in 8v8, there are fewer stimuli for anaerobic resistance, which at this stage of the development of the player has to be considered positive. Besides, despite the No. 4 ball's poor level of explosive power, it can be passed to any player in any part of the field, thus stimulating development of perceptive capacities.

8. The job of the youth coach, who generally is not very experienced, is much easier. He or she learns under simpler conditions (fewer players but more ball contacts, less-complex game situations) to analyse the players' performance and the team as a whole, as well as how to facilitate programming the contents for the next training sessions. The greater facility in analysis makes it easier to find appropriate solutions to problems.

9. Most coaches play with three front runners, three midfield players, a free defender and a goal-keeper. Due to the shorter length of the playing field (33 metres less than the official pitch), the midfield players often go up to attack and the forwards move downfield to defend. That is why 8v8 football prevents an early specialisation of young football players.

10. What is valid for the coach is valid also for the referee. Putting a logical progression of youth competitions into practice will also, without doubt, benefit the level of umpiring in the long term. Like the coach and his or her young players, young referees also grow slowly—by facing increasingly difficult and complex problems—into the full game, ensuring that they feel capable at each stage of their referee development.

11. Spectators, especially parents, really enjoy watching an 8v8 game more than the traditional one because it is easier to follow. Because there are more goal opportunities for both teams, it is more exciting. Moreover, because of the larger penalty areas between the centre-lines and the 16.5-metre line of the full field

(almost 40 metres deep and 55 metres wide), fair play must be practiced to not give away penalties to the opponents. That is why far fewer injuries occur when the rules of 8v8 football are applied. Last but not least, parents see their daughters and sons in possession of the ball more frequently; they see more successful interventions than in the full game—and more possibilities of scoring.

> **'What is defeat? Nothing but education; nothing but the first step to something better.'**
> —*Wendell Phillips*

A solid bridge between learning more complex situations and applying them again is presented in this chapter. Here a great variety of simplified games and their corrective exercises mainly help to fine-tune the technical aspects, but in addition the chapter constructs a link with understanding particular situations and with applications in an official competition (8v8 football). Training and competition are always viewed as a unit, one being tightly linked to the other. Game-orientated practice found in this chapter stimulates young players more than do instruction and training sessions (as are so frequently observed in other approaches to youth football) whose contents are isolated from the competition.

Taking Football
Into the Future

The football of the past we have to respect, the football of today we must study, and the game of the future we should anticipate.

Bora Milutinović

Players should encounter training that is enjoyable, effective and appropriate for their age as soon as they set foot on the pitch. This is the only way to develop healthy, happy, talented football players. Any attempt to rush the natural development of young football players or have them confront the demands of the full game too early has to be considered detrimental to their development and future performance.

Bringing the Game Out of the Middle Ages

Neil Postman, a professor of sociology at the University of New York, states in his well-known book *The Disappearance of Childhood* (1994) that modern society often does not allow children to distinguish their mode of living from that of adults. 'They are eating the same food, they are watching the same television program, commit crimes like adults, and take alcohol at an early age as well as drugs'. He further states, 'The world of labor is also getting out of control. Girls between 12 and 17 years of age are, today, among the world's best-paid models, and there are children that, at the age of 8, are already multi-millionaires (e.g., actors or pop stars). It is impossible that these children are behaving and will behave in the future as normal children would. . . .'

According to Postman, it is very dangerous when society does not notice much difference between the world of children and that of adults. He believes that children must discover the mysteries of life slowly and step by step, always in accordance with their mental stage and their present capacities.

The environment that children move and play in today has suffered an enormous transformation from nature to urban jungle. This development has denied children the chance to learn from and follow nature. Instead they are more often forced to move against their own nature (e.g., to cross the road only when there is a zebra path or play computer games instead of outdoor games in fresh air). Since children have lost the natural setting, which influenced the education and development of their parents and grandparents, they should be given modern surroundings for learning and gaining experience on their own that can replace the former ones. This is why having organised sports in schools and clubs is so important for the quality of life of our youth!

Our world of football reflects the current situation. Instead of children being able to practice their particular games as in the past, in the streets or other natural settings, the increasing urbanisation of the landscape does not allow most of them to make use of the natural surroundings that their grandparents had for play.

Besides having to play the game on artificial grass fields far away from their homes, in our advanced society young boys and girls—in many clubs and schools—must maintain rigid training methods and competitions that in no way respect the laws of nature or the children's actual mental and physical capacities.

Everywhere children are obliged to train and compete like adults, forced to adapt to rules originally intended for adults. The rush to introduce talented youth to the adult game has frequently resulted in their acquiring bad habits that later limit their performance on our senior teams.

We know that when an institution organises competitions for 8- and 9-year-olds as well as 10- and 11-year-olds that require them to play with the same rules as the adults', it determines to a high degree the objectives, contents and methods of the children's training and learning process. That means that if the structure of the competition is wrong, the way the coach trains them must also be incorrect.

Experience shows that coaches of young players are seen positively by the parents and club officials only when the kids demonstrate success or winning. But to achieve this kind of success in a traditional competition, coaches must train them in a very similar way to adults, with more or less the same contents and methods.

Beginners in such a system are obliged to compete every weekend in a match where success is conditioned mainly by one specific skill (the long pass) and often by destructive or negative tactics. This forces the coaches, in the limited available practice time (generally three hours a week), to concentrate almost exclusively on match-winning aspects. They are afraid to waste time in developing the children at the initial stage through a wide range of physical activities and problem-solving situations. But it is only in this systematic way that a sound level of coordination and conditioning capacities can be acquired. And these, as we all well know, are indispensable for the further improvement of young players' performance.

Although all sport scientists agree on this developmental model, few sports federations are making use of the important recommendations these professionals make. Instead of copying nature and patiently developing all the necessary capacities, through training and competitions tailored to the children's capacities, many coaches of young players still force them to play like clones of an adult.

Modifying Postman's words slightly we might affirm the statement, 'Once we give the children access to the forbidden fruit of adult information [competition], we expel them from the garden of infancy'. It does seem as though, in many parts of the world, there are too many teachers and coaches of young football players still living in the Middle Ages. Why call it that? In the Middle Ages society knew only infants and adults. By 6 or 7 years of age, a person was already considered adult because he or she participated in adult activities: The child worked, ate, dressed and behaved as an adult. How long can we allow the ignorance of these coaches and administrators to continue to obstruct the natural development of the next generation of football players?

10 Rules for Continuous Improvement

1. Be prepared to give up your way of thinking.
2. When you teach, always question what and how you teach and what you have done up to now.
3. To overcome certain weaknesses of a player or a team, it is not enough to detect and diagnose the problems. You must seek their roots and apply the corresponding remedies.
4. To prepare a fine performance in the next match, consider and perfect every small component of the performance; small details may change the circumstances dramatically.
5. Progress step by step.
6. A 100 per cent solution is difficult to find.
7. The difference between a good performance and an excellent one is putting in some more effort.
8. The best preparation for tomorrow is doing an optimal job today; the final victory results from a series of small, daily successes.
9. As none of us knows so much as all of us, working in a team ensures better results.
10. The process of continuous improvement never finishes.

You have a step-by-step program here, designed precisely to match young players and to nurture their motivation to grow and develop in the game. Through this development model, you can help them flourish, year by year, as better and better players on the way to the wonderful adult game. You can foster their love of sport and good football playing.

References

Almond, L. 1983. 'Teaching games through action research.' Pp. 185-197 in *Teaching Team Sports*. Roma: Comitato Olimpico Nazionale Italianio/Scuola dello Sport.

Andresen, R., and G. Hagedorn. 1976. *Zur Sportspiel-Forschung*, Band 1. Berlin: Bartels und Wernitz.

Blázquez Sánchez, D. 1995. *La iniciación deportiva y el deporte escolar*. Barcelona: INDE Publicaciones.

Bohm, D., and F. P. Peat. (1987). *Science, Order, and Creativity*. New York: Bantam Books.

Diem, C. Lectures author attended at Deutsche Sporthochschule Köln, 1960s.

Dietrich, K. 1968. *Fussball Spielgemäss lernen-spielgemäss üben*. Schorndorf (Germany): Verlag Hofmann.

Dietrich, K., and G. Landau. 1976. *Beiträge zur Didaktik der Sportspiele*, Teil 1. *Spiel in der Leibeserziehung*. Schorndorf (Germany): Verlag Hofmann.

Durand, M. 1988. *El niño y el deporte*. Barcelona: Ediciones Paidos.

Filippi, C. 'Análisis de los 52 partidos del Campeonato Mundial en 1994.' *Il Nuovo Calcio*. Número 112.

Gallahue, D. 1973. *Teaching Physical Education in Elementary Schools*, 5th edition. Philadelphia: Saunders.

Gallahue, D., and B. MacClenaghan. 1985. *Movimientos fundamentales: su desarrollo y rehabilitación*. Buenos Aires: Ed. Médica Panamericana.

Gould, D., and M. Weiss, eds. 1987. *Advances in Pediatric Sport Sciences*, vol. 2. Champaign, IL: Human Kinetics.

Halliwell, W. 1994. 'The motivation in team sports,' *Apuntes de Educación Física y Deportes*, no. 35 (Barcelona), 51–58.

Leitner, S. 1991. *So lernt Man lernen*. Freiburg (Germany): Herder Verlag.

Leitner, S. 1972. *So lernt Man lernen*. Freiburg (Germany): Herder Verlag.

Mahlo, F. 1981. *La acción táctica en el juego*. La Habana: Ed. Pueblo y Educacíon.

Martin, D. 1982. *Grundlagen der Trainingslehre*. Schorndorf (Germany): Verlag Hofmann.

Millmann, D. 1979. *The Warrior Athlete—Body, Mind, and Spirit*. Walpole, NH: Stillpoint Publishing.

Morehouse, L., and L. Gross. 1977. *Maximum Performance*. New York: Mayflower Granada.

Mosston, M. 1988. *La enseñanza de la educación física*. Buenos Aires: Ediciones Paidos.

Ostrander, S., N. Ostrander, and L. Schroeder. 1979. *Leichter lernen ohne Stress–Superlearning*. Bern: Scherz Verlag.

Pierce, W., and R. Stratton. 1981. 'Perceived sources of stress in youth sport participants.' In *Psychology of Motor Behavior and Sport*. Champaign, IL: Human Kinetics.

Postman, Neil. *The Disappearance of Childhood*. 1994. New York: Vintage Books.

Robbins, A. 1987. *Poder sin limites*. Barcelona: Ediciones Grijalbo.

Spackmann, L. 1983. 'Orientamenti practici per l'insegnamento dei giochi.' In *L'insegnamento dei Giochi Sportivi*. Roma: CONI–Scuola dello Sport.

Thorpe, R., and D. Bunker. 1983. 'A new approach to the teaching of games in physical education curriculum.' In *Teaching Team Sports*. Roma: CONI–Scuola dello Sport.

Thorpe, R., D. Bunker, and L. Almond, Eds. 1988. *Rethinking Games Teaching*. Loughborough, UK: Loughborough University.

Wahlsten, J., and T. Molley. 1995. *Quality Ice Hockey*, Vol. 2. of *Understanding and Learning the Game of Ice Hockey*. Helsinki: Finlands Ishockeyförbund.

Wein, H. 1999. *Fútbol a la medida del adolescente*. Sevilla: Federación Andaluza de Fútbol.

Wein, H. 2005. *Developing Game Intelligence in Soccer*. Spring City, PA: Reedswain.

Whitmore, J. 1997. *Coaching for Performance*. London: Nicholas Brealey.

Wilson, V. 1984. 'Help children deal with stress factors found in competition.' In *Momentum, Journal of Human Movement Studies*, Vol. 9, no. 1 (Edinburgh): 26–28.

Ziglar, Z. 1986. *Pasos hacia la cumbre del éxito*. Bogota: Editorial Norma S.A.

About the Author

Horst Wein is perhaps the world's foremost mentor of football (soccer) coaches and trainers. He has taught the coaches of institutions in 53 countries covering four continents and has written 31 sport-related textbooks, including four on football.

Wein, an Olympic silver medal winner as a coach, was the first coach from the Western world to be invited to train top athletes in the former Soviet Union in the late 1970s. He also has served as a consultant for two Olympic Games, the Asian Games, and one of the most important football clubs in the world—Internazionale Milan.

Currently, Horst Wein works cooperatively with the Center for Research and Studies (CEDIF) of the Royal Spanish Football Federation. He also travels extensively, helping others adapt the game of football to better suit their young players. Recently, the United Nations asked him for help in designing their project of Football Schools in Central and South America, and Nike United Kingdom appointed him as head coach for their famous Premier Football training programme. He resides near Barcelona, Spain.